"At the beginning of this year," Mary Rose O'Reilley writes in *The Barn at the End of the World*, "I had no idea why I felt led to light out into the unfamiliar territory of sheep farming and Buddhist practice." By the end of this remarkable book, she finds the "deep peace of animal creation" and a way to live consciously in the world.

Praise for *The Barn at the End of the World:*
The Apprenticeship of a Quaker, Buddhist Shepherd

"O'Reilley, a Catholic-born Quaker who practices Zen Buddhism, has created a memoir that is as delightfully unconventional as her approach to religion."—*Dallas Morning News*

"A memorable spiritual autobiography. . . . *The Barn at the End of the World* is in three parts, quilted by 99 brief essays ranging from barn ecology to the religion of natural process. Worthy ideas—many expressed with elegance, many comedic—are on every page."
—Colman McCarthy, *Washington Post Book World*

"The life and death reality of raising sheep provides a reality to her spirituality that most people do not have."—Temple Grandin, author of *Thinking in Pictures*

"This is a delightful book, penned by a teacher determined to bring spirituality down to earth. . . . In the end, her book is an open-ended inquiry, a wonderfully humble and good-natured and perceptive gift, that will appeal mightily to anyone who yearns for a simpler path."
—*NAPRA Review*

"Read it and laugh. Read it and weep. Read it and grow. This is a flat-out fabulous book!"—Parker J. Palmer, author of *Let Your Life Speak: Listening for the Voice of Vocation*

"O'Reilley builds a narrative in short essays that focus on a midlife turning point. A certain amount of humor creeps in: Buddhist monks accuse her of animal abuse for giving beer to slugs in the vegetable garden. . . . We are given a range of meditative approaches to social and individual change from a bright fellow traveler."—Sandy Primm, *St. Louis Post Dispatch*

"I was entranced, amused and educated by Mary Rose O'Reilley's beautifully written spiritual memoir."—Mary Anne Grossmann, *St. Paul Pioneer Press*

"There was no putting it down. Four readings later I still can't. . . . What she has rendered is experience embraced with such fervor, verve and grace that she leaves me, at least, with only one request: keep on going, and write for us what happens next."—Susan Gardner, *Women's Review of Books*

"It is all incredibly serious, wonderfully funny, full of the texture of being alive."—Paul A. Lacey, author of *Growing into Goodness*

The Barn
at the End of the World

The Apprenticeship of a Quaker, Buddhist Shepherd

To Carol

Mary Rose O'Reilley

Mary Rose O'Reilley

MILKWEED EDITIONS

Cloth edition published 2000 by Milkweed Editions
Printed in the United States of America
Cover and interior art by Beth Crowder
Cover design by Adrian Morgan, Red Letter Design
Interior design by Donna Burch
The text of this book is set in Granjon
      03 04   5 4 3
First Paperback Edition

Milkweed Editions, a nonprofit publisher, gratefully acknowledges support from our World As Home funders: Lila Wallace-Reader's Digest Fund and Reader's Legacy underwriter Elly Sturgis. Other support has been provided by the Elmer L. and Eleanor J. Andersen Foundation; Bush Foundation; Faegre and Benson Foundation; General Mills Foundation; Marshall Field's Project Imagine with support from the Target Foundation and Target Stores; McKnight Foundation; Minnesota State Arts Board through an appropriation by the Minnesota State Legislature and a grant from the National Endowment for the Arts; Norwest Foundation on behalf of Norwest Bank Minnesota; Lawrence and Elizabeth Ann O'Shaughnessy Charitable Income Trust in honor of Lawrence M. O'Shaughnessy; Oswald Family Foundation; Ritz Foundation on behalf of Mr. and Mrs. E. J. Phelps Jr.; John and Beverly Rollwagen Fund of the Minneapolis Foundation; St. Paul Companies, Inc.; U.S. Bancorp Foundation; and generous individuals.

Library of Congress Cataloging-in-Publication Data

O'Reilley, Mary Rose.
      The barn at the end of the world : b the apprenticeship of a Quaker, Buddhist shepherd /
      c Mary Rose O'Reilley.
         p. cm.
      ISBN 1-57131-237-4 (cloth), 1-57131-254-4 (paperback)
      1. Farm life—Religious aspects—Buddhism. 2. Sheep ranchers—France— Religious life. 3. Human ecology—Religious aspects—Buddhism. 4. Buddhism— Doctrines.
      I. Title.

      BQ5480.F37 O74 2000
      294.3'092—dc21
      [B]
                                                                                    99-016274

This book is lovingly dedicated to Robin Fox,
in harmony

The Barn
at the End of the World

PART TWO

Clearing Land for the Lotus Pool

PART THREE

I Saw a River Rise

Acknowledgments

I'D PARTICULARLY LIKE to thank the man identified here as Josef for giving me generous and free permission to write about my experience at Plum Village: "We'll know it's only your opinion," he assured me. I've quoted extensively from my notes on Thich N'hat Hanh's dharma talks, in hopes that they might be as valuable to others as they were, and are, to me: I'm grateful for the privilege of having been there, while others could not be, and feel a responsibility to pass on what I recorded. However, the best source of information on Thay's teaching remains his own vast and accessible series of books, beginning with *The Miracle of Mindfulness,* most of them published by Parallax Press.

I'm grateful, also, to my sister Peg Plumbo, my friend Robin Fox, my children, Jude and Julian O'Reilley, and my colleague Bob Miller for reading early versions of the manuscript and offering helpful suggestions. Without Bob's astute and sensitive emendations, in particular, I would be even more afraid than I am to let this book out of my sight. Thank you, dear friend, for so many years of patient, loving counsel.

I gratefully acknowledge the assistance of grants from the Bush Foundation, the Minnesota State Arts Board, and the University of St. Thomas, which helped me to live and record the story that's told here.

Introduction

I GREW UP at the intersection of narrative and silence, as most of us do; in any relatively normal family, there are those who tell stories—stories about themselves and the life of the family—and those who do not: some, too, who listen, and some who do not. At the kitchen table of our little cottage, long after my grandfather had gone off to his carpentry work, my grandmother's stories would roll: The Day My Twin Died and His Spirit Came to Me, The Girl with Lice, Florence and the Ouija Board, My Vision of the Angel of Death, and so on. My mother, too, especially in the midst of canning or jelly making, was full of family narrative. But the silent members of the family exerted an influence as well, the aunts who sat wordlessly rocking, the ones who chose not to speak or were silenced, their stories controlled by others. I had a photograph, once, of a nineteenth-century male relative, a handsome, quite rakish face above a clerical collar. Sadly, in one of our many moves, the photo was somehow thrown out in the trash. When I am dead or demented, no one will remember this man, and then he will truly be gone. I try to call his face up onto my mental screen as often as I can, an act of faith and repentance.

Having grown up this way, with responsibilities to the past, I must write also from the crossroads of speech and silence. Writers, my kind at any rate, are rather like field biologists: they want to understand, quite simply, the *quality* of a given life. Nothing much needs to happen; merely to see and feel the shifting light of a

moment suffices. *The Barn at the End of the World* grows, in part,
out of years of teaching spiritual autobiography, and lamenting, at
least in the classic texts of that genre, the suppression of the body
and the created world. To be a spiritual person, do you have to
climb out of your body? It's a long climb and not worth the trouble.
This book attempts to view the issues of spiritual autobiography
from within the world. It's full of the names and habits and habi-
tats of created things, and the point of it is (in Philip J. Bailey's
words) that "All who breathe mean something more to the true
eye than their shapes show; for all were made in love and made to
be beloved." A thesis like that is not really "arguable," so the book
is structured more like a long poem than a short treatise. Themes
are introduced imagistically, then recapitulated in story, and sometimes, if the matter is appropriate to that inquiry, framed in a few
words of discursive argument. Whatever is going on elsewhere, or
available to read about in books, my Quaker religion obligates me
to a unique discipline: speak only from experience. From early
times, spiritual autobiography has been central to the Quaker path;
it constitutes a body of experiential theology. Nobody knows
much, really, about how the universe is put together in its private
parts. We can only speak about what we ourselves have witnessed.
Being an academic, I have a habit of trying to frame things in a
broader world of ideas and some of that goes on here, too—I hope
not too much.

I've spent a lot of time arranging, rather than organizing, this
material. Writing is rather like quilting, in that you have to use
the materials at hand and, at the same time, discern the pattern in
them. There always is a pattern: that's how the mind works. But
one wants to avoid controlling the outcome; to do that is to miss
the revelation, both for reader and writer. Having written this
book, I "know" what happens, but then my job is to go back and
arrange the material so that the reader can take the same journey

I took. For a year, I've been living with a soft old quilt in various shades of brown and rose, and night after night I follow the needleworker's journey over what at first seemed a random design. By the time I figure out the point of this soft golden patch, this heathery shift, I am, in a way, *friends* with this long-dead quilter. Similarly I hope the reader will be my companion on this road.

I'm trying to lure the reader into participating as I introduce a theme, then drop it behind the fabric — hoping the subconscious will retain it and perk up when it comes forward again. The spiritual life is full of paradoxes: finding the self and losing it, rest and motion, presence/absence, solitude and community. The human mind and body can hold together these opposites, but argument cannot. A poem can hold them, and on one level, much of this text must be read according to the logic of images. On another level, it's a "how-to" (or "how-I-did") book about raising sheep. When you do any craft well and consciously, however, you explore the whole structure of the universe. When you pick up a piece of any ancient pot, you know something about the whole pot, the potter, the culture that produced it, and yourself.

The personal essay is not an exercise in self-expression as much as it is an exercise in perspective. As a Buddhist practitioner, as well as a Quaker, I try to negotiate my teacher's repeated admonition, *"Are you sure?"* No, I am not. If "I" am not entirely congruent with the self who speaks here, even less can I speak with authority about the lives of others. My sister, for example, read an early draft of this manuscript and commented, "We grew up in different houses." Well, certainly, we did.

All that's told here is true, true at least to the perspective of the narrator. However, I've changed the names of anyone who isn't a public person (like the Venerable Thich N'hat Hanh) or a member of my family and intimate circle. In one or two cases, I've altered the details of an incident sufficiently, I hope, to prevent embarrassing anyone who might otherwise be recognized. It pains me to do this, especially in the case of my fellow workers in the barn, who are such heroes to me. I'd prefer to honor them, but they are unassuming people and would hate the publicity.

The Barn
at the End of the World

PART ONE

Flight School

Surrender

Restless, I go down to the barn and attempt to dissect the
concept of "peace..."

As I help Anna clean out the lambing pens, my skirt pinned up
under an apron, mind and body begin to alter their usual relation
to each other. I cannot think about "peace"; I cannot think about
anything. This is a natural consequence of doing the kind of repetitive work called "mindless" by those who disdain it. Yet my mind
is not so much absent as still. It's not at its usual station in my head,
but diffused throughout my body. Or, slid beyond the body, even,
to encompass all that's going on in the barn.

My hands are efficiently chucking down clean straw and, as I
watch the ewe position herself for the scrambling lamb, my nipples
contract in the reflex of a nursing mother. If I were not well past
the childbearing years, my blouse might be soaked with milk. This
is a passing, negligible sensation, a product merely of being present.
I do not stop working to examine it. A casual dissolution of boundaries body-to-body happens when you work in the barn. With
animals, it's safe, and pertinent, to have no edges. It helps you to
manage sheep and them to manage you. If I bother to retrieve my
mind, I find it shared out among the ewes, who have made good
time with it.

There is deep rest in this loss of self. Peace, which implies stillness, and ecstasy: every hair in motion. Thus lovers and people
who read each other's poems breathe the other, if they love or read

well. Thus music. If you play the fiddle, no matter how badly, and you go to hear a great violinist—as last month I went to a concert of Isaac Stern's—you hear the performance in the hollows of your own body (or has it ceased to be your body?)—that lilt of Stern's at the tip of the bow is in your fingers. If I am flowing in this moment through one pride of skin and not another, it's accident. And I test the limits of this bubble as once I tested the limits of the womb.

When you go down to the lambing pens you can tell from the doorway if something's gone wrong: a ewe whose lamb is dead will have slipped back in the fold with her sisters. Most animals are pragmatic and have little patience with weakness—perhaps you have seen how a mother cat will favor her strong, aggressive kitten and paw aside the runts. Last night Anna struggled till 3 A.M. to save a lamb too short to reach the teats, tubing colostrum into her stomach, then bottle feeding every two hours. This morning the lamb came to me with her tail shaking, a sign of health, and took two ounces of formula. In the barnyard, I try to volunteer a shift with Anna, sparing her the night work since I'm fresher.

But—"I don't think we will have to stay up tonight," she says. Her tone is the oblique and respectful one used by my dad and his pilot friends when refusing to pronounce the word *crash.* Over her shoulder I see four ewes in the fold where three had been standing.

We put the dead lamb in a plastic bucket, later to bury. "Poor little mauser," says Anna. "Still, she had some good hours."

Philosophers make distinctions between varieties of dispossession; it cannot be the same, they say, to surrender to love, to music, to animal creation, and to prayer. (But stand with someone you love, palm to palm, eyes closed, and sing a perfect fourth . . .) Since I experience these slips of consciousness as similar, I can only speak from what I know. Intensity of presence is the common element, though in the next moment one could say, intensity of absence.

Without presence, the violence would be unthinkable: of God, of Zen practice, of lovemaking, and certainly of the farm. How disquieting to fight so hard for the life of a lamb and tomorrow meet its cousin tucked up in the crockpot. *Namaste:* I honor the god in you.

Disquieting, anyway.

8 A.M. in the Sheep Barn

"SHEEP PROLAPSE THEIR rectums because they cough too much..." Ben, the barn manager, was telling me as we headed into the morning's task, trimming necrotic tissue from the rectums of five two-hundred-pound Hampshire ram lambs.

I am capable of dithering for years over some foolish decision; but at other times, important shifts come with absolute authority, in the time it takes to sink a basket or fall dead. One day, after I came back to America from Anna's sheep farm in England, I found myself brooding over a question of lamb nutrition. "Phone Hank," a farming friend told me. "He's a professor of sheep science."

Incredulously: "Sheep science?"

"That's what they call it at the college."

A subsequent conversation with Hank about colostrum and intubation fascinated me so much that I blurted, "If I want to find out more about all this, what should I do?"

"Be at the sheep barn, 8:00 tomorrow morning," he said.

"OK," I said, and there went my plans for the next year and a half.

Hank put me under Ben's tutelage. Ben was a senior agriculture student, strong and competent, who had grown up on a sheep farm in western Minnesota. He had white-blond hair and wore a feed cap that said "I Care About My Animals."

"What makes them cough?" I wanted to know. Anna's sheep in England rarely coughed.

"If you could tell me that . . ." Ben's voice trailed off as the stench of necrotic tissue wafted up from the hind quarters of the ram we were working on. "What I don't do for you guys," Ben said to the sheep.

The rectum is a straight tube of intestinal tissue, and when a sheep coughs repeatedly, the tube is pushed out and protrudes from the anus like an angry sausage. When that happens, our task is to wrap a heavy rubber band around the protrusion, cutting off the blood supply and necrotizing the tissue. First we plug the rectum with a syringe casing (there are always a few left over from routine inoculations). Through the casing, open at both ends, the lamb can continue to defecate. After a few days, when the tissue is dead, you cut it off. That's what we're doing today.

I hand instruments to Ben and hold the grunting lambs in the metal cradle that flips them with their feet in the air, bum presenting. This procedure does not make the lambs too happy, but they leave in better condition than they arrived, with a walk similar to the postpartum swagger of women on the delivery floor.

Bolting out of bed at six that June morning, I had suffered a fashion crisis. What to wear on a Minnesota farm? The older farmers I know wear brown polyester jumpsuits, like factory workers. The young ones wear jeans, but the forecast was for ninety-five degrees with heavy humidity. The wardrobe of Quaker ladies in their middle years runs to denim skirts and hiking boots. This outfit had worked fine for me in England. But one of my jobs in Minnesota will be to climb onto the industrial cuisinart in the hay barn and mix fifty-pound bags of nutritional supplement and corn into blades as big as my body. Getting a skirt caught in that thing would be bad news for Betty Crocker.

My favorite cotton shirt is printed with sunflowers and celebrates Organic Gardening Week in big green letters. I've decided this shirt might be impolitic. Organic gardeners are about as welcome in production farming as bird watchers in logging country. Finally I settled on lightweight cotton pants and one of my son's V-necked undershirts. This ensemble turns out to be perfect for trimming rectal tissue, and is soon covered in lamb shit.

When Ben gave me my inaugural tour of the barn, he made it clear that his major interest is in lamb production. Our Polypay flock, a mixture of Dorset, Targhee, Finn, and Rambouillet, is bred to bear young almost year-around. He doesn't encourage dependency. "When I started here," Ben told me, "the ewes would come up to me and groan and want help with the lambing. I make them lamb on their own. My goal is to make every animal in here independent of me."

Ben's hard-ass pose makes me think he would not be sympathetic to organic gardeners and vegetarians. I want to stay anonymous in my affiliations if only to avoid being stereotyped as the lamb-hugger I am. I long to be accepted as a worker among workers.

In return, I try not to stereotype Ben. He works hard, seems to love it, and is a natural, hands-on teacher.

I consort with a lot of liberals who are animal rights activists, and, while I respect their positions, I find they often do not know much about the practical order. In fact, investigating the essential facts of food production is one thing that's drawn me to the barn. One professorial friend recently scolded me about the "perverse and unnatural" business of breeding animals year-round. I don't know. Maybe. On the other hand, many third-world people, mostly women, depend on lamb production to make their living. I could count my English friend, Anna, among these marginal women. She runs about twenty sheep and each one is an individual to her, living out a fairly normal ruminant life except, of course, for the lambs, whose sale has put her sons through university.

Yet even slaughter—I do not shrink from the word—can be accomplished with respect. Anna takes the lambs to her local butcher two-by-two in a small van, because she believes the large cattle trucks frighten them. The butcher renders them unconscious with a stun gun and then cuts their throats. They are hung immediately and the meat is perfectly tended. Anna believes it's a mark of reverence for the animals to take perfect care of their meat and to waste nothing.

I told my friend that if I wanted to have an effect on animal rights, I would be inclined to follow Anna's reasonable example...

"Mary!" Ben snaps across my line of internal chatter. "Stop thinking. Flip that ram for me, will you? Your body knows how to do it. Don't try to do it with your mind."

Ben has, in some cosmic transaction, accepted the position of my Zen master.

As If

I WOULD NOT SAY I am looking for God. Or, I am not looking for
God precisely. I am not seeking the God I learned about as a
Catholic child, as an eighteen-year-old novice in a religious community, as an agnostic graduate student, as—but who cares about
my disguises? Or God's.

In childhood, exiled by rheumatic fever to a back bedroom,
I existed for months in boredom so exquisite it approached, as it
now seems to me, the threshold of *satori*. Next to my bed was a
table, and on the table lay a thick glass to protect the wood surface
beneath. Propped on pillows, a child could stare slantwise into a
half-inch angle of refraction that disappeared into infinity. I longed
to slip into this world under glass and drift through the dense sea
of light where (something told me) no gravity governed the operation of things. Yet sometimes the prospect of liberation terrified me;
tumbling into sleep, I would waken in horror at a dream of falling
into a void between the glass and the table, drifting forever without even the minimal distractions of my confined life: soap operas
on the radio, lunch, arithmetic worksheets, fear of the doctor, the
click of my mother's heels when she came home from work.

When the temptation comes over me to say I am looking for
God, this primal scene sometimes returns. Other recollections
crowd in as well, many of them from childhood; all of them have
in common the sense of brushing (with longing and fear) against
a parallel universe. The young exist quite naturally in a liminal

world; consider how children's books retain this intuition of possibility: that in the back of the wardrobe or through a wrinkle in time, down a hole in the garden, on the back of a sparrow, or in the company of Mr. Toad, you can simply chuck the grown-ups and *be there,* where things count. Plato, I believe, had long periods of indulging a similar whimsy. And so do most poets. "There are things I tell to no one," writes Galway Kinnell (telling):

> Those close to me might think
> I was sad, and try to comfort me, or become sad
>   themselves.
> At such times I go off alone, in silence, as if listening
>   for God.

I am saying these things to explain why, in the middle of my life, I found myself *wandering away,* as children do, sometimes alone, sometimes in silence. I went to Anna's sheep farm in England, to a Buddhist monastery in France, to a parsonage in rural Maine. I completed a certification program in spiritual direction, learning to talk to people who wanted to talk to God. I went back to serious work in my first college major, music, and traveled around singing and playing fiddle duets with Robin, the man who has long been my music partner and life's companion. My university job no longer interested me as much as it once had. Teaching English is (as professorial jobs go) unusually labor intensive and draining. To do it well, you have to spend a lot of time coaching students individually on their writing and thinking. Strangely enough, I still had a lot of energy for this student-oriented part of the job. Rather, it was *books* that no longer interested me, drama and fiction in particular. It was as though a priest, in midcareer, had come to doubt the reality of transubstantiation. I could still engage with poems and expository prose, but most fiction seemed the product of extremities I no longer wished to visit. So many years of Zen training had reiterated, "Don't get lost in the dramas of life"; and here I had to stand around in a classroom defending Oedipus.

Or maybe it was twenty-five years of Quaker discipline that had made me suspicious of fiction; Quakers have, after all, some theology in common with that clique who shut down the theaters in 1642. The Society of Friends, with its practical focus, has tended to produce natural scientists, botanical illustrators, and manufacturers of chocolate bars. Quakers seldom write fiction and I can't, offhand, think of any who write it well. Our rather unimaginative testimonies about literal truth lead us away from what we, erroneously, take for its opposite: story. Once I was staying at a Quaker community that suffered flooding in the night from an ice dam on the library roof. Fortunately—or as it turned out, ironically—one of my goddaughters was staying with me, a young woman employed professionally as a museum preservationist. She sprang into action. "I'll call a friend of mine who knows how to dry out books," she volunteered, looking at the sodden volumes, many of them rare. "Oh, don't worry about it," the librarian told her. "It's only the fiction section."

I would not have majored in English and gone on to teach literature had I not been able to construct a counterargument about the truthfulness of fiction; still, as writers turn away from the industrious villages of George Eliot and Thomas Hardy, I learn less and less from them that helps me to ponder my life. In time, I found myself agreeing with the course evaluations written by my testier freshmen students: "All the literature we read this term was depressing." How naive. How sane. One night I begged Robin, a scientist by training, to watch Arthur Miller's "Death of a Salesman" with me on PBS. He lasted about one act, then turned to me in horror: "This is how you spend your days? Thinking about things like this?" I was ashamed. I could have been learning about string theory or how flowers pollinate themselves.

I think his remark was the beginning of my crisis of faith. Like so many of my generation in graduate school, I had turned to literature as a kind of substitute for formal religion, which no longer fed my soul, or for therapy, which I could not afford. With therapy, given luck, time, or medication, the neurosis wanes and one no longer makes appointments. Teaching English, the neurosis wanes as well, and then ... well, why do you think so many English teachers become administrators, or throw themselves into abstract contemplation of critical theory? For my part, I became interested in exploring the theory of nonfiction and in writing memoir, a genre that gives us access to that lost Middlemarch of reflection and social commentary. Quakers are, as a group, pigheaded individualists. George Fox, the founder of the Society of Friends, issued a famous challenge to his followers: "Christ saith this and the Apostles say this, but what canst *thou* say? Art *thou* a child of Light and hast thou walked in the Light? ..." What could be more validating to the journal keeper?

I do not think, however, that a memoir is intrinsically more truthful than a novel. Indeed, the diarist should remind herself daily how subjective her occupation is, because she has the overwhelming advantage and responsibility of inscribing her version of events. She should keep in mind, at least—as should her readers— the old country-and-western song, "We live in a two-storey house. She has her story and I have mine." One kind of nonfiction is, I think, a subspecies of poetry, and poetry is a way to honor the stream of things by observation. Poetry affirms the hunger of our condition: for each other, for comprehension, for God, for the landscape outside self. But it is not botanical illustration.

Having come to doubt the reality of (literary) transubstantiation, I needed, as I do in any crisis, a practical focus. So I became a shepherd: a *hireling* shepherd. It's a job with good Biblical antecedents. I went to work in the agricultural division of a land grant college and took on two hundred sheep to be my spiritual teachers. It was a toss-up between that and joining an enclosed contemplative order. *"Ora et labora,"* the Benedictines teach: work and pray. That's what I wanted to do. Though what would it mean to pray? I had no idea.

Thoreau—whom I could still read with pleasure—under similar duress had formulated his famous pronouncement:

> I went to the woods because I wished to
> live deliberately, to front only the essential facts of
> life, and see if I could not learn what it had to
> teach, and not, when I came to die, discover that I
> had not lived. I did not wish to live what
> was not life, living is so dear . . .

Lovers of *Walden* will observe that in my quotation I have stopped short of Thoreau's full agenda: the part about sucking out the marrow of life, living sturdily and Spartan-like, cutting swaths and shaving close, driving life into a corner. Even as a tubercular thirty-year-old, he had more energy than I, as well as more tolerance for austerity. Besides, it was not my first foray into living deliberately: convent life had wakened that impulse in me. Marriage, bearing children, divorce, single parenting, work: all had confronted me with certain essential facts of life. I wasn't even unhappy. The fact is, living (somewhat) consciously, like eating wonderful food, had given me more rather than less of an appetite. I had found living so dear that I wanted to do it full time.

How is one to *act as if?* Start with what you know. What are your deepest instincts? What have you long denied? Over and over, through the years, I had denied the deep peace that came to me in a barn full of animals. I think that, to the extent we're well socialized, we habitually ignore impulses in our lives that don't fit the cultural script. Yet people frequently tell me about longings that arise as though from nowhere—the stock analyst who wants to write film scripts, the lawyer with a dream of building houses for the poor. When my friends tell me these things, I feel that I've been put in the presence of a tender mystery, yet they often reveal their hearts with a sad, dismissive laugh: "Oh, I know it's just a crazy fantasy." We fear these impulses because they have the potential to disrupt our social house of cards, our livelihood, our families. A fellow teacher who longed to sing opera made fun of herself this way: "It's as crazy as Zelda Fitzgerald wanting to dance ballet."

Cultural wisdom says, "Don't quit your day job." Yet I think these desires represent our psyche's stretch toward wholeness. And to be whole, as many religious traditions teach, is to make manifest a unique face of God in the world. We don't want to be irresponsible, yet for every accountant who deserts his family and sails for Tahiti, ten American men have heart attacks at their desks, after hours. And so I usually say to people who bring their longings to me, "Is there a way you can incorporate this need into your daily life, on a kind of trial basis, to see where it leads you? Take singing lessons, learn Italian?"

These kinds of conversations often happen in the course of spiritual direction—by the way, coming out of an egalitarian Quaker tradition, I prefer the term "spiritual companioning." Whatever you call it, it's different from psychology, but it makes a parallel effort to translate the subtle codes of the unconscious. I could not, back when I made the decision to tend sheep, understand the language of my desire. I didn't know what the barn was "about." In fact, I think it's a mistake to be too literal in our response to inner directions—it's when we're too literal that we make regrettable mistakes about sailing to Tahiti. Before you can follow your heart's desire, you have to examine your heart closely. It's a subtle instrument of inquiry, the examined heart.

I don't know why Thoreau went to the woods, rather than to England or to the Carthusians or to some nineteenth-century Mall of America. Neither could I say why, precisely, I went to the barn. And why did this need for deliberate life well up just then, in 1845 or 1995, for Henry David or for me? Thoreau, who elides as much as he tells, says he wished to transact "some private business with the fewest obstacles." And what was he looking for? "I long ago lost," he says, "a hound, a bay horse, and a turtle dove and am still on their trail."

Oh, yes. I know them. They slipped me, too.

Thoreau's brief catalog of longing and desire seems to me as unpretentious, tentative, and proportionate a description as I have ever come across of the condition of someone going on spiritual business. How unyielding, on the terrain of this delicate work, seem to me the hard-edged names of God. Years ago I resolved I would go to seminary if only I could somehow stand aside from theology's relentless dissection and categorization of holy things— a worthy activity for people of a certain temperament, but antithetical to mine. The study of spiritual direction, by contrast, grows out of contemplative tradition, where all the names of God rapidly become moot. *"Contemplare et contemplata aliis tradere,"* says Thomas Aquinas: Gaze with love on God, share what has been seen with others.

Facts

To say, in a work of nonfiction, "I was born in such and such a place, in such and such a year" seems pretentious. It makes one's individual life appear very important—when what matters are not the facts of a life but the quality of the feelings and affections—what is universal, that is, instead of what is merely local and historical. My individual life could not be more insignificant, and I venture to speak about it not because anything particularly interesting has happened to me but simply because *life* has happened to me, and it has happened as well to everyone who reads these words. Every book that I care to read or write is a book about the texture of being alive, and only incidentally about the facts of a particular historical moment or gender or ethnicity or skin.

Yet the facts of a life are strings that hold it to the ground. The government is interested in these facts, to be sure, and so is any fair-minded reader who wants a context for evaluating an individual view of the world. Besides, as I think about the scraps of life one shares from day to day, over coffee or traveling into the dark on trains, I realize that the details of my oddly fragmented life present a conundrum to many. "Sometimes you come across like the typical college professor and then you switch on the country-and-western music," a friend may complain. "Sometimes you seem so solitary, sometimes surrounded by a vast extended family. . . . Are you a Catholic? A Buddhist? A Quaker?" With apologies, then, but in the interests of clarity, I produce the following facts:

I was born in Pampa, Texas, in an Air Force base hospital, in 1944. My parents were, as parents often were in those days, very young, and they had little money. After the war, we went back to a blue-collar east side neighborhood in St. Paul, Minnesota, and lived for several years in a fourplex on Case Street. We shared the house with grandparents, aunts and uncles, and, best of all, cousins—five or six of them so close to me in age that I had all the advantages of growing up in the middle of a huge family. My mother had come out of this neighborhood, out of this very fourplex, and her family, the McManuses, were people of note. On the east side, in those days, that was likely to mean you had a job at the telephone company; but in fact, my maternal grandfather and his brothers were even more exalted in station: they were engineers for the Great Northern Railroad.

One day, shortly after the birth of my sister, a moving truck came and made me, for a day, the center of neighborhood excitement: we were going to live in a new house. I did not understand, at five, how permanent this break would be from my fleet of cousins, the wonderful city dump we played in from morning till night, the music of my cousin's piano, the camaraderie, the protection—and that I would awaken for the next fifteen years or so in a tract house in suburban Roseville, a place that felt as dry to the spirit as if it had been wrung out by huge, impersonal hands.

Like many people after the war, my parents were looking for safety and stability. Their children would not burrow in amusing dumps, they would not be at the beck and call of every manic aunt. Like all the best childhoods, mine was shaping up to be, on Case Street, a machine for producing terror and ecstasy: my parents hoped to put a stop to that. They sought a protected space, planted turf on it, and strung out flowers in manageable lines. It's possible to control a life, so long as you keep it small and take no chances. The war had exhausted, at a young age, many grown-ups' interest in taking chances.

I still spent lots of time with my paternal grandparents, who divided their lives between a one-room apartment in the city and a one-room cabin in western Wisconsin, as well as with the maiden aunts and uncle who had raised my mother: their names were Mamie, Sadie, and Boo.

My grandparents were, in retrospect, odd company. Grandpa hardly spoke at all and worked from early in the morning till late at night building beautiful, intricate things in his workshop, inlaid tables primarily: he had been a carpenter all his life. My grandmother was musical, psychic, and a gifted storyteller. And in their presence I was what every child needs to be for however long it takes to put down the roots of a strong spirit: the object of love unlimited. Similarly, Mamie, Sadie, and Boo spoiled and petted me. Boo, in particular, would take me to the dime store every visit and bring me back with my pockets full of plastic treasure and my cheeks bulging with sweets. Left in the care of my aunts, I learned to roll pies and eat them right up with ice cream. Left with Uncle Boo, the cuisine was simpler. "Cooking," for Boo, meant buttering a slice of Wonder Bread and covering it with syrup. We'd eat it, then pick up the plates and lick them clean. When I hear words and phrases like "grace" or "the mercy of God," my frivolous mind composes a dinner plate glazed with Log Cabin.

But it was only a few years ago, when I turned fifty, that I realized how disconnected I felt after the move to Roseville—cut off from what Carson McCullers called "the we of me"—like a pup taken out of the litter and set to train on a cold cement floor. After one summer moving day, I never again saw my warm-hearted Italian uncle, Tony, my cousin, Denny, who marauded the countryside with me, Rosie and Joanne who looked out for all the younger ones and brought Denny and me home safely when we stalled on some great dump adventure. Behind, as well, was the upright piano I had lain behind from babyhood, absorbing music through portholes in the soul. A piano would not fit into my parents' decorating scheme for many years and, when it did, it would be a tinkly spinet with the pinched soul of furniture.

That week I turned fifty, my children got hold of an old photo album, looking for pictures of mom as a child. They found a snap-shot of me, tiny among cousins, so uncharacteristically surrounded. "Who are these people?" they asked. Without thinking about it, I al-most gave the response my parents had taught me when I wailed for that lost family: "They're nobody special to us." The bare words seem cruel, but the underlying sentiment was, I think, merely ele-giac: our blood connection was uncertain, we want to put that life behind us, something happened that doesn't concern you . . .

Instead, the little black-and-white photo blazed its revelation: the "we of me." The answer, perhaps, to a number of miscellaneous questions: why I keep trying to live in community, why I married a man who was the eldest of ten children, why my house has accom-modated, over the years, such odd lots of people, why, still, I keep wandering around looking for "the rest."

Roseville, the merciless subdivision: Levittown of the prairie. It must have unrolled as though from a traveling puppeteer's bag of tricks, sidewalks, tarmac, chain-link fences, and the ugly houses with their false brick fronts and aluminum siding: *unreal city.* It did not take me long, transplanted from the delightful squalor of Case Street and fourplex living with my cousins, to start howling. My parents, I'm sure, were thrilled to be there, which illustrates the economies of cosmic intelligence. Why provide space for both heaven and hell when in two thousand square feet both can serve their respective inhabitants?

I love city life, its ruthless push of body on soul, the exacerbation, the grinding down. Sometimes. Often. And I love deep country, lakes lit like white fire. But nothing in my soul responds to suburbs, from which life has been sucked through a stellar straw. As though we were an experiment in the making of black holes.

Worst was the green and loathsome grass. People in those days did not understand the folly of monocropping the fussy *gramineae* family: how the pesticide washing over temperamental grass would kill not only dandelions and plantain (a handy medicinal plant, called "nature's bandage" in the old herbals: this is a commercial message) but also the tiger swallowtail and luna moth, the earth-worm, and probably my dad who died of cancer in 1991 after fifty years of dusting everything green in sight with a chemical cocktail called 2–4 D. It will probably compromise my sister and me as well, who walked barefoot on that grass, as well as our children, who carry our poison in their veins. But nobody knew, or believed what they had been told by the likes of Rachel Carson—for, tramping around old barns, I often come upon stores of the same chemicals stockpiled (I assume) by guys of my dad's era. They've heard some kind of bad news about this handy chemical mix and—having ex-perienced Prohibition—they instinctively hoard.

I still labor with my city neighbors over the dandelion issue. I've caught dear (in other respects) friends sneaking over at night to spray my yellow miscreants. And I have to head for the basement every spring when clouds of vapor drifting across the neighbor-hood catch me unaware. A tank truck has pulled up next door, a happy golden truck painted with children playing in the poisoned gramineae, eating their dissolution. Once I accosted the sixteen-year-old driver of the golden wagon labelled "Robolawn," or what-ever they call it these days. He had stopped to spray, and to tack out the little signs that warn whichever animals are literate.

"Excuse me, but I'm a mom, and so I have to ask you why the company doesn't provide you with a respirator and whether you know what you're breathing in there?"

"I have no idea," he responds to the latter question. "And they decided it's bad for business if we go around wearing gas masks while we spray."

"May you be safe, may your body be well, may your mind be at peace." This is an ancient Buddhist prayer for sending *meta,* compassion. May your hormones not be altered. May your children be capable of reproduction. May they see, some sunset, the pale green elegant line of luna moth.

Having survived the war, just about everybody in Roseville was trying to put death behind them, but fortunately I saw enough of it, like the child Siddhartha, to get me thinking.

The crow had been slit by a cat, I guess, and it lay beside the chain-link fence that edged our garage. The contents of its stomach had silted out beside it on the ground, undigested bright corn. I had never before witnessed this particular dialog of assimilation and dissolve. If a huge vulgar bird could simply eat corn and die, the universe seemed to my seven-year-old mind an implacable place.

The bird's death had occurred a little beyond our property line, where it was not subject to my father's relentless maintenance. So I could watch through a month of summer, as though at the July Academy of Desire and Longing, its slow decay. First the bright eyes went, then other scavengers plucked the corn from its gullet. Finally, the thing just mummified. I shared the drama with no one, but simply visited this summer school every day and pondered its lessons. It was during that July I began to cart home every bone and skeletal fragment I could find while ranging the neighborhood. I would label these old cow teeth and weasel skulls and put them on shelves in my room, which did not make my parents happy.

Death became a concern of mine. That was the winter I had been knocked out with rheumatic fever and exiled from school. Children do not grasp the whole picture of certain finalities—death, divorce—as quickly as they seem to. A young farmer I know, who niche markets lambs to the upscale restaurant trade, was determined to raise his children with a full and generous understanding of barnyard life and death. He hated to think his children might grow up with the idea that "meat" sprang cleaned, cut, and shrink-wrapped into the supermarket case. In the interests of education, he led his five-year-old to participate in the life cycle of one sturdy wether named Jimmy, from birth to lamb chop. Parturition went fine, gamboling proceeded as usual. From time to time the little boy was reminded that Jimmy would ultimately go to the butcher. The day came, the boy said good-bye, and a week later the family went back to retrieve the packaged frozen lamb. The boy seemed to follow all his dad's patient explanation till, as they drove the meat from locker to farm, he suddenly exclaimed, "Dad! We forgot Jimmy!"

So children do not always get it. As much as I knew I got from watching a crow decompose in the weeds by a suburban fence, and when it disappeared one day, no doubt in the mouth of a dog, I did not think it had gone to heaven.

Catching and Flipping and Shearing

F LIPPING SHEEP is a major component of barn management. You have to flip them to shear them, to perform any vet work (as we call the inoculations and small surgeries of everyday work), or merely to get their attention and remind them that they're sheep and we aren't. Perhaps I should mention what everybody takes for granted: you have to catch them first.

When I say "lambs," most people think about cute little wooly animals, but in our barn we are moving market lambs and wethers, big castrated male sheep that run two hundred pounds. We also have around a hundred ewes at the moment, our breeding females, and several huge ram sires. Catching any of these animals requires skill and strength.

"Don't you use a crook?" my friends ask, picturing perhaps a quaint shepherdess on an embroidered field of wildflowers. We don't, but I don't know why we don't. Maybe it's considered effeminate. Ben, of course, can easily head a sheep out of the flock, grab it under the chin, and get a purchase with the other hand on its tailbone. For my part, I'm slow, a little arthritic, and like to save my hands for sawing pitifully on the violin. I can't reach from the chin to the tail of a large animal. Mostly I slide around in sheep shit to the delight of anyone in the barn.

"Don't run around so aimlessly," Ben sings out, as we pull sheep in for shearing. I'm black and blue all over. My instinct is to sink my fingers into the wool and hold on, at which point the rams just gather steam and pull me over.

We shear constantly, for one reason or another, in the summer simply to keep the animals cool. Our Polypays and Hampshires produce a poor wool staple, so we don't bother with the classy shearing that might be done for the handspinning trade. Sheared wool is, however, separated by color, bagged, and sold for mattress-stuffing and blankets.

The rules of shearing are (1) keep the skin stretched; (2) don't cut off the teats or nick a ewe's vagina or cut off a ram's sheath; (3) watch out for the Achilles tendon; and (4) hold the clippers flat and clip close. In my first few attempts I did not cut close but neither did I excise any vital organs.

While we shear, Ben, the extrovert, tells me more than I can absorb about genetics, breed characteristics, and the gossip of sheep production: which breeders are well thought of, who are suspected of having "spider" (a genetic malformation) in the DNA of their animals. Much of it goes right by me. At this point, I can authoritatively pick out a Dorset from a Hampshire, but a "classic Texel look" is lost on me. I'm merely happy I've reached a point where not all sheep look alike.

But as the summer days go by, I'm growing discouraged. My bones ache; my mind throbs and misfires over calculations about feed ratios. I wonder if I am too old to take this new direction, or if, like so many things, it's a matter of focus rather than of strength and agility.

Green Pastures

D ID YOU READ YOUR HANDOUT on sheep parasites, Mary?"
Ben asked as he loped from the office to the barn. I trotted
behind him like an anxious puppy.

"Yes."

"Then tell me how we would know to look at them if these
sheep were infected?"

"Ummm. They'd be anemic and have diarrhea and be off their
feed."

"How would we know if they're anemic?"

"The pink part under their eyes would be more white? . . ." I
ventured. This is how moms know that children are anemic.

"Their gums," said Ben, "would stay white when you push on
them."

Without pressing on any gums, we could see that these sheep
were infected. They were scraggly looking and their backsides
scoury (that is, covered in shit). First we shaved bottoms, a charm-
ing job. Then we caught and inoculated them with vermifuge.
Last night I practiced flipping my border collie, Shep, so I have the
moves down and can trip these feisty little fifty-pound Texel bucks
without too much trouble. I easily flipped and inoculated fifteen
without being inoculated back.

The sheep have parasites because they have been on pasture. We
are conducting an experiment to compare sheep raised on pasture

with sheep who have access only to the barn and its neighboring yards. One pastured sheep is blind from eating milk vetch.

"Factory farming"—often defined in terms of keeping the animals more confined—is a major political issue in Minnesota. Huge pig farms, in particular, with holding tanks of manure that sometimes leak and pollute the water table, are especially controversial. Observing this experiment, however, I see that some degree of confinement may be more comfortable and healthy for the animal.

Health Food

I BEGAN MEDITATION PRACTICE at eighteen when I entered religious community. We were taught a lot about prayer and given hours a day to work on it, but much of my best instruction came from a book passed on to me by a senior novice. In those days, we postulants (as young women in their first year were called), slept three to a room under the eye of a senior novice (women in their third year of religious life). The senior novices were exotic figures to us aspirants; while we wore knee-length black skirts and blouses, black capes and stockings, they wore the full religious habit, which in those days meant a floor-length serge dress, white wimple, and long veil. We retained our "civilian" hairstyles, pixie or flip: their hair was cut short and, even at bedtime, tucked in a white cap. We were called Jean Hanson or Susie Smith; each of them had disappeared into the identity of Sister Macaria or Sister Paul Joseph—gender and family erased as cleanly as possible. "If you ask my name," wrote Appolonius of Tyre, "say that I lost it on the sea. If you ask my family, say that I am shipwrecked. . . ."

The senior novices represented what we postulants most longed for and feared. We watched them covertly and constantly, collecting little bits of data about each one, speculating, mourning when one or another left the community before profession, occasionally falling into austere, wordless love.

For we were not, in the ordinary course of things, allowed to speak to them. Merely by presence, the senior novice monitored behavior in each little room, but the rule forbade interaction between nuns and postulants. Indeed, in the bedrooms, postulants were not allowed to speak to other postulants, even their roommates, excluding illness, emergency, or the vocal prayer that signaled dawn: "Let us bless the Lord!" the novice would intone. "Thanks be to God!" each postulant responded, unless she had gone into a coma.

Denied normal concourse, we grew as clever as dogs at interpreting a frown or tilt of the head. We could pick out each novice sitting in chapel merely by the way she pinned her veil; we knew who came late to refectory by her footsteps. How extraordinary, in this environment of perfervid observation, to come upon Sister Michael Ann sitting like a Buddha, cross-legged in the middle of her bed. At first I saw only her shadow—for each bed was curtained—felt her peculiar stillness. Then, as days passed, I would flounce in from late study in the postulate, throw myself on the bed, and catch a glimpse of her as the bed curtains danced in the breeze of my unrecollected passage. She would be sitting there cross-legged in her black night robe and white cap, eyes closed, hands palm up on her knees.

It was months before I could ask what she was up to: Christmas or Pentecost—one of the holidays on which we were given permission to speak to the novices. She told me she was sitting zazen. Amazing. I had never encountered such a practice, outside of the most esoteric texts in comparative religion. Certainly it had nothing to do with *our* religion. Perhaps it was forbidden by the First Commandment. That was the point on which Sister Michael Ann set me straight. She gave me a book by an Irish Jesuit who had spent his life in Japan, and whose work involved a careful mediation of every aspect of Christianity and Buddhism. It was an unusual introduction to Eastern meditation practice, taking place in a contemplative Christian community and utterly dissociated from any understanding of Buddhism itself as a philosophic system. Sister Michael Ann's journey was later popularized by such a famous, male, and surely orthodox monastic as Thomas Merton, but I think that in those days she was almost alone on the zafu.

And I learned to sit there, too.

An oddity of Zen Buddhism, as distinct from the rituals of most religions, is that it has a *practice* distinct from a *belief system*. You can "sit"—as meditators say—and remain a Jew or a Catholic or an atheist. So my early Zen training kept me in place, on the zafu, through all the religious inquiry of my later years—for it was not long after I left the novitiate that I stopped attending Mass. One of the great gifts of Catholicism, paradoxically, was a Buddhist meditation practice. I laze away from sitting now and then, sometimes for months, but I always return as though to home. It's a place where invisible spirits put food in front of me and feed my soul.

They feed it now, as I try to muster enough concentration to handle three-hundred-pound sheep . . .

I'm getting up with the sun these days, so I can do yoga and have some meditation time before driving across town to the barn. It helps me to focus better and not get stomped, bitten, or killed. Imagine the indignity of being killed by a sheep. How hard it would be on my grown children to have to say, "Mom was killed by a sheep. . . ." Always that little snicker.

Today a man named Mabu came and bought eight lambs, which we herded into his Dodge Caravan. The lambs were happy to board and left with their noses up against the glass like tourists. It would make a great commercial for Dodge Caravans. I'm told that Muslims, like Orthodox Jews, slaughter in a ritual way that requires reverence for the animal as well as thanksgiving for a meal.

As I wave good-bye, I think about a phrase my son uses when we have discussions about the ethics of food production: *meat that has been read its rights.* After he evolved this position, we bought our beef and pork from a local farmer whose operation we knew well, and chickens that were labeled "pareve." But as time went on, we came to shrink from the sight of beef. Pork disappeared from our diet after my daughter raised piglets one summer. I will not admit to being a vegetarian; I've lived in too many third-world countries, where even roadkill is retrieved as a gift of the gods, to espouse— I am chattering to myself—such a bourgeois fashion. Excluding a strict religious orientation, Hindu or Buddhist, one can only be a vegetarian from a position of privilege. Besides, many foreign visitors come to my house, and I like to serve them what they crave . . .

That is to say, I was rationalizing, standing there in the dusty road waving to a Dodge Caravan full of sheep. "Doesn't it bother you at all?" I ask Ben.

"They die, we die." It's one of his koanic little sayings that I go home and ponder on my zafu.

Five young people in the high-status beige jumpsuits of vet students are coming up the road. Our major job today will be collecting blood samples from eighty sheep for a scrapie project in the nearby school of veterinary medicine. The vets are studying whether the disease can be discerned on the DNA chain. Every shepherd dreads scrapie, an appalling neurological catastrophe that causes the animal to go crazy, rip its own wool, and chew its flesh. It's rare in the United States, but more of a problem in England (where I never heard it mentioned).

Ninety degrees again, and ten degrees hotter in the barn. My job is to catch and hold for the vet students, which can only be done by straddling and climbing the sheep like ponies. Often they get away and bash me into the walls. On the larger ones, my legs don't touch the ground. I only get smashed underfoot once, which marks progress in my sheep-busting ability.

Afterwards we flop in the office kitchen, have a couple of beers and a round of pizza and donuts—good Minnesota health food.

Stopping for Coffee

I SELDOM THINK ABOUT how young Ben is, because he's smart and competent and worries at the skill level of a forty-year-old. But he recently made a few days' holiday of turning twenty-one and getting married to a girl he met in Future Farmers of America. She's from a cattle family. Then, at the beginning of the week, he called me with a note of urgency in his voice: "I'm back! Come in and help me deworm." I'm honored by this panicky call from the Real: to be valued as a common worker calms my spirit, agitated by too much abstraction. What Ben tells me daily, though not in words, and what the sheep tell me in their own language is, *you are enough*.

After our little hiatus, I relish the patient work with animals—patient, if not always perfectly skillful. Leaving the barn, I carry a sense of groundedness and practical focus that seems to improve even my driving. Tending sheep is a more symbiotic relationship than anything except perhaps motherhood. In some odd way I need these sheep to feel wholly myself.

We drenched about forty ewes and rams, quite large ones (eighty to three hundred pounds). I discovered that if I managed them in a small pen, I could control them easily (this being another operation where you sometimes have to sit on them). Drenching is an alternate deworming procedure; you suspend the vermifuge like an IV and slide the nozzle of the drench gun, which resembles a caulking gun, along the animal's tongue and insert it deep in its throat. Unpleasant as it sounds, the sheep don't seem to mind this much and it's a quick procedure. One squirt and off they go. It was relatively easy, and I proudly drenched most of the flock on my own while Ben went about his business.

Then I cleaned the shit off my pink high-tops and drove home, stopping for an espresso at the coffeehouse across from the college. Men and women were hunched over copies of Jean Paul Sartre and writing in their journals. Most wore the thin-rimmed tortoiseshell glasses favored by intellectuals. Their clothes were faded to a precisely fashionable degree: you can buy them that way from catalogs now, new clothes processed to look old. The intellectuals looked at me in my overalls the way such people inevitably look at farmers.

I dumped a lot of sugar in my espresso and sipped it delicately at a corner table near the door. I looked at them the way farmers look at intellectuals.

Choirs of Seraphim

Today I attempted my first solo shearing. Rather like the society hostess who broke a teacup to set her clumsy guest at ease, Ben nicked the demonstration animal five or six times before handing me the electric clippers. He told me he had cut the ears off two ewes yesterday and had to suture them back on. My first shearing took about an hour and left half an inch of wool all over the animal.

Next, with light, relentless rain beating on the corrugated iron roof of the barn, we accomplished step one of fixing the prolapsed rectum of ram #5004. First Ben cut the syringe casing with hoof trimmers and wrapped it in surgical tape so it would stick inside the sheep. The sheep's rectum, when we had him flipped over in the tipping cradle, protruded four inches. Ben slid the casing into the protrusion and banded it with the elastrator, a device we use for castrating. Then he squirted everything in sight with Betadine and gave the sheep 5 cc of penicillin in each glut. (The ram is also on cortisone to impact its coughing; we have to medicate these sheep a lot.)

Ben is going away for the weekend and leaving me in charge of feeding, chores, and ram #5004.

I have just finished reading *The Hot Zone,* a biomedical thriller about an outbreak of Ebola virus; while Ben, with no gloves on, paws around in the sheep, while rectal tissue flies all over and lands on my favorite overalls, I tell him about how viruses jump species.

"The blood of an infected monkey can be absorbed through the skin," I report, handing tools like a good surgical nurse.

"If I'd been gonna get it, I'd 'a got it," Ben drawls. This is his response to most of my hygienic proposals.

As we wash up in our minimalist way, in the same sink where Ben does dinner dishes and tosses the syringes to soak, I evoke rolling hills and farms, villages, and little cities of viruses all living on the head of a pin. Rolling around in an intricate dance. Choirs of microscopic seraphim.

I can see that my exhortation has gotten to him. "That God would allow that," he mutters. "It makes me wonder why I go to church."

On Call

I GOT TO THE BARN at eight-fifteen this morning, but Ben's new wife, Marge, had already done chores. She was waiting for me, the big sheep specialist, to inoculate #5004 with cortisone and penicillin. So I did. As we were herding the rams back into their pens, Marge picked up a revolting object. "What's this?"

"Whoops. That's #5004's butt plug." Obviously, he had coughed out the syringe casing.

"Ben will have to fix it on Sunday," Marge said.

A dangerous possibility loomed, however, which Ben had warned me about: that the ram could shuck his casing without getting rid of the elastrator band. The band would then strangulate the rectum and allow no egress for fecal material. "I'm afraid we'll have to fix it now, otherwise he'll be impacted by Sunday," I bravely told her.

Before he left, Ben had given me a lecture on retrieving the green rubber band by snicking it on the prongs of the elastrator and cutting it with a bandage scissors. (A blunt crochet hook would be the ideal instrument for this, and from now on, I'll never leave home without one.) I had listened to Ben's instructions with the attention one gives to stewardesses on transcontinental flights who drone about the remote possibility of a loss of cabin pressure: surely I will not be called upon to deal with this.

Ram #5004 is so vexed with us that he has thrown himself full tilt at the slats of the feeding bunk and wedged his head. This turns out to be a fine position for us to work on his bum. Marge bends down to look at the black fringe of necrotic tissue and says hopefully, "I think the band has slipped off."

"Marge, you are in denial." The laws of physics dictate, I believe, that the band—wound tight around the rectum—will have been sucked up *inside* the ram.

I slip my sensitive violinist's fingers into the sheep's anus (naturally we are out of surgical gloves), whisper a charm against anthrax, and feel for a tight rubber band. It's there, and it's easy to catch with the elastrator, easy to snip. I have, in effect, reversed Ben's earlier procedure but assured #5004 a comfortable weekend. We squirt the anus with bright yellow Furazolidone and leave behind a happy sheep.

Then we go into the kitchen and wash up. "I could never do what you just did," Marge tells me. Then the farm bravado kicks in. "I could if I had to."

"Sure you could." I wash in the kitchen sink for five minutes, then wash in the bathroom for five more. Then I go home and scrub my hands with bleach.

I have heard Ben say he fantasizes the stink of necrotic tissue all day. I believe it is not an hallucination but some mechanism of the biology of smell: pheromones or something remain on your body. All the bleach of Araby will not sweeten these little hands.

But at least these hands have been useful, for a change.

Nature

Ben came in this morning after being away since Friday to find one of the ram lambs dead—not the one we had been fussing over all weekend but one that had seemed perfectly healthy. We loaded it onto the pickup and Ben drove away to dispose of it at the medical waste facility, leaving me to feed the stock.

I double-check my work and tend to move slowly with the feeding, so by the time I was halfway down the barn the hungry old rams were in a snit. The biggest, whom we call Butthead, a three hundred fifty-pound ram with the face of a camel, managed to push through a wired gate and get out. I hurried to secure the doors so he wouldn't head down a freeway, or worse, turn over our huge delectable tank of molasses—then tried to get him back in the pen. By then, the other big rams were making their way out. I stuck my knee into the wedge they were coming through and got a painful compression bruise out of it as a big vasectomized ram pushed through. He got out and among the young rams, where a butting contest ensued. Bloody and panting, the old ram, who has bad lungs, had to cede.

By this time, Butthead had his face in the corn and was hard to deflect. Finally I maneuvered him into an unoccupied pen.

Ben's truck on the gravel. "Mary, can't I leave you alone for a minute?"

With one sheep dead, I have become more than usually observant of the actions of the rest. One of the rams was hunched over, moving convulsively. "Ben! Is that ram sick?"

"He's ejaculating, Mary."

I think I spent too much time in graduate school.

Buddhist tradition tells of a monk bathing in a river, where he comes upon a drowning scorpion. Tenderly he lifts the scorpion out of the water and the scorpion stings him savagely. The cycle of rescue and attack repeats itself as the monk tries to get the scorpion to shore before it kills him. The other monks try to intervene but, "He is acting according to his dharma," the monk tells them, "and so am I." The word *dharma* here means a kind of internal wisdom: what Quakers call the Light, or sometimes the Inner Teacher. There is an old saying, "Live up to the Light that thou hast and more will be given."

Last night when I checked the animals around dusk, two men were walking an unleashed husky near the pens. I hate huskies. Half the time a child or a small animal is attacked by a dog you'll find a husky in it: this is part of the rural Minnesota belief system.

"Last year," Ben told me, "a husky chased a ewe lamb straight to the end of the paddock, tore off her udder and ripped her vagina."

The owner refused to accept any responsibility, saying, "It's just her nature."

Ben went on, "If I see that owner around here again I'm going to rip his ass. It's my nature."

Acceptance of the Present

I T WAS LAST APRIL in the north of England, one of those moments when it felt like I'd been traveling for about thirteen
years, jazzed on homeopathic fright pills. I was telling myself that
yoga is at root a practice of acceptance: acceptance of the body from
moment to moment, day to day; people, situations, and events as
they occur. *Softening* to whatever comes. I was having these thoughts
while trying to surrender to a chilly bed in Birmingham, at a community where I was doing research. The mattress was the kind of
penitential hump with a ridge running down the middle that forces
you to deposit half of your body east and half of it west, divided
precisely in two lest one side overbalance and you slide to the floor.
The damp cold seeped into me as I lay watching the dark like a cat
at God's mousehole. Part of me delivered rational comfort: it will
be warm in a minute, I'll be asleep. Another part wailed, "There's
been a mistake! I've been buried alive in Birmingham, and this is
the cold of a deep grave I can't whine my way out of!"

Yoga mediates between these two voices. This moment is as it
should be. This moment is my teacher. If I struggle against this
moment, I struggle against the flow of the universe.

Finally I got out of bed and found my long underwear and a
stash of those overwashed community blankets that lie on you like
tacos, letting in drafts from all sides. I hoped the homeopathic fright
pills were specific for being buried alive. Then I slept or fell down
a coal chute till 5 A.M. truck traffic on the Bristol road committed

me to the day. The pillow jammed under my head repulsed me
with its smell of exotic hair oil, male and tropical. I pushed off the
hump and made for the shower. The water was lukewarm, and I
caught, shivering, the scent of a peculiarly British brand of disin-
fectant. Olfactory sensations go right to the glands of memory; I
was back in an English youth hostel, adventurous, displaced, and
twenty-four. On the skylight above me a spongy, plopping sound
began and I sensed the peculiar light of snow.

But I was not twenty-four, I was unstuck in time, and in a few
hours I was due to be in Manchester to meet the man who has been
the companion of my life for some fifteen years.

The one given me to love, I think, fondly—sometimes—when
he drops his socks on the floor. For to have someone to love is worth
the price of admission to life; not even Birmingham could shake
my soul on that point. Robin and I met in church, as Abby Van
Buren recommends, or rather at Quaker meeting. And then we met
again, singing. Both of us belong to a group that sings in a colonial
American tradition called Sacred Harp or shape note. In fact, it's
music business that brings Robin to England: he will be teaching
Sacred Harp singing to English choral groups and directing a national convention. Let me try to give you a picture of how strange
it will be to transplant this raucous, unsubtle music into the ironic
idiom of British choral singers.

Bound for Canaan

YOU CAN HEAR the singing at a Sacred Harp convention twelve blocks away, I'm told. My children say twelve blocks isn't far enough—*death metal folk,* they call it. For my part, I think it sounds best when you are standing in the middle of the hollow square, with one hundred fifty singers around you in full voice.

Sacred Harp, or shape note singing, comes out of a religious music tradition going back to early New England singing schools. If you look into the big red Sacred Harp songbook that Robin and I carry with us everywhere, you may think you're looking at medieval chant, because the music is notated in triangles, circles, and squares (hence "shape note"); each shape represents a note in a modified solfège system. Sacred Harp was devised to teach music quickly to those unaccustomed to sight-singing and it contains, in contrast to the usual do-re-mi system, only four syllables (fa-so-la-mi). Unlike chant, the music is polyphonic and unsubtle; its conventions, indeed, are unlike any mainstream Western tradition. Singers belt out the pieces at full volume, singing first the shapes, then the texts; academic musicians often tell me contemptuously that it contradicts everything they were ever taught. Maybe that's because it's not precisely—or not only—music. It has elements of religion, therapy, sport, and catharsis.

How does one describe a sound? "Death metal folk" is one attempt. I've heard it called "white gospel" by those trying to get across the flavor (though black people sing it, too). It has a medieval feeling in its minor tonalities, its resonant fourths and fifths. "Wondrous Love"—a song that often makes its way into modern hymnals— is a typical Sacred Harp piece. If you've heard William Billings's eighteenth-century American music, you've heard a bit of the shape note style—though probably not at the volume and level of idiosyncrasy that characterize a Southern country "singing." For it was in the rural South that this music survived, often in Primitive Baptist communities where, today, the average singer is likely to be over sixty. It reflects a religion so fierce and elemental that its only other objective correlative (alternate Sundays) might be snake handling.

The conventions of Sacred Harp singing are many and subtle. I don't know what goes on in other sections—treble, tenor, and bass: I can only describe the contours of my alto world. Altos need to be big (in some physical or metaphysical sense) and loud; they tend to squabble over the front row of seats. Singers sit in squares, by section, facing a song leader who stands in the middle. Conducting a song—which any member of the group may do—is something of a collaboration between the one who has gotten up to lead and the front-bench singers. The front benchers are responsible for keeping the beat, roaring out the part, and communicating, by means of some psychic energy, the song leader's intentions. These singers are not appointed, anointed, or elected: they assume their places with a sense of *noblesse oblige.*

In a weekly singing group, rank is barely discriminated. Strong singers, responsible for carrying the part, tend to head for the front seats, but at weekly meetings, a beginner may sit up front without incurring the wrath of some senior alto. At a regional convention, by contrast, confident indeed would be the new singer who seated herself in the front row, unless she were simply, as I was at my first convention, ignorant of the forms. Many singers have national reputations and carry themselves with the dignity of *majas.* A southerner at a Yankee convention would always have pride of place, of course. Or an elderly singer, even if the voice is gone.

Still, an innocent youngster may break for the first row, perhaps assuming that newcomers learn better in front of a rank of good singers; this reasonable assumption happens to violate Sacred Harp etiquette. By the first coffee break, she will realize—something deep inside will tell her—that she must take a lower place.

❦

I had come late to my first big Midwest convention, back in the 1980s, and took the only chair available: row six. A steady row-two singer at home, I wanted to get a little closer to the front. Returning from lunch, I saw that a vacancy had opened in the middle of row one. Tempting, but out of my league. Still, most of the other singers had already taken their places . . .

"Does anyone want this chair?" I ask humbly, for humility becomes my station: a slight presence among these goddess altos. People seem to smile encouragement, so I place my big red book on the first-row chair.

There is a tense silence.

Then a great voice soars from the area of the coffee machine. *"Oh,* are you going to take that place? I suppose I should have put my book on the chair."

She is a tall, hawk-nosed, red-haired woman in ebony silk; she is from Detroit. Waters of treble part before her as she sounds. I leap to my small feet. "Do you want this place?"

"There are some very strong singers here." It is blackly spoken. High Noon on the alto range. But she chooses to toy with me. "Maybe you'd like to switch at the break?"

"Sure," I say, but my submissive whinny goes unheard as the

front-row singer next to me rises and cedes her own place to the alto from Detroit. The psychic space she requires scrunches me up against the bass section.

Her voice is a great dark bell. There will be no contest here, such as contentious tenors might engage in. Certainly no splendid entente, as when two mighty altos play off each other. She will simply punish, vanquish, and destroy me with sound, like that poor pickpocket caught in the ringing of *The Nine Tailors*.

> Lord, when thou didst ascend on high
> Ten thousand angels filled the sky.
> Those heav'nly guards around thee wait
> Like chariots that attend thy state.

The piece—a great collaboration between Isaac Watts and William Billings—has lots of wild ornamentation and the leader is taking it at warp speed. Sight-reading, I miss notes and fuguing entrances. The Detroit alto runs over me like an earth mover; she sings every shape no matter how fast the runs, how strange the rhythm—none of your la-la-la cheating.

One of our tenors, renowned for giving out the opening pitches, gets up to lead.

> Will God forever cast us off?
> His wrath forever smoke?
> Against the people of his love,
> His little chosen flock?

This is meat for his little chosen altos, lots of big round fifths. We claim our ground. The leader smiles at me as he cues our side. "I think we have not heard as much as you can give," that tenor once said to me.

No prophet speaks to calm our grief,
But all in silence mourn;
Nor know the hour of our relief
The hour of thy return.

I give it away.

I did not always have this alto voice. Does that sound like the beginning of a folktale? It came about in this way. Seven years ago, my dad died after a long illness. He was a great tenor—though he always complained that the Air Force had ruined his voice by making him yell too much—who used to stand in the front doorway on summer evenings and sing "Jerusalem" for the edification of Roseville. Music meant a lot to him; in the course of his last illness, he chose his funeral music with precision and one of the songs he wanted was "Amazing Grace." In the end, however, the priest wouldn't allow it. "It's a Protestant song," he told us. My sister and I didn't fight the decision. My dad had wanted a lot of things from us: that we be ladies, and sopranos, and married, and Catholic. Here we were, failing him again.

Public occasions in our family tend to tumble into black comedy. For starters, the undertaker had to explain to us, with a great deal of pausing and shuffling, that there seemed to be no place to bury my father. One of our relatives had gotten hold of the deed to the family plot at Calvary and sold it. So, on short notice, we had to take dad out to the national cemetery. In the end, he fell back into the arms of the Air Force. My sister and I got out of the funeral limousine, teetering on our unaccustomed high heels, and were surprised to meet five old men in uniform with rifles on their shoulders.

"Do something," my Quaker children whispered.

"Don't make a scene," said my mother. Across dad's slick blue cadillac of a coffin, my son caught my eye: his look said, *give it away.* By then, guys in jets were staging a screaming flyover, veterans of my father's generation, maybe, or young pilots getting a day's pay.

It's hard to sing "Amazing Grace" over five jets and a volley of rifle fire. But that's the way I got my alto, and thank God for the brave cousins who came in before I crashed in flames. Before that I had—to quote one of my choir directors—"a very little voice." My dad, smitten with sound, had tried to remedy my weakness with singing lessons, but the music chosen for instruction embarrassed me into diffident trilling. It was all romance and foolishness. At some level back then I was longing for a good wailing Sacred Harp text:

> Must death forever rage and reign
> Or hast thou made mankind in vain?

A question worth answering, a song worth singing out the front door. But my music teacher offered twittering madrigals and something about how, in Italy, in Italy, the oranges hang on the tree. He treated me—the humiliation of it—as a soprano.

These, by contrast, are the six elements of a Sacred Harp alto: rage, darkness, motherhood, earth, malice, and sex. Once you feel it, you can always do it. You know where to go for it, though it will cost you.

In Sacred Harp we are always singing for our fathers, our mothers, our lost. We altos hug the ground, splay out our legs, and cry from the belly; we are suspect even among our own. "I can't sing next to one of *them*," complains a pretty treble, moving down the square.

> And did He rise? Did He rise?
> Hear it ye nations, hear it all ye dead!

They can't miss it. The trebles—who sing a descant line composed of ecstasy, light, purity, jet contrails, and self-surrender—
have by now burst the bonds of earth. They will all call in sick on
Monday.

An old singer has come up from Alabama for our convention
and tells us how southerners feel about Sacred Harp. "This is not
pretty music," he says. "The people who first sang it had hard
lives." Did the music make them feel better, I wonder, did it provide a metaphoric encounter with plague, starvation, mania, and
passion? An encounter they could win, until the voice broke?
Sometimes I leave the singings exhausted, sometimes energized
for days, occasionally scared. Is it something about the breathing?
Something Zen? Is it that music affects your synapses? I'm told
that listening to Mozart makes you smarter. I'm told that when
some communities of Catholic monks stopped chanting plainsong
in the wake of Vatican II, they began to suffer depression and
lethargy.

After dinner—a two-hour banquet of fried chicken and meat-
balls and pie (tofu available on request)—we stop for the Memorial
Lesson, remembering those who have died that year. Midwesterners
are a new community, mostly under forty years old. We have only
Winston's grandmother to remember. The southerners, by contrast,
have a long list and sad stories. Harper, who gave out the opening
pitches, has passed on. Harper who never looked up and you better
be ready. . . . A child has been run over by a car. A girl who had a
twin sister . . .

> I'm fettered and chained up in clay;
> I struggle and pant to be free:
> I long to be soaring away . . .

Moved perhaps by the Memorial Lesson, the mighty alto from Detroit inclines to me. "Where you're confident," she says, "you can hold your own."

The day after the convention, sitting at my bedroom window in a kind of crystalline exhaustion, tears spring as a phrase, merely, goes through my mind: "O had I wings, I would fly away and be at rest."

Singing this music is something like what I think psychologists call "abreaction"—when they flood the system with psychoactive drugs or stab a probe into the lizard brain or do whatever they do to cause a complete reorganization and downloading of the mental systems. The singing over, we drop like birds who have been buffeted to the edge of the oxygen zone. We have barely escaped with our lives.

In those days, I was beginning to go home with that tenor famous for his pitches—Robin, it was. We would part awhile, then start singing for each other across the room, then get to the point where promises were made: "When you're dying, I'll sing for you. . . . If you get dementia, I'll prop you up in the square."

Once on the Saturday night of a weekend convention we went home and climbed into bed, and I said, "Tell me something about your father."

"He had a childlike, transforming smile. He was very gentle, he always did what he promised. He wasn't interested in any material thing. His graduate students loved him. A week before he died he had a vision of animals walking in a circle. He was profoundly, strikingly gifted. He died on Christmas Eve. . . ."

Then we cried, the music breaks you open so.

I also love Gregorian chant, which I sang daily for two years in a convent community trained by a monk from Solesmes. But this music is the precise opposite. Plainsong is safer, though not safe. It stations itself on a wide plain at the edge of the abyss. Standing patiently in the comprehensible world, it weaves a daily net of attention. Wise music. Sacred Harp, by contrast, flings itself over the edge. Driven by the relentless rhythm, the singers spend themselves. "O Canaan, Sweet Canaan! We're bound for the land of Canaan—" we shriek, giving it, giving everything. We are caught up in a fury of dispossession, for immolating ourselves. We reiterate at full volume the impossible: "I'll fly—"

Well, we won't. We waken on the Monday after a convention, thirty hours of singing, stunned to see that the sun has risen, that we have to teach school, sell cars.

I'm four pounds lighter on the scale.

The Shelagh

IN BRITAIN, wailing and praying out loud are not on the daily menu, and we were not sure how our music would be received. Yet the British singers, too, give it all away. I say this with respect and diffidence, not affirming some vulgar public catharsis, but rather an elemental artistic event, close in spirit to what Federico Garcia Lorca called "Deep Song." "These black sounds," Lorca wrote, "are the mystery, the roots fastened in the mire that we all know and all ignore, the mire that gives us the very substance of art." Mostly in music we husband our resources, color within the annotated lines; we have to live to sing another day. One of my teachers wrote me a note once, during a concert: "Don't put all your musicality into every phrase—" That was one of my most important artistic lessons, and the one most quickly forgotten, especially in the hollow square. Lorca speaks of the singer who in extremity can but tear the voice, there is no other option; she must search out "the marrow of forms, pure music with a body so lean it could stay in the air." This is what he famously calls the *duende*. It may not be a loud moment; perhaps it is encompassed within a pure chord, when the shell of a human seems to open and slide as if it were made for that.

Once, in a dream, my father came to visit me from the country of death. "What is God like?" I asked him. He said, "The condition of music." In the waning hours after singing, you can see on the faces of the British singers the look of people coming slowly back from a struggle with the soul.

It's now a couple of weeks into our trip to England, and Robin and I are trying out the interval of a fourth in an abandoned eleventh-century Romanesque church on the Welsh border. The night before we had tested the acoustics of a sea cave on the Cardigan coast: it's an obsession singers have, I guess, or people who find God in harmonic progressions.

What puzzles us more than the resonances of the little church are the pagan carvings around its eave, or corbel. I use the word *pagan* as advisedly as I use the word *God,* for I've talked in my time to many people who kneel in odd spaces, like the lady in Deer Park, Wisconsin, who receives the Blessed Virgin on the off-channels of her TV. For my part, I used to feel quite comfortable among the Guatemalan Indians who went to Mass on Sunday, then burned offerings to the Mayan gods on the church steps. It made sense to me; my religious nature is omnivorous. I can worship just about anything that occupies a certain slant of light. *Pray always*—the old injunction goes—and, it must follow, *to anything.*

This little church was built by Celts with a similar—perhaps progenitive—religious imagination to mine. We discover a "green man" disappearing into stonework fretted like the illustrations in the Lindisfarne Gospels. Over the main door is carved a horse surmounted by a cross. A guidebook, written by the former vicar, identifies it as an "Agnus Dei," but I know lambs too well to mistake them for horses; I'm pretty sure the horse is a symbol for the Celtic goddess Rhiannon. These were folk, who like the Guatemalan Indians, knew how to hedge their bets.

Given this sensibility, what are we to make of the corbel carvings? There are men falling from the sky, male figures embracing. Who can they be? Lovers? Choirboys? A number of carvings represent various occupations and trades, but no coherent thread links them, no story I know. Here's a story I do know: a representation of a squatting woman with her legs spread, swollen genitals, a wild smile on her face, and a distinctly *alto* quality. Obviously she has just given birth—perhaps the icon is simply an advertisement for the local eleventh-century midwife. The guidebook says I'm wrong. She's identified as "an erotic female figure," the Shelagh-na-gig who so often turns up in ancient Irish architecture.

I suspect the scholars are wrong about Shelagh. Men, even genteel male clerics like the one who wrote our guidebook, tend to see a woman's genital presentation only as it affects them. But I do not think this figure would puzzle a woman from traditional culture, used to giving birth in a reasonable squat, with hands clasped around her knees to help the womb open. I'm not an art historian, but I am a needleworker, and I know that stylized versions of this same figure occur in the weaving and embroidery of most indigenous cultures. Ukrainian girls, for example, used to work a version of it on the bed curtains they sewed for their dower chests.

Some feminists have tried to reclaim the Shelagh as a "goddess figure," but I don't think traditional women made such a separation between the sacred and the profane. How did such icons come to be? It seems natural that a pregnant woman, thinking about her swelling body and the ordeal to come, would fashion for herself an image of happy birth—or her mother would make it, or her husband, or the local midwife—and her fingers would return to it for reassurance and her eyes would want to seek it on the corbel of the church where the hopes of all the village gathered. I wonder if ancient worship was not all "natural" in this way. Things go well or badly without explanation, but our humble vision of a good outcome (call it prayer) turns the will of time.

This religious expression seems organic and logical to me. These people knew many faces of God and did not trouble their minds with theologizing and the agonies of "belief."

British singers—confronted by the radical presence of Sacred Harp texts—will sometimes shyly ask if we're "believers," Robin and I. It's a hard question. Often, as soon as someone says, "I believe in God" or "I don't believe in God," I fear that I will not be able to talk deeply to that person. The fierce, unyielding word *believe* suggests—though not inevitably—that such a person views the issue within an analytical frame that is relatively meaningless to me. It is "believers" who so often take an uncompromising and fundamentalist position as though to defend the wheels and cogs and flysprings of their mental processes. Yet in the last few days, people have opened their hearts to me with just this bashful phrase. Perhaps it is more an incantation than a theological query.

Certainly I believe whatever I am singing for exactly as long as I'm singing it.

> Show my forgetful feet the way
> That leads to joys on high,
> Where knowledge grows without decay
> And love shall never die.

Thus Robin and I were wailing away in the middle of a deserted Welsh forest. We like the last two lines so well that we bawl them out again: *and love shall never die!* Suddenly about fifteen Welsh people materialize out of their hidden fastnesses and begin to applaud. But what they are clapping for, I don't know—perhaps, being Welsh, the interval of a fourth.

Knowing God is rather like experiencing a deer by her scent, when she has passed before you a moment earlier on the trail. I know a woman in Vancouver who can sense bears this way. The experience of God is that subtle and that destabilizing: deer or bear? One crosses into the woods warily and tries to make a lot of noise.

Ordinary Time

W HILE ROBIN AND I were in England, Ben got the results of
the ram lamb's postmortem, which showed hemophilus
pneumonia, and, now that I am back, we are puzzling over what,
if anything, to treat the others with.

The last two days I've been doing morning barn chores by myself. I love to be outside in the early light, the pasture covered in
mist. This morning as I brought corn out to the ewe lambs behind
the shed, two big sheep bashed me from behind and pushed me
against the feeder, then stuck their heads into the metal interstices,
pinning me by the leg. I had to lean on them and push with all my
might. Then I climbed to freedom by crawling across a shelf of
wooly backs. These animals try all kinds of things with me they
wouldn't try with Ben. It's hard to boss the big lambs while carrying two buckets, seventeen pounds of corn each, and keeping noses
out of it till I get across the pasture to the feeding station.

We have twelve skinny white-faced Polypay ewes in the barn
setting up a racket, running their thin pale tongues out and bleating madly. They're being weaned from their lambs. They get
nothing but hay for forty-eight hours—no corn, no water. Tears
rise to my eyes as I deal with these animals, caught in the ordinary
suffering of life. Sentimental? Yes, but you see, my youngest
daughter, Julian, is going away to college next week, and I feel
all too keenly the plight of these bereft ewes. Ben and I call them
"the church ladies." With their fringe of white perms and incessant

vocalization, they remind us of a certain stalwart type of Lutheran woman.

This morning when I came in, I was surprised to discover two Simmental heifers, a cow and her calf (the kind of French-looking beef stock painted by Rosa Bonheur) grazing behind the barn. And several handsome Suffolks as well as a beautiful Dorset ram, just washed. Today's job was to "show shear" and wash these animals for a judging up north.

As I was feeding, a sudden violent storm came up, the barn lights went on, and rain crashed on the tin roof. The cows with their deep low seemed to be trying to pacify the ewes, still running skinny tongues out over their perfectly spaced and false-looking teeth in a panic of bleating. The wall of rain slid between us and the city; we had become the barn at the end of the world. All the animals, myself included, quieted down like a congregation hearing bells.

In the lambing barn, where at this season we usually park our cars, Ben had the beautiful Dorset ram lamb up on the fit stand, currying it. With their white poll, short ears, and stocky bodies, Dorsets look like the lambs Polish people mold out of butter: the kind depicted in church windows with a victory flag under the right front hoof, the kind of which D. H. Lawrence wrote, "I like lambs too much to have them stand for something."

Sweeping

I HAD DRIVEN THROUGH another thunderstorm blown up out of the relentless humidity, sheets of water flooding into the north end of the barn as I arrived. The outdoor sheep were lurking in their sheds, looking like extras from a Christmas crèche. Even Butthead, even the ever starving Polypay ewes, seemed subdued as I rationed out corn and soybean mix and freshened the hay. The ewe lambs in the pasture get thirty-two pounds of corn divided between two metal feeders, but the feeders were full of water. I couldn't dump it all out; I wasn't strong enough to lift the bunks, so the sheep had to tough each other out at one feeder.

Frost, the barn cat, came along for a ride on the hay cart as I worked inside. She is a focused killer who regularly swipes birds out of the air.

Sweeping the floor is one of my chores.

This is how it went: first, the broom annoyed me and I began to analyze and comment to myself on its nasty plastic American uselessness. Next, I began to fantasize how a good old-fashioned broom would sweep that barn clean. I carefully considered the possibility of getting psittacosis from the dust of pigeon shit. I lamented that seventy feet of the barn remained to be swept. A third of the way into the task, as about a third of the way into a Zen session, I thought I would have to quit or snap: that is the edge you always have to lean against. Then I began to get into a rhythm and a swish of sound that pleased me, and at the same time I became more efficient. Halfway down the barn rose another temptation to get off the zafu: I'm tired, fifty feet is enough, my shoulders ache, it doesn't look any cleaner than when I started, why am I doing this? I could be cooking dinner, playing music. Does this even need to be done?

I lean on my rotten broom and think: I am paying good money to sweep this barn with a lousy broom. I have paid eighty dollars in tuition for an independent study in animal science, much as I might pay eighty dollars at the Zen Center to experience the discipline of silence and manual work, to clear my mind of ideas, most of them wrong. The silence, now the rain has stopped, is worth the tuition. Pacified by hay, water, and corn, the animals are lying down and breathing as calmly as bodhisattvas.

I go back to my broom. How Ben would laugh at my inexorable patient sweeping. I have not earned much in my life, but I have earned this work, the right to sweep patiently.

Thus I thought while trying to let go of thought, and then for one sweep of the broom I was not thinking.

Is It Necessary to Have a Plow?

TㅎIS MORNING I sheared a Suffolk ewe with a bad attitude. I still have a hard time catching sheep, never mind shearing them. I chased four ewes around the pen for half an hour until suddenly one went down on its knees in the corner, terrified not by me but by the sound of Ben on his Bobcat cleaning out the pens at the north end of the barn. Even at that, I could not get her onto the stand. Ben had to strap her in for me. But I managed to shear her without taking off any body parts. I few weeks ago Ben asked me to paint a sign for the sheep barn at the state fair and I have been working at that back home on my kitchen table. Today I discovered that hours spent drawing sheep paid off in practical knowledge of what curves lay under the wool: it improved my shearing.

I took her off the stand and she booked away, jumped the fence, and tore off down the pasture. I spent the next hour trying to head her out and pen her again. A huge Simmental bull residing in the barn for the state fair watched us with an expression of vast disdain.

Ben, interested in all trades, wants to know why I'm a writer. "What do you write about?" he asks as we curry another lovely Dorset.

What did Montaigne say? "Myself." Writing essays, writing poetry, is a solipsistic occupation, much harder to justify than sheep farming. But I wanted to answer Ben's question as conscientiously as he answers mine. Our lives and backgrounds have brought us to different choices, but we're transacting the same private business, he and I. At the beginning of *Terre des Hommes,* Antoine de Saint-Exupery says, "A man discovers himself when he measures himself against an obstacle. But, in order to pay attention, he has to have a tool, a plow or . . ." a Bobcat or a pen. "Just now, I'm writing about work, and how people experience their lives spiritually," I said.

"Why?"

"Well, in a way, to get a grip on what I feel and know. It's only after I've written about something that I see patterns, bring things to light." In one of her poems, "The Chance to Love Everything," Mary Oliver speaks of something outside her tent, "pressing inward at eye level." Strange and mysterious things press on the tent of consciousness. I want to bring them in where I can love them, or at least acknowledge them mine.

Comb. Comb. Comb. Farming is one of the few remaining reflective occupations. It's inward, solitary, and yet social. "If they don't do chores together, how does a man talk to his boys?" wondered my friend Conor, a dairy farmer with a small herd. After he said that to me, I went home and got rid of the dishwasher (somewhat to the chagrin of my children). When I look for an image of the writer's life, I remember Conor on his knees in the dairy barn, his long listening look as he monitored the milking machine. Writing would be merely an act of crazy hubris were it not a means of discovery, cunning and patient.

"What if I carve some speed lines in this guy's wool, or maybe the barn logo?" I wanted to know.

"I'd say, if you do that we'll lose show points."

Chaos

Today the barn was in chaos when I got there at eight-fifteen. Half the pens had been cleaned out and all the west side sheep were on the east side, a number of wethers were missing, and some odd faces peered out here and there. Butthead, in his fancy Sam Browne belt, had been put in with the ewes and was looking unusually pleased with himself. The ram's belt, or mating harness, contains an oily red chalk, called raddle, which marks the ewes when he mounts them. This ancient system helps us keep track of the revels and predict our lambing schedule—it's hard to tell when sheep are pregnant because most of the lamb's growth occurs in the last three months. I could see that our happy Butthead had done his duty by these raddled ewes.

One of the vasectomized rams, by contrast, was in ill humor and kept trying to get behind me as I crossed the pasture to check water. I would be walking sturdily along, then sense an air current behind me. As soon as I turned, the ram would stop and look as innocent as any politician. Then I'd walk ahead and he'd charge.

This morning, it was taking me forever to mix feed, because I was not sure of what the plan was. Giving out the wrong feed is no small mistake when we're fattening lambs for market, drying up ewes, etc.

Finally around nine-thirty Ben came in, madder than hops from a meeting with the auditors. They want the barn to become financially self-sustaining, despite the fact that Ben's superb management has retired a colossal debt from earlier years. "Where does the money go?" Ben wants to know.

"Lots of administrators sitting around playing with themselves," I confide. It's rare that I know something he doesn't know. "They have meetings and devise projects that they then need to have more meetings to talk about, though most of the projects are unnecessary, destructive, and show no common sense."

Ben gives a disheartened snicker. Ben is a real person doing real things, at the mercy of unreal people doing unreal things.

It reminds me of teaching, a job I used to do long ago.

Later we played an elaborate game of "Run, Sheep, Run" all over the pastures, rounding up a bunch of ewes we are getting ready to breed. They have to be dewormed, inoculated, and fed with "weigh back"—a mixture of corn, silage, hay, soybeans, and nutritional supplements we get from the dairy barn after it has been processed through the cow stalls. The idea is to get the ewes into the best possible condition for bearing their young. Luring them in from the pasture was half the battle, since they were perfectly happy to remain there. Inside, penning thirty Hampshire ewes meant repenning a number of other sheep, none of them in favor of our plan. In the process, half the outdoor sheep had jumped the inside fence following their friend the vasectomized ram. Vasectomized rams are put in with the ewes in order to make them start cycling, then removed (to their chagrin) when the breeding ram (e.g., Butthead) goes in to do his work. You can imagine what the vasectomized ram thinks about this and how it affects his temper. His is one of those weird karmas; it's like being a eunuch in a harem.

When Ben calls the sheep, he croons to them with the same call I've heard Yorkshire farmers use: "Com'la', Com'la'."

He instructs me on the nuances of sheep language. "Don't say 'go!' to them," he chides. "They don't know that word. They know *Hai!* They know *OK!* They know *Hai-up, you goddam sonsa bitches!*"

"I see."

"Those words are for *driving before*. Com'la' is for *calling in*."

Animal songs, like lullabies and clapping rhymes, must be among the oldest sounds in the language. Every man must invent his own love-talk but speaks a common dialect to his animals: "Co'boss! Sooey!" These words, a linguist once told me, can be traced back to the time of Beowulf.

After we penned the ewes, we drenched them with vermifuge and shot them up with anti-overeating medicine. Without this medicine, sheep, if they happen to get their noses into some illegitimate corn, will eat themselves to death. Hand under the muzzle again for control, shoot, drench, mark with orange chalk. Bye for now, she's jumped the outer fence and headed back for the pasture. "Don't shoot too near the spinal cord," Ben cautions, "or I'll make you take her home in a wheelchair."

I'm never happier than when biting off the cap of a syringe and giving shots or performing some minor surgery, simply because I'm competent at it. I suppose this is why doctors get into trouble performing unnecessary procedures: the good of the patient can be overshadowed by the pleasures of craft.

Space

THERE IS A BENCH in the back of my garden shaded by
Virginia creeper, climbing roses, and a white pine where I
sit early in the morning and watch the action. Light blue bells of
a dwarf campanula drift over the rock garden just before my eyes.
Behind it, a three-foot stand of aconite is flowering now, each dark
blue cowl-like corolla bowed for worship or intrigue: thus its common name, monkshood. Next to the aconite, black madonna lilies
with their seductive Easter scent are just coming into bloom. At
the back of the garden, a hollow log, used in its glory days for
a base to split kindling, now spills white cascade petunias and
lobelia.

I can't get enough of watching the bees and trying to imagine
how they experience the abundance of, say, a blue campanula blos-
som, the dizzy light pulsing, every fiber of being immersed in the
flower. "No intention," as John Cage said of his music, or nothing
but intention.

A wren dropped and died here last night, while I was pruning
roses: a chick who couldn't get the knack of flight. It lay in the dirt,
shaking wings that ought to have gotten it airborne, but didn't. I
lifted it into a part of the garden where it would be safe from cats
and where I wouldn't have to watch it die.

Last night, after a day in the garden, I asked Robin to explain
(again) photosynthesis to me. I can't take in this business of *eating
light* and turning it into stem and thorn and flower . . .

I would not call this meditation, sitting in the back garden. Maybe I would call it eating light. Mystical traditions recognize two kinds of practice: *apophatic mysticism,* which is the dark surrender of Zen, the Via Negativa of John of the Cross, and *kataphatic mysticism,* less well defined: an openhearted surrender to the beauty of creation. Maybe Francis of Assisi was, on the whole, a kataphatic mystic, as was Thérèse of Lisieux in her exuberant moments: but the fact is, kataphatic mysticism has low status in religious circles. Francis and Thérèse were made, really made, any mother superior will let you know, in the dark nights of their lives: no more of this throwing off your clothes and singing songs and babbling about the shelter of God's arms.

When I was twelve and had my first menstrual period, my grandmother took me aside and said, "Now your childhood is over. You will never really be happy again." That is pretty much how some spiritual directors treat the transition from kataphatic to apophatic mysticism.

But, I'm sorry. I'm going to sit here every day the sun shines and eat this light. Hung in the bell of desire.

Barn Talk

There is a rhythm to barn conversation. You speak a few sentences. Then you have to be quiet for ten minutes, throw some straw around, and think about it. People new to Minnesota think this is evidence of our stupidity, but I think it signals a natural contemplative bent.

"What religion are you, Mary?" Ben asked one day.

"Quaker."

Ben laughed. Then he turned red and bashful. "You're not kidding."

"Nope."

"I didn't know Quakers were still around, except, you know . . ."

"Uh huh. Cereal. Motor oil."

"Heck of a deal."

"Uh huh. Imagine Catholic puffed rice."

"I thought Quakers wore funny clothes."

"Some might say they do." Ben is always making fun of the denim jumpers that cover me like a tent while I change into my overalls in our unisex locker room. "Bet you're a Lutheran," I say to him.

"Missouri Synod."

Religion is one of our big topics, along with marriage, child rearing, where you can get secondhand clothes, and of course every aspect of animal husbandry and sheep gossip.

Ben's brother Tom has brought his beautiful Simmental heifers in for the state fair. The bull, with his leery rolling eye, hangs out in the far southeast pen. Last night (Ben told me) he escaped and climbed halfway up the baled hay in the shed. The sheep who are going to the fair have been washed, shorn, and covered in red and blue tabards—decked out as for a medieval pageant.

In the afternoon, I helped Ben shear a couple of rams.

"Tom saw a terrible accident coming in on the freeway," he told me. "Someone had a heart attack during rush hour and went out of control. Another car rammed him from behind and a cattle truck shot over the top and the whole thing burst into flames."

Wool is slipping off the ram's flank in a smooth bat under my clippers. "Are the animals all right?"

"Only one broken leg," replies Ben.

Later Hank came in and Ben retold the story. "Animals all right?" Hank wanted to know.

"Yup. One broken leg. It was on the ten o'clock news. Did you see it, Mary?"

"Can't watch TV. The girls have burned it out watching *Days of Our Lives*. Now we can't get any reception at all. We're wondering about what happened to Hope."

Ben chains a big ram into the fit stand. "Hope got back her memories, but then Bo asked her for a divorce because he's still in love with Billy, the one he married after Hope was killed and before she came back from the dead. Sammy had an accident and dreamed she had the abortion. Oil your clippers, Mary. I can hear 'em running slow. . . . I don't think she wants the abortion. She's just tormenting Austin. Would you catch me that ram with the shaggy head, Mary, and try not to just chase it till it goes down on its knees. That stresses them."

"Why do they go down on their knees anyway?"

"Because they're sheep—"

"And we're not."

Normal Suffering

J UDE TURNED HIS HEAD and shot me his characteristic look of
canny intelligence ready-to-be-amused. He was a few minutes
old and looking at me from a glass box next to the delivery table.
That gaze remained distinctive, accentuated by the glasses he had
to wear from the age of thirteen months.

I had married foolishly in the world's terms but wisely in the
heart's economy. We were broke and struggling the whole nineteen-
year course of the marriage; it was a traveling circus, and we were
tumblers in love. Jude was born in a big Catholic hospital ward full
of teenage moms who talked on the phone incessantly in Spanish.
When the priest came to give communion, they would simply turn
their heads away from the phones, stick out their tongues for the
wafer, and go back to the conversation. Jobless and without prospects
in that tight economy, we went to live with my husband's family,
sharing a room with the two youngest of the ten children. In a few
weeks, however, we were able to move into our new home, a converted school bus. And the circus rolled on.

Julian was born into a situation of more security. My sister, a
nurse midwife, delivered her. The birth—in contrast to our first
main ring event—had been contemplative and private, and she
was a quiet baby who would spend hours turning and watching
her own long fingers in the air.

We'd lived in Maine, in a fishing community, after Jude's birth,
surrounded by men in waders fighting and cutting each other's float

lines. Without any women to tell me how to mother, I got my advice from Jane Goodall's books on chimpanzees, which I was reading at the time. Chimps seemed to hold and nurse their babies a lot, and as a result the young ones grew up brave and independent. I settled on this as a philosophy. Our children never suffered separation anxiety: it was *I* who balked at every stage of their leaving home.

"And *she will not be here.* That's all I can think about: not how much space I'll have in the house, or how I'll be free to travel. She will not be here," I am sobbing to Peter on the phone.

My friend Peter Crysdale and I, over ten years ago, entered into a relationship that we called "spiritual companioning." We agreed to talk to each other twice a week, like crotchety old desert abbas and ammas, about our spiritual lives. We might have consulted a priest or nun, but we felt too imperfect and we had too much to say about sex. Both of us were living, at the time, in a Quaker community called Pendle Hill, near Philadelphia, where people came (and still do come) to deepen their spiritual lives.

Even though Peter and I have moved five hundred miles from each other, the conversations go on, as we try to decode for each other the ways of spirit.

"You will be able to have a beautiful relationship with your daughter now—" Peter tells me. "College changes everything."

"But she will not be here." Her size twelve shoes will not lie in the doorway, her beautiful profile will not lean over a book, her long fingers will not touch my face in kindness or condescension. She will not leave corn on her plate, sleep till one, neglect her housework, steal my sweaters and poetry books. Her leaving looms like an engagement at the hospital, a surgery from which one may not awaken or not awaken as oneself.

I am distracted with grief, like the church ladies, those silly ewes who do not know we're taking care of them, that we have their good at heart. I am incessantly bleating.

"She's setting you free. You will be able to live any life you choose," Peter tells me.

For one day after the lambs go, the ewes are inconsolable. The next day they bleat less and in a week they have forgotten their own young. But human beings suffer relentlessly for what is lost. Before and after the marriage ended, our house was always full of people—relatives, loose kids, exchange students. Even Julian, while I was in England, "adopted." She phoned me in London: "Jane's coming to live with us. The social worker said OK."

But now the house is a shell and I am a hermit crab. Martha is married and living in Portland, Jude works for a company in New York, Carolina and Zoe write only at Christmas, Jane's mattress is stowed under a bed. Only the current Japanese student remains, a quiet girl who bides in her room.

I have tried to reason with myself. It's foolish to fuss over a giddy girl packing for college. But perhaps I'm also in mourning for my own life. She will not be here, and therefore I will not be here, either. Without her, who will I be? Who will I care for? And where is the "we of me"?

Endangered Species

THE POET OLGA BROUMAS recalls Gary Snyder saying, "The most difficult discipline is that of following your own desires."

The day after Julian left, I drove down to Decorah, Iowa, and visited a farm engaged in preserving rare animal species: not, in this case, snail darters and whistling swans, but pigs and cows and chickens. Selective breeding, such as we do to get more and better meat, militates against biodiversity. We forget that what's genetically important today may be worthless tomorrow. We forget that animals are not put on earth merely to suffer our manipulations. Such breeding often yields at the end an inferior product, ill-adapted to slight changes in agricultural practice—cows, for example, who upon being invited to rotational grazing, cannot physically endure the walk from barn to pasture. So the Decorah farmers raise mule-foot hogs, Navaho Churro sheep, Jacob's sheep, and Fjord horses—sturdy old beasts who look like studies for a Flemish painting.

The word *farm* still calls up in my mind the little spreads of my childhood: a few cows, a few sheep, chickens, a hog fattening at the bottom of the garden. Is it only nostalgia, or is there an intrinsic rightness to this picture? In the fifties, farmers became increasingly convinced of the economics of monocropping and many got rid of animals altogether, unless committed to beef production or raising turkeys. Be a specialist, not a generalist: the same fashion ripped through academic life, through medicine. Profitable, maybe, in the short term, but soul destroying.

And perhaps not even in the long run economical. Wendell Berry says that the small farm, like Anna's ten acres in Oxfordshire, needs to exist as an example of conscientious stewardship because nothing there can be wasted and problems must be solved with the utmost intelligence rather than with money.

The Decorah farm has given me a vision of the kind of life I would like to lead and a kind of farming that could be dependent more on preserving species than slaughtering for meat. But it is so hard to figure out the difference between a "leading," as Quakers say—a prophetic vision of what God is calling you to do—and a crazy fantasy. Next year, for example, I have a contract to go back and teach school. . . . My novice mistress used to say that God's will is found in the *here* and *the duty*. It's good advice; at least it's good short-term advice—it kept me married for nineteen years. Maybe, as usual, I missed some important fine print in the message. What if those wise virgins in the Bible, who dutifully sat up all night keeping their lamps burning, had decided, "Screw this, it's a waste of fossil fuel." That would have made a different story, and I can imagine Jesus telling it on a different day.

Peter is right. With all my children raised, I, too, am free to leave home.

"I'll launch my boat upon the sea," I sing to myself, driving back from Decorah. "This land is not the land for me."

Dominant Species

My method of catching sheep at present is to stare at them until their nerves crack and they do something stupid, like put their heads through a fence and stick there. It's handy that, whatever my deficiencies, sheeps' nerves break before mine do.

As I wheeled my hay cart down the aisle, I saw that a sprocket had broken on the fence between the Hampshire rams and three fluffy white show-groomed Dorsets, a ram and two ewes. The partition crashed down even as I watched and all the animals milled together. I managed to pen the three Dorsets outside in a corner by confining them between the broken fence and the sliding door, but that left Hampshire ram #5001 inside the Dorset pen with no intention of vacating.

I caught him easily, but I could not move him by

1. herding
2. getting behind him and pushing
3. yelling "hai!"
4. clutching him around the neck and dragging
5. getting on his back and pulling up his chin
6. getting on his back and clutching his shoulders in my knees while dragging myself and him hand over hand down the wire fence
7. bribing him with corn
8. pulling his feet forward one at a time

I worked with him for one-and-a-half hours while both of us exchanged smells. Finally I left him, sprinted for the dairy barn, and yelled for a man or a five-year-old child to help me, and sprinted back in time to kick him off the ewe before he ejaculated (I hope). The cow vet, whose name was Doug, came along to render assistance.

Here's what he did to help: walked into the pen. Here's what #5001 did: shot out the door I'd been aiming him toward. Here's what the vet said: "I'm not going to tell you how we men do that."

Then I fixed the pen as well as I could with baling wire I found on the floor, since the office was locked and I couldn't get at the tools or my shearing equipment.

Desire

"WHAT IS YOUR PRAYER LIKE?" I asked Peter on the phone. This is the kind of question spiritual companions are required to ask.

"Kind of like the prayer of an adolescent boy hanging around the pizza parlor."

Prayer of longing. Undifferentiated longing perhaps: for pizza, for girls, for life to begin, for something to happen. Augustine says, "Thou hast made us for thyself, O Lord, and our souls are restless until they rest in thee."

As an adolescent, I knew I was restless, but I didn't believe that it could be for God. Nor was I self-deceived enough to think it was only for marriage, a job, money, children. If I could have articulated my desire then, perhaps I would have longed for a fuller understanding, an identity, instead of the tin of nuts and bolts and mismatched bicycle parts I seemed to have been issued instead of a self.

It's what I still long for. The heart longs to be free-running, instead of dammed up, transfixed by selfishness, compulsed around some anxiety.

Buddhism tells us to transcend desire. Christianity, by contrast, flaunts its longing like a coat of many colors. Christianity, in this respect, is more congruent with natural process. This is what we see in the barn: longing and groaning. The ram for his desire, the panicky passion of the drying ewes for their lambs, the wrenching desire of the shepherd to explain things to his sheep, especially things that from the sheep's viewpoint are painful. The flocking instinct, the night gathering, the sleeping together instinct, the keenness to follow, the frisking wish to stray, the desire of the shepherd to serve.

Buddhism asks us to detach from desire; Judeo-Christian prayer, by contrast, concerns the education of desire. Consider, for example, the archetypal formula of that great Rabbinic text, the Lord's Prayer. Simone Weil used to recite it daily in Greek and daily be transported into a mystical state. (I think this only works in Greek.) The idea of a "father in heaven," whom the prayer compels us to address, has been somewhat contaminated for me by listening, as a child, to Burl Ives singing "Big Rock Candy Mountain." This was my earliest idea of afterlife: lemonade springs, soda water fountains. The Greek text, though, seems to open wider vistas, space to get lost in, the pink nebula in Orion.

Most of us independent characters also have trouble with the phrase, "Thy will be done." Peter keeps trying to explain this to me. He is a great reader of Rabbi Abraham Heschel, who writes about God's longing for mystical union with creation: may holy desire be fulfilled. Hasidic Jews pray not "Thy will be done," which Christians have been known to mutter in an agony of abasement, but rather, "Thy longing be satisfied." God's desire pursues us, Rabbi Heschel teaches, and that is what makes everything run smoothly—to the extent it does—in the universe. This is prayer that prays us beyond our hearts' own limits. Think of Bernini's Teresa of Avila in ecstasy, clearly over the top.

How can this be? Still, as shepherd I have felt a similar agony of desire to communicate my intentions to a suffering ewe. As above, so below. Creation moves according to its longing, the sunflower for light, virus for host, we for God, and God for us. One day soon, after weeks of austere reflection in a zendo in a foreign country, sweeping the prayer hall at dawn, insight will come to me like reverse satori: *I do not wish to transcend desire and longing.*

Lots of people fear spirituality because they think it incompatible with natural happiness. They think surrender to God will take something precious away from them. It's no wonder they think this, of course: many religious practices violate our instinctive wisdom. Some skinny guru, covered in ants at the mouth of a cave, does not speak to our survival instincts.

Part of our problem is that we want more than food, clothing, and shelter, we want Pop-Tarts, designer jeans, and four thousand square feet of house on five acres—what I've heard people call a "starter castle." I've just heard about a new abomination called a "princess suite," which realtors are advertising these days: a separate wing for the eldest daughter with bath, dressing room, and vast closets. Still, if that's the light you have, go with it, and no doubt your little princess can become a good woman anyway; such is grace.

I've never had much truck with asceticism. I don't feel led to give up anything I can't give up "for joy" like that merchant tracking pearls in Matthew's gospel. Self-abnegation, when your heart isn't in it, easily leads to self-righteousness, self-punishment, and disdain for creation. Me, I'm on the Pop-Tart path.

But when you have your eye on some prize, possessions begin to weigh heavily, junk food slows the steps. Surrender, at that point, is a natural process; it's what we do to attain the vision we have come to long for.

When I lived in intentional community with my young children, we had to negotiate periodic bursts of "simple living" fervor on the part of other community members. Someone would decide we all needed to have a day of fasting, a weekly "third-world meal"—clear soup and bread. The first time this happened, my son, coming in from a cross-country run, scarfed down his bread and helped himself to seconds from the sideboard. An elderly lady in the community rebuked him: "The spirit of simple meal is to take only what's provided, not go around looking for leftovers."

After that, I hiked the children out for pizza and ice cream whenever the community got into one of its fits of self-abnegation. I didn't want my children to associate religion with an empty stomach.

Jesus, I'm told, spent a lot of time carousing and picnicking, which is how he got in trouble with the religious leadership. He was always feeding people, as full of kitchen tricks as any house-wife. If you hung around with Jesus, you had good wine and your boat would be full of sunfish. When he wasn't feeding people, he was putting his hands on them and getting them on their feet. Most of his counsel, like the Buddha's, was about how to be happy in a difficult world.

Into the Woods

I'M NOT THE SORT of person who is much given to religious experiences, certainly not of the mystical, visionary kind. Indeed, I cherish the nondramatic, everyday quality of spiritual life: to paraphrase a Buddhist aphorism, "No big deal." But most of us get so used to living a hectic life that even the present moment, with its vast spiritual resonance, is unavailable to us. This is less true of the solitary, quiet workers whose company I have treasured; they seem to be living in a different psychic space from other people on the evening news. I do not mean farmers alone, but my grandfather in his carpentry shop, or Robin, when he comes home from a day of tuning pianos (which is how he makes his living). Such people may not know that their daily experience—contemplatively charged as it is—is different from other people's. When something, like a trip to the mall, brings the disjunction to their awareness, they may fault themselves for being "out of it." A day in the city looking for a couple of shirts can fry the brains of a normal country person.

Last weekend I went to the woods for forty-eight hours of retreat. It became an opportunity to watch myself pass through these alternate worlds we inhabit. I felt like a diver descending. I usually go to the woods with plenty of reading material, beads to string, or letters to write, so I can keep happily paddling on the surface. This is my psyche's defense against too much reality, which T. S. Eliot says we cannot bear. Besides, my car is always close by, ready to get me out if I need to rush off and buy something. But last weekend, two strokes of fortune intervened. A friend, who needed my car, volunteered to drop me off, so I had no way out. And, in my distraction, I forgot the companionable basket of sewing. There I was in the woods with nothing to do but tell one leaf from another.

For the first five hours, I thought I'd have to walk miles to the nearest—oh, whatever, bait shop. Boredom hit. I was so restless it was hard not to run full tilt into an oak tree just to cause a sensation, be sure my nervous system was functioning.

I went for a walk. Down the meadow, as though determined to navigate its hundred and fifty yards, ran a small beetle. The sand stretches were easy for him, but then he came to grass blades and whole clumps of tangle, a quick puzzle each: over, around, through? How athletic, how trying, and what could he have in mind? Six hours into my sojourn, I could sit still long enough to watch.

Perversely, I planted before him my inexorable shoe. Perhaps he alone of the millions of hatchmates running this meadow has *seen* a shoe. What will he make of it? Nothing. The shoe was simply too much for his antennae. He stopped not a moment. Burrowed under.

How long will I stand here, make him work? I could be the death, merely from strain, of this beetle. I could sap his life in twenty minutes but I do not, more uninterested than merciful. He has no clue, running on, what he's escaped: how high the shoe, what towered above the shoe, the stalk of carbon atoms topped with alien perception. Prescient, from his view, beyond imagining, yet more ignorant than he of why or how to cross a meadow.

Retreating onto this high prairie reminds me of going into the desert last spring with a generous man named Donn Rawlings. This wilderness of sand was about seventy-five miles north of Phoenix near Prescott, Arizona, where Donn showed me the pink-purple spiral face of a barrel cactus and also: ocotillo, saguaro, choya, paloverde, yucca, ferruginous hawk, red-tailed hawk, shrike, northern flicker, acorn woodpecker. I had to take these words and hold them carefully in my mouth until I got home to Robin, who would want to hear each one and ponder them.

Donn also gave me Edward Abbey and his book *Desert Solitaire,* marking for me the page that read, "I believe that there is a kind of poetry, even a kind of truth, in simple fact." Abbey was a park ranger, broken by tourism and bureaucracy. When he died, his friends stole his body and buried him in some unmarked place of sand, ocotillo, saguaro, choya. . . . "I dream of a hard and brutal mysticism," Abbey wrote, "in which the naked self merges with a non-human world and yet somehow survives intact, individual, separate."

By 8 P.M., drugged with watching micromeadow life, I lay down to watch the various greens of pin oak, birch, and aspen leaf deflect the light, a full-time job before tumbling into thirteen hours of sleep.

And so the hours went until my friend met me on the road, blinking like a badger turned out of her river bank. Surely it can't be time to leave?

Across the Face of a Clock

SOLITUDE CREATES A SPACE for ghost ships to rise up out of the depths of personality. One sees—perhaps not the precise truth of things—but more of what's there to be apprehended. One longs, inevitably, for insight, but dreams merely chaotic dreams. Still, things have loosened up inside and, in the days and weeks after retreat, the new order slowly manifests and the dreams can be read.

When that inner process is going on, I can get very nasty.

Coming back from the woods, I fell into such a vortex of emotion that it's difficult to reconstruct the "real" events. Strong feeling floods the mind and makes for confusion, so it's hard to sort out what's happening—the nerves feel by turns frozen, stung, shut down, and throbbing with infection.

Returning to the empty house, I found myself in so much grief over my daughter's absence that I could think of little else, though I was trying to do whatever my appointment book had in mind for me. In the middle of this reorganization process, Robin made some slight demand on me and, in an instant, the grief shifted to fury. Fury that literally blinded and choked me. I was afraid I'd scream. Writing this, I realize it's a version of the old Minnesota joke: "I was so happy I almost smiled." I was so angry I almost let on.

I did let on, finally, and, trying to break the block between us, Robin and I sat down to meditate together. Slowly a little of the blind rage lifted and I was able to tell him how I felt and also to cry out in grief, "I miss her so—I can't bear not to see her, that her junk

isn't all over the place and nobody raids my closet. And besides missing her, I feel that my life is over. And I long, long, long for her."

Furthermore, I want no demands on me whatsoever. I want to
be the baby! I want to be held! It's shaming and humbling to admit
such neediness, but also curative. So the tumult of feeling was a
catharsis of sorts.

Left alone for only a few days, my large garden has turned into
something along the lines of a rain forest. So this week I must practice one of the disciplines of gardening: *nothing too much.* I'm one
who overdoes, rather than underdoes, tears into a project, and
faints in the heat of the day. The slow and steady plod is hard for
me, and in athletic terms I'm a sprinter rather than a long-distance
runner. So every day I ration myself in the garden, one hour early
in the morning, no more. It's difficult. As I uproot the quack grass
and creeping charlie that's invaded the perennial gardens, I hear
each raspberry behind the alley fence crying out, "Save us!" while
bindweed and Virginia creeper encircle the ripe fruit. How fast
can I get there? Can you hang on till Wednesday?

"The tranquillity of order"—another Augustinian phrase I relish. I love to see well-groomed plants perking out of neatly mulched
soil. Balance and symmetry. Maidenhair fern in soft contrast to wild
geranium, the elephant ears of summer bloodroot. I even trim the
long purple flower forms off hosta because it looks unkempt to me.

Within doors I long for similar order, my drawers neat, my
books dusted, my closet color-coded. Fortunately, my tall children
think nothing of lifting me up by the armpits and saying, "Quiet,
you tiny, fussy thing!"

How I admire messy individuals. What orderly minds they must
have. I require clean spaces without to mediate the chatter within.
My mind, unlike my dresser drawers, is full of mismatched socks
and odd kitchen implements.

By contrast: a woman friend, who invited me to dinner recently, spent hours in delightful chat, then suddenly roused to hunger at 8 P.M. We began to ransack the kitchen, finding ourselves at last atop kitchen chairs peering into the highest shelves. "I *know* there were some sardines up here," she mourned. This strikes me as gutsy detachment from the snares of the world. She deserves to be clothed like the lilies of the field, and fed by Elijah's ravens.

Bastard toadflax, an invasive weed, named obviously by a mortal enemy of bastard toadflax. To be truly present, weeding this bed, and indifferent to the one I will not reach till Saturday, is hard practice. My border collie, Shep, comes to lie down, preferably on the most delicate begonias. Her calendar reads only Today! Today!

Buddhism commends to us this relentless attention to nothing but the present. Like many spiritual disciplines, however, it's more important to practice than to perfect. Years of gentle trial gift you with momentary vistas of space behind space, a few stories about breathing, a kind glance, the lime green wing, with its lyrical bend, of luna moth: nothing special. Someone—a bank teller who interrupted my panicky scramble after something in my purse—gave me a fine present this week that I've been trying to pass on. "I have all the time in the world," he said.

Time and space are weird elastic materials: is that what Einstein's dream amounted to, that insight? I can sign on to such a physics. Time oppresses me, I crawl to God across the face of a clock. Spaces want cleaning, color coding. Yet certain magic incantations throw the whole system into misrule. This is one of them: I have all the time in the world.

And this week of patient weeding heals my mind of its tumultuous longing.

Dirty Stab Wound

H<small>ANK—OUR SUPERVISING PROF</small>—has asked me to help him teach the upcoming fall quarter sheep techniques class. I'm so proud. It is because he's desperate for help, rather than because I know anything.

All week we have been sorting and crutching and hoof-trimming to bring our pregnant ewes into safe haven and maximum physical peak. "Crutching" is a form of partial shearing that trims wool off the udder and the vagina to facilitate maneuvers during delivery. Udders are sheared because a lamb will suck on a dingleberry (that is, a lump of fecal material) as soon as on a teat. These ewes run about two hundred and fifty pounds and are hard for me to handle. I have overcome my disinclination to grab with my bare right hand a sheep's "go button," the tailbone—where a big piece of wet shit is inevitably clinging to the wool—but I can't predictably get them to "go" for me. My short arms barely reach from muzzle to tail and leave little left over for leverage. By contrast, I am pretty good at holding them with my leg muscles while Ben shears.

You have to squat—never kneel—to trim hooves. Then, if the sheep kicks, you will naturally veer rather than freeze there, a stationary target. Ben tells me he learned this from his dad while changing tires. Modern tires seldom explode, but sheep occasionally do.

Fortunately I was squatting, rather than kneeling, when a very tall, heavy, pre-vet student drove her big shears through my upper lip as I was teaching her how to trim hooves. It's nice to have students a little dumber than I, but not too nice. After stabbing me with this filthy instrument, which she had been using to dig impacted shit out of the sheep's hoof, the student began screaming, which on the whole I felt to be my prerogative. Hank smeared me with some penicillin salve we use on the animals and then it was off to the emergency room because I hadn't had a tetanus shot in recent memory.

The nurses seemed very pleased to be writing "dirty stab wound" on my chart and to carefully script details about "large pruning scissors used to trim sheep's hooves, contaminated with feces." The doctor was also pleased. But he asked, "At fifty-one years old, why are you studying agriculture?" I told him as conscientiously as I could.

He said, "You are a very interesting person." That is so true.

Or maybe I have contracted scrapie and will soon start chewing off my own wool.

When Ben came in later and found blood on the barn floor, he was relieved to know it for mine. "I was afraid somebody cut the bag off one of my ewes."

Attachment

WE ARE STILL bringing pregnant ewes from the north pasture into the barn, then separating the very pregnant from the less pregnant. Those about to deliver are held in the barn, while the others go back outside. This involves cutting the waddlers out in the pasture, then getting them past their feeding station without a rest and finally into the barn without any curious aunties flocking along.

Sheep charge past me. "Ben! Ben! How do I tell which ones are pregnant?"

"The little skinny sheared ones *aren't*."

He looks at me with exasperation. No doubt I am pointing at ram lambs with testicles as big as cantaloupes. Ben sees each animal as an individual he knows by number, parentage, and date of birth; I still see undifferentiated masses of fleece, especially when I'm under pressure to make a fast call. I can easily mistake a small udder for testicles as an unsheared wooly creature blasts in my direction.

"You think too much," Ben says (Zen masters always repeat themselves) as I let a ewe slip behind me to gambol at the automatic feeder. "Your body knows how to move sheep."

Right: I am standing at the gate (too far out) going through my mental checklist. Has it got an udder? Bigger than a breadbox? My body does *not* know how to move sheep. After years of being kept in for recess after my bout with rheumatic fever, I never even learned how to hit a volleyball. At fifty-one, why am I doing this?

Ben's body knows how to move sheep.

Ben tends to give orders with his face turned away (watching ewes) and to rely on the handy counters of *this* and *that:* "Get that over here down there." When my son, Jude, was two years old and just developing language skills, he invented an all-purpose locution: up-here-down-there.

"Where's the cat, Jude?"

"Up-here-down-there."

It makes me laugh to hear the doctors shrieking so explicitly on TV hospital shows: "Hand me that #2 French! Let's tube him, STAT!" In a real hospital, I'll bet they say, "Hand me that thing up-here-down-there!"

Most communication is nonverbal, but the nonverbal language has to be encoded in the recipient. Otherwise your ewes will have their noses in the corn.

"Don't get attached to that goat," Ben says of a little angora I find penned in the barn. "He's going to be eaten by the Muslim Student Association."

Cast a cold eye on life, on death. "I don't get attached to animals," I reply.

Ben does the only double take I've seen him do.

"OK, a little, sometimes."

But not a lot, really. I rarely eat meat, can no longer stomach cooking it: though a corn dog at the state fair still exerts its comforting recollection of childhood. If I needed to eat meat, I would, and when I want to, I do, but I want to less and less. I'd like to get through life without causing other species to suffer.

But still, I send the lambs off to slaughter without regret. It seems to be part of the deal they have been cut, as my fate reflects the deal I have been cut. Farmers are always, at some level, rehearsing their own deaths: they die, we die. When you work with sheep every day, you have to honor their completeness, their lack of the fruitless striving and imagining that plagues me. In this respect they are my teachers. Why are we such *incomplete* animals, our souls restless? Sheep are "finished" every day, whole and coherent. We are only finished when we lie down to die.

Eight ewes have lambed, including two sets of twins, fewer than we'd hoped for, probably because of some being artificially inseminated. One Rambouillet mix is particularly handsome. We crutched up four or five big ewes, still concerned that the lambs not suck on a wool tag or piece of shit and starve. Inadequate nutrition is the major killer of lambs. I go around pulling new lambs to their feet, showing the students that if it stretches, arching its back like a cat's, that's a sign of well-being and a full belly.

One ewe is not well. Ben thinks one of the evening workers overfed her. "If you bring 'em on to feed too fast, they get sick," Ben mutters. Absent any clear etiology of disease process, it's handy to blame each other.

Then I spend a few hours shearing, holding the ewes at attention between my knees while clipping the delicate udders, with their frail distended veins.

Feast of St. Francis

WE HAVE TEN LAMBS, two sets of twins, most born Sunday night. When I came in for the sheep techniques class, the sick ewe was breathing stertorously. We were teaching the class drenching and inoculating techniques, so things were busy.

While the class was drenching under Hank's direction, I worked with some weak twins and in the course of that heard the ewe behind me stop breathing. I didn't want the students to know. I couldn't bear the spectacle of that hyper woman who stabbed me with the hoof trimmers starting to yell and keen. So there ensued the ridiculous exercise of continuing class with a dead sheep in the middle of her jug. Nobody noticed. The lamb was curled up confidingly next to the dead mother's head.

We carried on teaching the bloody-minded business of ear tagging and tail docking the lambs. The ear tag probably doesn't hurt any more than an earring hurts a human, but if your hands are small, the staple gun is a bit cumbersome. Be prepared to exert leverage at the end of the instrument, where you won't have perfect control, in order to make a fast snap and cause the lamb little pain. Ben has warned me that some students will refuse to dock (and then he will kick them out of class).

Eventually all the students finished their tasks and left while I remained behind to work with Paul, a short, stocky, quiet pre-vet whom I like to teach. He's steady and has good rapport with animals without squealing over them. He doesn't show off, as I do. The docking made him quite pale. The instrument used is like a big shears, of which one blade is a red-hot iron. You position the tail to cut just where two folds of skin flare, between the vertebrae rather than in a position to crush it. Then you squeeze and calmly hold it in place while the iron sears the skin, gently rotating the blade away from the vulvar or rectal tissue, which you don't want to burn. The lamb winces at the cut, but usually shows no reaction to the burn, which sears the "meat" exactly as it would sear on a grill, thus preventing a bleed or infection. You smell burning hair and skin.

As Paul's face lost color, I asked him, "Are you OK with this?"

"Yeah. I just try to do it quickly and cleanly."

"That's the way."

And later, Ben sends us to haul out the dead ewe. "I'm just not used to it," Paul says, rubbing a hand through his hair.

"You never get used to your animals dying," I tell him.

Hank, for example, I find washing implements at 9 P.M. when I come round to check the barn. He is still storming and swearing over the dead ewe. "She was coming along fine, no problems lambing, she gets a little sick, we hit her good [inject her with penicillin], and *bam*. You always think there's something more you could'a done." He repeats his maxim: "A sick sheep is a dead sheep."

I helped Hank build a kind of wooden stocks in which we confined the front quarters of a lactating ewe. We put the orphan lamb in with the new mother, hoping that if she couldn't see which lamb was nursing, she'd foster the orphan, "forgetting" that it wasn't hers.

Next morning, however, we saw that her milk was still not good, so I bottle-fed the lamb and he took it well.

We had about four new lambs and I was busy feeding, watering, stroking udders to bring down milk. In general we never name lambs or ewes but I couldn't resist calling one set of fragile twins Francis and Clare, for two saints who loved animals; these two needed a miracle. Clare, to my eye, was already half-dead. She had no sucking reflex at all when I tried her on my little finger (though the mother had a good bag), so Hank and I intubated her. First we milked the colostrum from the ewe and poured it into what looks like a big syringe with a long, thin red hose attached. Hank threaded the hose down to the lamb's stomach—you have to avoid the lungs or you'll kill her outright—then we had a conference about whether we could hear lung noises or not. If you have most of the hose down her throat (measure it first along the length of her body), you probably have it in the stomach. Gently squeeze in the colostrum. The effect on little Clare was instantaneous: tail-shaking perkiness.

Rumors fly that the accountants are seriously on our backs about finances. I asked Ben how many ewes we have to sell, but he evaded the question. "I don't know what's going on and I don't want to know."

Then home to celebrate the Feast of St. Francis. Robin and I took our dogs to a service at a local church that has a big blessing of animals on this day. Then we went home and let all our pets have a special meal on top of the picnic table.

Shep prefers to steal food—I had adopted her from an elderly couple who forgot her needs for days at a time. (Once she gobbled two loaves of unrisen bread dough, set out for the Catholic Worker. The fermentation in her gut might well have killed a lesser animal; Shep merely got drunk and sprang around the kitchen for hours on end.) So our invitation to the table befuddled her completely. She lurked, cringing, on the outskirts of the feast, until we left the yard. With the illusion of doing mischief returned to her, she could forage in peace.

Fidelity to Objects

THE SPIRITUAL LIFE—or the writing life—depends above all
on fidelity to objects.

I wrote that sentence and looked out the window. It has rained
for three days and in today's sun the late roses strain, soggy as wet
tissue, toward light coming just in time. Fidelity, I was saying, to
objects . . .

Whatever your eye falls on—for it will fall on what you love—
will lead you to the questions of your life, the questions that are in-
cumbent upon you to answer, because that is how the mind works
in concert with the eye. The things of this world draw us where we
need to go.

It doesn't matter how unprepossessing the world we look at,
though it may seem to the lust of the eye that blue sky and late roses
are more amusing to look at than dead winter growth. This mistake I make over and over.

On the first day of November last year, sacred to many religious
calendars but especially the Celtic, I went for a walk among bare
oaks and birch. Nothing much was going on. Scarlet sumac had
passed and the bees were dead. The pond had slicked overnight into
that shiny and deceptive glaze of delusion, first ice. It made me
remember skates and conjure a vision of myself skimming back-
ward on one foot, the other extended; the arms become wings.
Minnesota girls know that this is not a difficult maneuver if one's
limber and practices even a little after school before the boys claim

the rink for hockey. I think I can still do it—one thinks many foolish things when November's bright sun skips over the entrancing
first freeze.

A flock of sparrows reels through the air looking more like a
flying net than seventy conscious birds, a black veil thrown on the
wind. When one sparrow dodges, the whole net swerves, dips: one
mind. Am I a part of anything like that?

Maybe not. The last few years of my life have been characterized
by stripping away, one by one, loves and communities that sustain
the soul. A young colleague, new to my English department, recently asked me who I hang around with at school. "Nobody," I
had to say, feeling briefly ashamed. This solitude is one of the sur-
prises of middle age, especially if one's youth has been rich in love
and friendship and children. If you do your job right, children
leave home; few communities can stand an individual's most piti-
ful, amateur truth telling. So the soul must stand in her own mea-
ger feathers and learn to fly—or simply take hopeful jumps into
the wind.

In the Christian calendar, November 1 is the Feast of All
Saints, a day honoring not only those who are known and recognized as enlightened souls, but more especially the unknowns,
saints who walk beside us unrecognized down the millennia. In
Buddhism, we honor the bodhisattvas—saints—who refuse enlightenment and return willingly to the wheel of karma to help
other beings. Similarly, in Judaism, anonymous holy men pray the
world from its well-merited destruction. We never know who is
walking beside us, who is our spiritual teacher. That one—who
annoys you so—pretends for a day that he's the one, your personal
Obi Wan Kenobi. The first of November is a splendid, subversive
holiday.

Imagine a hectic procession of revelers—the half-mad bag lady;
a mumbling, scarred janitor whose ravaged face made the children

turn away; the austere, unsmiling mother superior who seemed
with great focus and clarity to do harm; a haunted music teacher,
survivor of Auschwitz. I bring them before my mind's eye, these
old friends of my soul, awakening to dance their day. Crazy saints:
but who knows what was home in the heart? This is the feast of
those who tried to take the path, so clumsily that no one knew or
noticed, the feast, indeed, of most of us.

It's an ugly woods, I was saying to myself, padding along a trail
where other walkers had broken ground before me. And then I
found an extraordinary bouquet. Someone had bound an offering
of dry seed pods, yew, lyme grass, red berries, and brown fern and
laid it on the path: "nothing special," as Buddhists say, meaning
"everything." Gathered to formality, each dry stalk proclaimed a
slant, an attitude, infinite shades of neutral.

All contemplative acts, silences, poems, honor the world this
way. Brought together by the eye of love, a milkweed pod, a twig,
allow us to see how things have been all along. A feast of being.

Ghost

WE INOCULATED A FLOCK of pregnant ewes with Lavaco,
against worms, largely without incident until Ben, holding
a syringe in his mouth, got a good dose of vermifuge. Then I broke
a needle in the wooly body of a sheep. Ben managed to find it. We
came upon a dead lamb in the shed outside, but couldn't find a
ewe with postpartum signs. A mystery. A virgin birth. We docked
Francis and Clare, Clare still holding her own, though tiny.

My mom and my sister Peggy turned up at the barn this morning. Peggy says I gave her a shock, for as I rounded the dairy barn,
she thought she was seeing Dad—me in my overalls and feed cap.
She says I walk like him, too. He has been dead seven years.

When Dad was in flight school, his exceptional skill immediately marked him for the bomber squadron; at the same time, his
gift for teaching made him too valuable to waste on warfare, so he
spent his service as a flight instructor. When peace came, he went
to work for a big airline, teaching again, and flying passenger routes.
He had found his vocation, but he lost it soon afterwards. Practical
voices grounded him (whose voices they were is a bit of a mystery),
and he started working for a mercantile corporation where he had
to call members of the founding family Mr. Henry, Mr. Philip, and
so on. He flew small planes, though, till his eyes gave out. He ob-
sessed over a huge vegetable garden. He sang out the front door.
At some level, he was furious, though he never let on, and baffled.

He would have laughed at the idea that work could give you

any kind of spiritual fulfillment, though he certainly knew its pow-
ers of erosion. When I was in the novitiate, he would write to me
about how lucky I was to live in a world without buying and selling.
He would park on the hill behind our cloister walk and try to get
a glimpse of us, for the visiting hours were so limited. Sometimes
I would see his little red car, but I was not allowed to wave. Anyway,
I don't think he was looking only for me, but trying to find a vision,
and something like the feeling of flight.

Tundra Swans

O LGA BROUMAS writes

> the body
> is that part of the soul
> perceptible by the five senses.

My cousin Jim, in Montreal, calls me now and then, usually in the middle of the night. Often decades elapse between his calls. Roused from sleep, I don't always absorb the message, usually gnomic, too well. It's rather like being summoned by an angel who commands, "Write this!" So I will: "You have to learn to relax and pay attention at the same time," Jim said, and hung up.

Robin and I were splitting an order of moussaka at our favorite Greek restaurant. "Do you have more trouble relaxing or paying attention?" I wanted to know.

Robin, when deep in moussaka, is hard to engage in philosophical questions, but he hauled himself out long enough to reply, "Depends."

"Depends?"

"On circumstances. Isn't that true for you?"

"No. I never relax." In fact my rheumatologist tells me this is why I have chronic joint problems.

Robin leaned back in his habitual pose of — relaxation. "OK,

I'll confess. Relaxing is easy for me. Though my animal part pays attention."

Robin, three hundred years of Quaker DNA trailing behind him, is the calmest human being I've ever known. He's exceptionally peaceful to be with, except when he does field biology from the car window while driving, and I have to reach over and jerk the wheel before we hit the shoulder of the road. Most of the time we're a good team. Today we have been making our annual pilgrimage up the Great River Road to a long slough where the Buffalo River slides into the Mississippi west of Alma, Wisconsin. At this time of year, thousands and thousands of tundra swans fly in to scream and hoot on their annual migration. They fly around in parties of four or six or eight—a few singletons move alone, adolescents maybe, or males cut out of the great dance. I love to watch the moment when the birds descend—big paddles hang useless, or perhaps rudder the operation—then the skid. For just a moment, it looks like fatal, ungainly fall. Nietzsche said, "When you stare into the abyss, the abyss stares back at you."

Has the tribe of swan been observing the tribe of human, our slow aboriginal progress down Highway 35? I think not. Binoculars bring you wing to wing with tundra swan; after awhile you forget your body's weight and merge into migration. What comparable pleasure could we offer them? Hauled in by the eyes, I forget I'm not swan, rather as divers pull off their masks and take in a rapturous gill-full, not noticing death. I tumble out into widening light above water. Robin gives me a poke. "Are you relaxing or paying attention?"

There is a woman busily running around among the birdwatchers in a rain parka marked "Swan Warden." She is one of those sturdy, gray-haired women in wellies who love facts, and she is definitely paying attention. "We had a 2013 through here—"

she is telling us all, "—hatched at Carlos Avery, wintered in Galveston. Can anybody see that trumpeter's number? We'd be very grateful."

For a trumpeter swan has been sighted among the dusky tundras. She is bigger, and something rakish around the eye differentiates her from the others. However, her chief distinguishing feature is a large orange plastic tag the size of a milk carton. It has a number on it, we are told, imposed by earlier ornithology, which for the moment the swan refuses to flaunt. She disdains the warden's interest in her hatching, her wintering.

We had planned to camp out next to the slough, wanting to go to sleep with that deep, muffled hooting in our ears, but it has turned dramatically cold. So we check into the local hotel. Here's what you get for fourteen dollars a night: a good bed, though stinky with cigarette smoke, two windows overlooking a brick wall, one aluminum lawn chair, and a sink of your own. This hotel is much in favor with deer hunters. Downstairs in the dining room, we listen in on conversations like this:

"I took the scent glands off his back legs and rubbed it all over myself."

"Helps you out with the wife, does it?"

On the street outside, a line of pickups is parked, each with its deer gutted and displayed on the rear hatch in a gel of frozen blood.

Back in the room, we haul out the red book and sing 31-on-the-top. Then we carefully straighten the orange plastic paddles on our backs and go to bed.

Why I Am Plodding

O to be self-balanced for contingencies,
To confront night, storms, hunger, ridicule, accidents,
rebuffs, as the trees and animals do.

—*Walt Whitman*

LOW MOODS INCUBATE psychic distress like a still, shallow pond rolls out algae and bacteria. I begin the working day in a mood of depressed anxiety, then move on to blaming myself for being unhappy. Blame generates shame. Shame occasions a judgment about how stupid it is to feel ashamed. Stupidity generalizes into pervasive clumsy incompetence. I make mistakes and the mistakes make me angry at myself. There you have the whole knot of the human condition. At what point could I have stopped this inexorable progression into a seething ball of trouble? Looking for the answer to that is at least one of the reasons I am plodding along on a spiritual path.

There is a new woman, Lucy, who suddenly appeared on "my" shift, at "my" hours. She's an M.A. candidate in some aspect of reproductive medicine and has a farm and sheep of her own. She's bossy and competent and athletic; all Monday morning I slunk around bashing into things and walking two steps behind her.

By later in the week, I was in a better frame of mind and merely resolved to be present and humble, as befits my level of stupidity. We have a new ram, a huge splendid black Hampshire who's going in with our ewes. We spend a lot of time running around catching him, putting a halter on him, and letting him drag us through mud and shit. Yesterday we devoted most of our shift to coupling and uncoupling hoses to water the stock. It took two hours.

"What's that pretty saffron color on those new lambs?" I wondered out loud.

"That's meconium," snapped Lucy, seeming to add, "idiot!" Meconium is the substance fetal lambs defecate in utero.

O to be self-balanced!

The reasons I don't get along with Lucy are the reasons I don't get along with divided factions within myself. Though I've spoken occasionally of "being yourself" as though the phrase had some kind of objective reality, as though self were univocal, in fact identity seems to me rather more fluid. Socrates had only his "inner man" to contend with and bring into consonance with "the outer man" in order to be at peace, but I seem to hear a whole chorus of conflicting voices in what I loosely call myself. I don't, on the whole, go along with the academic fashion of social construction, which holds that we have no stable identity but merely a variety of roles: mother, daughter, teacher, churchgoer, assistant under-shepherd-teaching-assistant. Rather, integrity compels me to reconcile a variety of inner voices. It's a regular committee in there. When I was younger, it was like a loud family dinner, dominated by incompatible cousins. Some voices were so quiet they never got heard at all. Others bossed, and one or two knew they would get stuck with the dishes. Now we've learned to get along better, but the busy mother can still get cross-ways of the dreamy artist, just as Lucy and I spar about how to bring a weak lamb on to nurse.

You have to have a tea party in your heart, Peter tells me, and in your barn. Or think of society as being like a pond, an ecosystem. You need this anaerobic bacteria, that algae. Hold the phosphorus. We all see the world so clearly and crisply through our own glasses that it's a difficult imaginative leap to believe another person sees a different scene, logically incompatible with yours.

Later, after a few hours of Lucy practice, Ben took me into the barn office to work on birthing by feel. He covered a coffee can, open at both ends, with a towel and manipulated our lamb puppets through it in various presentations: normal ("Here's looking at you, kid, my two hooves tucked under my chin"), breech, footling breech, and, what's this—one head, two left hooves? He's trying to trick me again. A twin presentation, both trying to get through at once.

Thank God I was good at this exercise and good at telling what to do in each case. Be patient. Support the perineum. Ease a bad presentation back in if you can and turn it. If the vagina doesn't open sufficiently, massage with Esterall and gently dilate by spreading your fingers in the birth canal.

I'm beginning to understand that my journey in the barn has less to do with longing for the high things of the spirit than for simple physical competence. Folk wisdom tells us that you have to crawl before you can walk and that you can't skip stages. The part I skipped, as a kid deprived of recess, was time reveling in the natural physicality of children. I missed the moves that stabilize a baseball player, the spatial sense you learn playing tag. I stayed inside and read. I knew nothing practical. "She's no good in any crisis that doesn't require classical languages," one of my teachers used to say. My girlhood clumsiness and lack of common sense made me feel like a fool, a dumb poet; and that's why Lucy's competence abashes me.

I suppose in a different, artier ecosystem, I might have learned to value myself. And Lucy, for her part, glowers if more than two sentences come out of me. She's ill at ease with words.

Efficiency

TWO SLASHES WITH A SCALPEL takes off the bottom five–eighths of the lamb's scrotum, then you pinch his testicles and pull them out, dragging a vein, with pincers. Like medieval barber surgeons we work at speed: less blood, less trauma. When we are quick, the lambs seem to feel no pain. Many believe the modern method of castration, banding the scrotum with an elastrator, is more humane, but our barn's belief is that it causes the animal to suffer for days as one would with a rubber band around a finger. We band a few lambs just for practice. It's certainly a better summer method of castration and the students have to know how to do it; it's bloodless and thus reduces infection and the infestation of maggots called fly strike.

We dissect a testicle. "What's this, Mary?" Hank points. "Epididymis," I shoot back. "Right." It happens to be the only part of the testicle I know the name of.

"And this," says Hank, flicking his scalpel, "is the large part. And this is the other part." All the pre-vet students nod calmly.

Banding testicles is tricky. It's hard to feel the testicles, and if you miss them the first time, the lamb seems to learn to suck them up into his body. Of course, sometimes one or both are not descended. I founder a little in my presentation. "It's not like I feel testicles every day," I mutter. Hank gives me a look.

A couple of students really loathe today's work. Lorna, who hates castrating, still does it efficiently, a spirit I respect. "Go home and practice," says Hank.

From a Distance

DRIVING IN THE COUNTRY late at night, the illusion grows that the world around you has disappeared and a strange beast is mustering itself to lumber full of potential into your headlights . . .

Because I'm studying for a graduate certificate in spiritual direction, I'm filling in, these days, for various seminary friends who want a vacation from ministerial duties. Last night I drove out to a meeting of the Women's Missionary Committee at a small country church. We ate a lot of pie and discussed the best way to manage buying a motorbike for a mission in Sri Lanka. I sit through these events like an anthropologist from the Planet Mongo, studying how women in traditional societies have always gotten things done, the structures of matriarchy, how the next generation of leadership is trained, the role of elders, the composition of pie crust. On the whole, I love rural pastoring. Ministry has taught me more about the dignity and terror at the heart of life, especially in its waning years—for much of its daily work involves outreach to the elderly, or being reached out to by them. It's often a threat to the waistline (yes, thanks, I'll have another helping) and always a threat to complacency. I drop in on elderly ladies who live in houses neatly lined with bags of garbage and every copy of the *Minneapolis Star Tribune* published since 1935, or I am dropped in on by elderly ladies who preempt my visits, who don't want anybody to know how their lives have spiraled out of control ("Oh, Mary, I live way up a dirt road—you'll never find me").

Today, gray clouds, gray fleece, the long gray contours of the barn on its green hill, a freezing bluster out of the north. Watering sheep in the far east pastures, gloves soaked from coupling and uncoupling hoses, from threading hoses through fences, our fingers are cold to the bone. I look over my shoulder at the long line of the corrugated tin roof and recall how Thomas Merton wrote that whenever he was tempted to leave his monastery he would walk out on the far hill and see it from a distance, too dear to abandon. For years I have been searching for my own land in the country and have become a connoisseur of barns: red, old, heavy-timbered, round, or otherwise showing an interesting character attract me the most. Pole barns earn my disdain.

But from a distance, I see objectively that this barn I love so much and which is beautiful in my eyes is really an ugly old pole barn. When I look across the pasture, I do not usually look at its sheath of corrugated tin, but through it, into a pulse of life, the bleat and smashing of ram on ram, the peace of lights coming up in the rain, of evening lamb checks.

When the owners look at this property, however, they see an environment ideally suited for a machine shed.

Today we were engaged in the endless Tinkertoy task of moving fences, as we anticipate new lambs and a shipment of ewes coming in from a farm near the Canadian border. These northern sheep will no doubt arrive with frost on their wool and their bikinis packed for a southern vacation.

Whoever invented movable fences wins my praise. They are big steel toys that slip in and out of a peg-and-slot system. Our fences, however, are well rammed and jury-rigged with baling wire and twine and lengths of old halter. As fast as we rig one pen, the vasectomized rams bash it down in their fury to dominate the ram lambs in the next pen.

Cutting out a ram, "You're *meat*," Ben cusses. "You're going to the Muslims." This is his direst threat.

"Ben, I have to go away for awhile." I hesitate to tell him this
when we're so busy.

"To Wisconsin?"

"To France."

"What you going to do there?"

"Stay in a monastery." This is so hard to explain. "It's a Buddhist
monastery called Plum Village, founded by a man named Thich
N'hat Hanh."

Ben ponders the name as though it belonged to an unfamiliar
extension agent. He throws straw around for a little while. "Do
you think you could bring me back some Frisian ram semen?"

"How do you suggest I collect it?"

"The regular way."

"I'll try."

"No problem, then."

One of the reasons I'm going to Plum Village is that I met a
man named Luke Barker and his partner, Lee Paez, recent con-
verts to Buddhism, who invited me to dinner one night when I
was giving a faculty retreat in Dallas. Though meeting them for
the first time, I quickly moved to open my arms and embrace
them—they looked that kissable. Luke held me at arm's length.
"I'll teach you a meditation hug," he told me. "Go deeply inside
yourself and say *'Breathing deeply, I open like a flower'* —then hug.
Three times!"

After the hugging lesson, the evening continued with similar
unselfconscious pleasure in the rituals of their new religion. A chime
on the clock rang—we were invited to stop and draw within. At the
end of the evening they rang a temple bell and said a gatha: *Heart
and mind in perfect unity, I send my soul along with the sound of this
bell, may it awaken those who sleep in ignorance.*

Luke and Lee first put in my mind the idea of going to Plum
Village. Over and over it's been this way: people rise up before me,
as though evolved from mist, and show me the way I must go.

Thirty years ago, I was hanging out one night in London, wearing a black trench coat and smoking an unfiltered Gauloise—working, that is, on some more-than-usually-obnoxious false persona—when a woman approached me with her two teenaged children and began to chat. They told me they were Quakers, and in some mysterious way they attracted me so powerfully, despite the pretentious image I was cultivating at the time, that I wanted to *baah!* like a sheep and follow them home. Why? I don't know. I wanted to get into the soft light that held those people. So I understand how Jesus could say to someone, "Follow me," and they'd drop everything. Indeed, dropping everything is half the fun.

Of course, some places you can't get to from here, except via that wrinkle in time. Plum Village is one of them, though I did not know it then. But I will get there, slip through the right looking glass. It is customary in such places to perform mysterious tasks, be subject to great dangers and the promise of reward. I will cook and clean, stack wood, struggle with my ego, and receive a new dharma name. When I get back, nobody will know anything is different, and I will not find words to tell.

PART TWO

Clearing Land for the Lotus Pool

Cold

I DON'T LIKE TO TRAVEL; I cling to my homeopathic fright pills and so plunge into foreign countries like a crazy paratrooper. To most normal people, fear may seem incompatible with precipitate action, but careful planning just makes me more nervous; to shop tickets and pore over flashy brochures gives me time to think about how I hate to leave the green hills of my home. I'm usually willing to take the consequences of my spontaneous journeys. Fleabag hotels don't bother me. If I can't sleep in my own bed, I might as well be on a ledge in Tibet. For awhile, it seemed that was where I had ended up . . .

I arrived at Plum Village in time to eat the meal that had been set aside for me—clear soup and couscous—and to meet the American woman who would be my roommate. There were one or two other Western people in the kitchen, all of them speaking German. Everyone else was Vietnamese and most wore the brown polyester robes of Buddhist nuns, and brown knitted watch caps, like those favored in nautical circles, on their shaven heads.

After supper came an hour of sitting meditation with a walking meditation in the middle. The great freezing zendo is a converted stone barn, wood-floored, with a huge golden statue of Buddha at the head of the hall. Zafus and zabutons line up in front of Buddha. You sit in whatever approximation of the lotus position you can get into, face the wall, and try to climb it—or at least that is my approach. Yesterday I was raising sheep. Today I find myself squatting in the zendo praying that all beings, which includes my wooly pals, be brought to enlightenment. I smile to think what Ben would say about this project.

For my part, I'm not climbing the wall too well. It's composed of cold, loneliness, and a disappointment that is surprising, given the fact that I had plummeted in with few expectations. Probing this ache, I discover that I had anticipated at least the kindly welcome one typically finds in retreat communities—and a good library. The welcome has been distant and neutral. Worse, the lack of a library rears itself as a major issue, for I have brought no books from home. The bookish may wonder at this uncharacteristic oversight, but a friend who stayed awhile at Plum Village had told me there was a great library. Unfortunately, it's been closed. It's off-season in the monastery, and, as I will discover, the place has good reason to be a little unwelcoming to Americans.

Unexpected pleasures have also greeted me: the exceptional beauty of plain space. Stone walls, white pine. Nothing is ugly, nothing cluttered. Our beds, mats on the floor, are as comfortable as my futon at home, and it's blessedly warm at night. The water in the bathrooms is hot enough to make tea, so it gets my hot water bottle off to a good start.

But no books! No books! How can I survive a month with nothing to read?

Up at five-thirty for meditation, stumble through the dark. Be attentive to your breath in the Buddhist way; this is not difficult, since it's visible as steam on the freezing air. Breakfast is a feast of hot muesli, applesauce, cheese, and bread. We wait until the last comer has served herself or himself (this section of the monastery is for women only, but there are a few unexplained men around), by which time the food is cold. Soon I will master the trick of covering my hot muesli with my plate of bread.

After breakfast my first morning we all piled into cars and

drove to the "upper hamlet"—where the men live—for a dharma talk with Thich N'hat Hanh. I have sat Zen meditation for thirty-three years without a teacher and have come to Plum Village because this man's books have drawn me—his gentleness, his engagement with social issues, the practical simplicity of his practice. I should have been panting for my first glimpse of the master. But instead I was crabby and emotionally worn out. Thay—as he is always called (it is pronounced "tie" and means "teacher")—entered the upper hamlet zendo and everyone bowed as he walked in, a small, elegant, frail man of about seventy (I'm told) in the tacky brown habit and cap of his order. He is rather plain looking, has poor teeth and a kind smile. He sat down, we sat down, and I plugged myself into the wispy translation of his talk. It was a careful and conscientious exegesis of one word in Pali, Vietnamese, and Chinese, one word from the Five Noble Principles or the Twelve Precious Concepts or whatever. I don't know. I get them all mixed up. Two hours of that. I could barely hear the translator's whisper, though she seemed gifted—an Englishwoman, skeletally thin, who wore the habit of a nun. Someone called her Sister Angela. The only thing I got hold of was this gatha:

> I return
> to the island of self
> where Buddha, dharma, and sangha
> are always available to me.

"Island of self?" That seemed to me the opposite of the self-forgetfulness I was longing for. I tried out "island of solitude." *Dharma* was little more than an exotic word to me—the collection of sutras? The accumulated knowledge of Buddhist teaching? *Sangha?* The community of practice. I had no emotional resonance with these concepts. Indeed, I realized I knew next to nothing about the daily culture of Buddhism, which is why I was bored by this little lecture on comparative linguistics. Isolated from the main currents of American Buddhism and overfull, anyway, of theological concepts, I have resisted technical information beyond what's needed to semi-sit in the semi-lotus position and watch my breathing.

But I try to seek this island within. It is not a peaceful retreat. Everything pisses me off, especially the hierarchy, the food, the German-speaking, the unwelcoming attitude. Unfortunately, I've come during "lazy week," when no schedule is in effect and, as happens in busy communities, the staff is taking a rest from hospitality and the task of orienting guests. They are happy to tell you when you've done wrong, however:

"Why didn't you bring your forty-two hundred francs with you?"

"I was afraid to carry that much money [about eight hundred dollars] on the train."

"It's perfectly safe. How did you expect to pay?"

This blunt style of interrogation springs from no ill will but simply from lack of facility with the politer nuances of English. As a befuddled newcomer, though, I'm almost made tearful by its brusqueness.

"I had thought, perhaps, it would be possible to go to town, to withdraw money from my bank."

"You do not go to town."

Is this an injunction or a statement of fact? Both, as it turns out. The nearest village is a two-and-a-half kilometer hike, and there is nothing there but a tiny store with perhaps a few tangerines, biscuits, oddments. Larger stores are inaccessible, although some time, I'm told, it may be possible to hitch a ride with the "shopping team" as far as a supermarket with a cash machine. Besides, retreatants are encouraged not to go out in the world. I puzzle over how to get stamps, writing materials, and toothpaste.

Monkey Mind

MORNING MEDITATION BEGINS a half hour late during lazy week. Thay occasionally declares these periods of relaxed practice so that people can have the experience of doing without external discipline: return to the island of the self. Since arriving at Plum Village, I've begun sleeping with the enthusiasm of an animal burrowing deeper and deeper into its cave of safety. By contrast, my roommate, who says she is well rested and full of energy, reads most of the night by flashlight. "Lazy week" meets both our needs.

Coming out of the dormitory in the freezing dawn, we bow to a full moon caught in the western net of pines. This moon has become my great companion. She rises at night in the skylight over my bed and fills the room with soft light that I breathe in like oxygen. Now, before dawn, the stars are near, sharp and white in the lightening sky.

I attend my familiar wall.

A writer once commented about how, in a long period of Buddhist retreat, his wall would present him with a movie of wild sexual fantasy. My own wall is not so warming. I see only a procession of animal faces. As I sit in the freezing zendo, the sun rises slowly behind a bank of windows to my right. My white wall reddens. I try to breathe on Thay's recommended gatha: "Breathing in, I become a flower. . . . Breathing in, I become a mountain. Breathing in, I become water, reflecting all things. Calm water . . ."

By the time I have become a mountain, my mind is off chasing foxes, dogs, and rabbits among the stones. I am roused from distraction twenty-five minutes into meditation because that is the precise moment my legs fall asleep and the muscle under my lower leg becomes first annoyingly, then excruciatingly, cramped. I squeeze my leg muscles to return blood flow and arch my back a little. Cold has reached the dead center of my bones.

On Sunday, Thay talked about not adding fear to pain. I feel no fear, only pain and loathing for my situation. Although believing the act to be self-indulgent, I stretch out my leg. The bell rings.

We stretch for about two minutes on our zafus, exactly long enough to unkink my muscles sufficiently so I don't fall down when we get up for walking meditation. I pull myself up on the nose of a dog protruding from the wall. We walk solemnly around the zendo, left foot, right foot. Then we stop, bow, and get ready to clatter for the door—

No. It's to be another half hour of meditation. There are frequent changes in the daily order this week, so I never know what to expect.

In fact, I need the second half hour of meditation, as it's only then that I get a little quiet and clear, though what I get clear of or for I don't know. A thought rises with a lot of intensity of feeling behind it, streaking like Comet Kahoutec: *I have given this whole year to meditation and retreat and nothing is happening.* I let the comet burn itself out. The dream I was dreaming at dawn returns: I was at a party with my ex-husband and we began a screaming, embarrassing argument that ended with us squirting cans of whipped cream at each other and our fellow guests. In real life, we argued rarely and raised our voices so infrequently that the divorce amazed most people who knew us. An inner voice tells me, "You live with all the arguments you didn't have. They are buried inside."

Maybe yes, maybe no. I've learned to cast a cold eye on these insights that rise in prayer or meditation. They are rabbits, foxes, nothing more.

Once again, pain in my leg releases me from a deeper level of monkey mind. It is twenty minutes in. Today we chant tunelessly after finishing meditation, a (to me) meaningless hymn about the bliss of dharma. It is more tedious than the Catholic masses of my childhood. At least the Gospels had some action, none of this "Listen, Ananda, form is emptiness, emptiness is form, form is not other than emptiness nor emptiness other than form." Buddhism is so abstract. In all my years of practice, I have never gotten the point. Whenever someone starts to rant about darkness and the abyss, I start to dream of crème caramel, various shades of blue devoré velvet. My eyes fill with tears of self-pity, sensory deprivation, physical discomfort, and perfect confusion.

Casual

I THINK THAT WHEN you take on a discipline you should go at it whole hog, but I feel deep resistance in myself. Critiquing the system is my hereditary and traditional form of rebellion. At Plum Village, I carp (to myself) about the gap between ideal and practice. In any monastic community or utopia or political arena, this is a productive site for fault finding. So I allow the cliques to annoy me, the hard-assed attitude, the sanitary customs.

What would happen if I could surrender? I feel like the stone in Richard Wilbur's poem:

> As casual as cow-dung
> Under the crib of God,
> I lie where chance would have me,
> Up to the ears in sod.
> Why should I move? To move
> Befits a light desire.
> The sill of Heaven would founder,
> Did such as I aspire.

My roommate, by contrast, possesses a light desire. Everything pleases her. She plays on the swings. She has brought a bottle of soap to blow bubbles in the sun.

At an intellectual level I have chosen to be guided by Buddhism, but my Christian formation breeds rebellion. Here, in particular, I feel myself to be a Catholic of the blowzy, self-indulgent, holiday-making sort. I dream of Italy, so near, so full of treats.

When I plan to do something hard, I anticipate it like an athletic challenge. In fact, I expect to win. But the raw essence of challenge is that it takes you where you don't want to go. It presents the possibility of failure. It's not a challenge if failure isn't about 95 percent likely. The obstacles I face here are not the familiar demons of fear that often haunt me, but simple physical difficulties. I am cold, hungry all the time, and aching in every joint.

But today, Terry (one of the American women in the community) loaned me a violin and that will help. I went into the summer zendo, where, at a certain time in the afternoon, there is a spot of sun-struck warmth, and I played for an hour with my eyes closed. That is as close as I get to dwelling in pure abstraction, the abyss: a succession of notes and chords that mean nothing beyond resonance and because of that mean everything. *Listen, Ananda, form is not other than emptiness . . .*

This afternoon, out walking, I came upon two of the German women, one with her head in the lap of her friend, her long hair sweeping the ground. It was the first moment of tenderness I have seen at Plum Village, and I breathed it like air. In my complaints, I do not mean to imply that this is a cruel place; rather, I am outside its kindness. Not excluded either, but simply not in.

Nothing Human

WHEN I ENTERED A CATHOLIC novitiate at eighteen, friends who knew my lazy, self-indulgent ways predicted I wouldn't last a week. Indeed, many young women did check out of convent life after a three- or four-day sojourn. One kind, sentimental girl could not master her homesickness. Another had a breakdown. A third high-spirited postulant broke a sink by climbing on it and was asked to rethink her vocation. How I longed for such a revolving-door policy during my first week at Plum Village. But I was isolated in the country, the French trains had gone on strike, and the nearest cab stand, for all I knew, was in Paris.

Then I calmed down a little and stopped critiquing everything. My habit of submitting data to critical inquiry did not seem to be useful in the new environment, nor was my inclination to file and pigeonhole, sort and separate. Or maybe these Aristotelian habits were very useful indeed: they protected me from enthusiasm and premature conversion.

It was helpful for me, late in the first week, to share an afternoon walk with a young American from the upper hamlet who had lived a long time in Zen culture. I rolled out all my complaints, from vegetables to sexual repression. He said, "This is a monastery. Monastic practice is one thing, the world is another. I figure I don't have to decide for all time whether this is ultimately true or good, I just have to decide each day if I want to keep a monastic practice or leave."

That made sense to me. I realized that I had carried to France my Thomistic habit of lining up religious premises to see if they were worthy of assent and, if worthy, to choose, hopefully for all time. Buddhism doesn't (I don't think) involve these sorts of truth claims; it only presents a practice that will supposedly lead to greater happiness and tranquility in a painful world: give it a try, Buddhism says. This emphasis on *practice* is why Buddhism is compatible with Christianity; it doesn't ask to change your belief. You can go to Mass and then sit cross-legged chasing rabbits and foxes across a wall.

Mirroring this alteration in my inner weather, the outer weather suddenly got quite warm. Also, I began to know some of the nuns as individuals, some kind, some harsh of temper, some full of fun. Long walks in the countryside helped, too, though I always had to evaluate the number of calories I would expend and balance them with those I hoped to ingest the rest of the day. There was little fat in the diet and my hip bones had begun to protrude.

My roommate, who was on a different cosmic timetable, was already preparing to "take the precepts," which is a kind of commitment ceremony involving a dharma transmission and the conferring of a new name. The precepts involve, in summary: (1) protection of all life, (2) sharing of time, money, and resources, (3) responsible sexual behavior, (4) loving kindness in speech, and (5) refraining from ingesting toxic substances, such as alcohol, tacky novels, and (I dunno) corn chips maybe.

Nothing here that I don't as a Quaker incline toward, but (and this is also a Quaker trait) I resist anything phrased as a precept, commandment, or vow. Most Quakers put a high value on authenticity; my Catholic nature values hospitality, too. Shall I no longer serve wine at dinner? Am I required to speak kindly of those who annoy me? Deny my children their pot roast? There is even a disorderly part of me that needs to roll around and slobber in popular culture. If I don't do that, it seems to me I can miss what humankind is up to; I sign on to Teilhard's proclamation, "Nothing human is alien to me."

Kindness

ONE NIGHT, my roommate and I sat with Hilda and Josef, two members of the resident community, in their room for a long discussion about the kind of Buddhism practiced at Plum Village, the precepts, and how it all fits together. "Sat" literally, in meditation posture; if you visit someone at Plum Village or go to a meeting, you will be presented with a neatly swept room, a wood floor, and the familiar zafu. Zen sitting at meetings might be an idea worth taking home, as it would certainly shorten the length of time people would be able to endure the conversation. At any rate, indoor space here is enormously flexible—now a dormitory, now a zendo, now a seminar room. There's little to dust and fuss over so it's easy to maintain beautiful spaces and honor each occasion with a simple and perfect flower arrangement. This simplicity is one aspect of Plum Village I like a lot.

Josef and Hilda are a married couple, which is why Josef is to be seen going about our female world with his tool kit and his kind smile. I believe that in a former life these two were an engineer and a psychologist, respectively: they are an attractive, blonde, athletic-looking couple in their late fifties (I would judge). Their room is furnished in the familiar, spare white pine; they have a double bed and I happily think about them cuddling in it, but are they allowed to make love? We visitors are asked to refrain from sexual activity, along with drugs and alcohol, as part of our commitment to the monastery, but what are the rules for a resident couple? And why do I think their marriage is any of my business? Because I'm, on the whole, critical of asceticism, but I would like to better understand the rationale for espousing it.

Our conversation answered many of my questions about Buddhism, a subject to which Josef brings great intellectual energy and Hilda her illuminating, happy smile and psychological insight. I learned that practice at Plum Village is rooted in Mahayana Buddhism, which originated in India, made its way to China and, finally, to Vietnam. Mahayana is an ancestor of Rinzai Zen; I was shocked to discover that, since I have long nourished a prejudice against this form of Buddhism. One of my friends committed suicide during a Rinzai retreat. Well, it's just as well I didn't know about the lineage or I would never have come here. Some distinguishing characteristics of Mahayana Buddhism include shorter sitting meditation (none of those breakthrough twelve-hour sessions typical of Japanese Zen) and the priority given to walking meditation. There is no koan study. ("We have enough koans to solve in daily life," Josef quoted Thay.) Another eccentricity of Thay's teaching is its emphasis on social engagement; in fact, it's this social justice component that has attracted me to Plum Village, since I am trying to put together the threads of action and contemplation in my own life.

In particular, our conversation with Josef and Hilda was helpful in elucidating the Five Wonderful Precepts, as they are formally called, which govern ethical conduct for those who subscribe to them. "They are not commandments," Josef explained. "You can't *break* the precepts."

"You mean you can eat meat or drink wine?" I ventured.

Josef smiled. "You should hear the conversation we have with French people about that." The precepts, Josef explained in a puzzling and provocative phrase, are to be understood as "fields of awareness." Sometimes they are called the "five gates"; in German they are translated as "pillars of wisdom."

There is really only one way to be thrown out of the precept club, once you have "taken" them, and that is by failing to recite them at least once in three months. Then your dharma transmission becomes invalidated (whatever that may mean).

As a teacher and mother, I admire the logic of precept recitation. Thay does not require any set of actions; he merely provides principles and asks the aspirant to keep reading them and referring the questions of life to them. Conversion, then, involves a deep turning of the soul, not a choice made out of fear or enthusiasm or even intellectual commitment.

Pondering this pedagogy, I told Josef an old Quaker story. When young William Penn became a Quaker, he went in consternation to see the great leader, George Fox. His Quaker fellows had asked Penn, the new-minted pacifist, to stop wearing his sword; but Penn was an aristocrat, and wearing his sword was a badge of identity as well as rank. Would he have to lay it aside? George Fox ruminated quietly on the young man's quandary. Finally he raised his head and spoke: "Wear it as long as thee can!"

Josef laughed. "Exactly! A great story! It is precisely in this spirit that the precepts are to be understood."

I feel a lightening of spirit, the recipient of Josef and Hilda's kindness as well as of their wisdom. They ended by explaining to me that the precepts are the way to "stay in touch with Buddha nature."

Which is what? "The place where your deepest identity touches God or spirit," I hesitantly translated for myself.

"Yes," they nodded.

Practice Everything

IN THE MAHAYANA TRADITION, even sitting meditation is sub-ordinate to the "practice" of what rises in daily life. Thus the emphasis on walking meditation. Hilda has finally explained this puzzling practice, which usually splits our morning and evening meditation. (Josef and Hilda have given up their own "lazy week" to see my roommate and me through our beginner's work.) Walking meditation is not just a way to wake up your feet after sitting in the lotus position, but rather a way of expressing connection with the earth and training the body/mind to be present and alert to the world. We learn to go about the business of life, then, as if we were sitting meditation—with awareness, calm, and love. Or at least awareness. Walking meditation trains us for social engagement be-cause it is a transition between the deep presence of sitting zazen and the kind of practice one might try for while feeding the sheep or negotiating a union contract. In walking meditation, Hilda taught us, one breathes in while taking a step with the left foot, breathes out on the right. Touching the earth as a mother touches her child in tender reconciliation, allowing oneself to feel the love the earth has for her despoiling children, . . . it is in this spirit we are to circle the zendo for ten minutes morning and night; more impor-tantly, we should try to bring similar attention to our walking from dormitory to kitchen, to our daily work. Breathing is available, as long as we live, as a point of reference, a reminder to be pre-sent. Walking is almost always available. At Plum Village, we often walk very slowly in formal practice, but walking meditation can be done at a normal rate of speed. It's simply a matter of synchronizing breath and footstep, a matter of intentionality.

Much to my surprise, after Hilda's lesson I began to find walking meditation very calming, and I tried to stop hustling around. As it turns out, *everything* at Plum Village is understood to be practice: cutting carrots, carrying wood, riding in the bus on a special excursion through the Dordogne Valley with some visitors from Vietnam (which was this week's special treat). Having practiced lamely on my own and read Thay's books, I have mastered the concept (if not the practice) of mindfulness. I had hoped that at Plum Village there would be advanced instruction, something more than "smiling, breathing, walking." Fortunately, it is not to be. Instead there is deep, fierce, passionate emphasis on smiling, breathing, and walking. If you're angry, breathe. If you're cutting wood, cut it consciously. Thay often tells a story that emphasizes this point: "When I come into the kitchen and ask a nun what she is doing, if she says, 'cutting carrots, Thay,' I know she is not practicing well. If she says 'smiling and breathing, Thay,' I know she is practicing well."

But all is not well in our little loft room.

For the last twenty-four hours I have been smiling and breathing irritation with my roommate. Everything she does annoys me. I feel like that monk in Browning's "Soliloquy of the Spanish Cloister," greeting her every innocent and kindly gesture with some variation of "Grr, you swine!" What are her faults? She smiles constantly, she sings to herself. She skips and plays. Everything to her is "wonderful," "beautiful." She treasures every moment, while I glare in baleful resistance. She shares everything she has with me.

What's not to hate?

Josef has been quite clear about how we are to deal with anger. Realize that the problem is not in the phenomenal world but in your mind. We know that this is true, he says, if we consider how the same piece of music, or joke, or flower arrangement delights one and leaves another cold. Our mental constructions influence whether we choose to be happy, sad, or angry. "It is just an *idea* that something should be this way or that way."

Ideas in my mind tend to be followed by critical judgments. I have judged, for example, that someone who smiles all the time is not as "authentic" as someone who snaps at breakfast, just as I have decided that Rod McKuen's poetry is inferior to John Donne's. This *idea,* Josef would say, is making me unhappy. "However," I have said to Josef, "some ideas are the foundation of civilization. Ideas are not all equal. Some are bad and some are good." Since Josef is German, I have not brought up the case of Hitler, but no doubt he has heard the name.

"If the goal is to change society, as Thay worked hard to do in the Vietnam War days, we do not have to get angry to do it. In fact, anger makes us less productive." This was Josef's mild response.

When I heard that, my jaw dropped. My early days as a social activist were fueled by "righteous" indignation, and whatever mellowing has gone on since then convinces me that Josef is right. I am more useful in society when I operate out of a friendly acceptance of other views, a wariness about the splendor of my own ideas, a clarity about what ought to happen, and a detachment from who should get the credit. These are lessons of age as well as of Buddhism.

But I am not angry at my roommate, merely irritated. I practice irritation, I practice my irascible thin-skinned temperament. But it is *my* temperament, I am aware today. Josef would say, "The problem is in your mind, not in reality." My roommate is innocent.

Back home, I am sometimes full of aggravation about the behavior of one or another of my friends or sheep or colleagues. These seductive furies always present themselves as sane and rational positions: people *should* remove their wet boots before stepping on a clean floor. Workers in the barn *should not* bully the animals and make them run.

"It is possible to set these things right," Josef has told me, "with no show of righteous indignation."

I begin to see why people spend years at Plum Village trying to get hold of this simple concept.

Homesick

A NEW AMERICAN WOMAN has come to join the community of nuns, after serving her novitiate in California. Her name is Sister Edith and she is an anthropologist by training. Like me, she has grown-up children and an ex-husband. I can't for the life of me understand why she would be drawn to a vision of such austerity. She says she doesn't find it austere! There you are. Life at Plum Village often reminds me of the joke about a man who goes to hell and finds himself sitting in a room with an old couple who are happily showing slides of their trip to Florida. In agony he remonstrates with the devil, concluding with the final complaint, "And if this is hell, why is that old couple so happy while I'm miserable?" The devil smiles, "God and I hate to waste space. You're in hell but the old couple is in heaven." This is a good Buddhist story.

Sister Edith taught me something yesterday about listening. She was drawn to a certain Buddhist monk as a teacher. She had a problem she wanted to talk about and asked him for a consultation. He asked her out into the garden under a full moon, looked around slowly with appreciation of the scene, tucked his robes formally around him, assumed the lotus position, and closed his eyes. Then he breathed, "I am ready," and listened to her for an hour without saying a word. At the end he said, "I understand."

When you are listened to like that, she said, your whole life is up for grabs.

Today was Mindfulness Day, a weekly occurrence at which

Thay gives a dharma talk, the upper and lower hamlets mingle together, and we have a long, formal lunch.

Today, Thay talked for two hours about the *Sutra on Living Alone*. But first, he scolded mildly, "I heard the sound of a bell rung unmindfully!" There followed a half-hour's digression on the proper "inviting" of the bell. First the gatha: "Body, speech, and mind in oneness, I send myself along with the sound of the bell." Between awakening the bell (a muffled tap) and inviting the bell (a stroke) we breathe in and out. Breathe three times between each sound of the bell. Another gatha: "Listen! the sound of the bell! It brings me back to myself."

"We want the sound to be liberated, to fly up, not to be caught in the bell," he went on.

Then it was on to the subject of inner peace and the forces that disrupt it.

"What is it that makes you not at peace? we might ask a friend who comes to us in trouble. When we have heard out our friend's reasons, we can suggest a new way of living. Peace comes from the food that gives us peace. We can never be happy if we are eating the food that makes us anxious.

"But when we are depressed, we are weary and anxious. We must accept and recognize it. Look deeply into the suffering and discover the food that has fed that unhappiness. Take the path that puts an end to that suffering.

"There is another word for peace that means 'doesn't have waves.' We are at peace till a wave comes along: an idea, a thought that gives rise to desire, craving, thirst, wanting—*If I only had that I'd be happy.* Here are some of the waves that assault our peace:

Sexual desire.

Desire for fame.

Anger and hatred.

A wrong perception about the self and others—we are not number one, and we think we are. Or we think we are rubbish and we are not. Buddha talked about what we now call low self-esteem as a sickness. We must live in humility, yet each one has the capacity to be awakened. All of our practice is devoted to knowing who we really are. We must see the negative seeds and the positive seeds and be careful to water only the positive.

Suspicion and doubt—of ourselves, our path of practice, and our teachers.

Jealousy—notice how all these waves arise because we have wrong perceptions.

Worry and fear—anxiety about tomorrow, loss. Betrayal waters the seeds of fear. We see people laid off, love betrayed, and we worry. *Life is impermanent.* We are at the mercy of advertising: *If you buy this you will have no anxiety.* But the burglar alarm will not protect you. You can guarantee nothing. Only dwelling in the present moment can make us free of anxiety. Our practice is to bring us peace. We have to look into our suffering, our craving. And when we see its face we will smile: you can not make me your prisoner any more. We have to ask our sangha and our teachers to cast light on our aggravation. Peace is every step. It is realized in every moment."

⟋⟍⟍⟋

The rain abating, we went for a long mindfulness walk under the gaze of huge French cows who live on the next farm. There are three dogs living in the lower hamlet, two huge rough-coated mastiffs (the generic dog of rural France) and an overgrown terrier named Benji. The monks brought down their young Alsatian and we all trekked happily through the mud. Thick, sucking, foreign mud, like nothing I have ever tried to drag a boot through. Thay seems to take a farmer's pleasure in hiking through his plum orchards and taking a long look at the place. Ben would understand that.

Then we had a delicious, freezing cold plate of vegetables and rice.

I went back to the dorm and wrote a letter to Joan, my dear friend back home, about how I hate it here. My roommate, ever helpful, has put a quotation from Thay's new book, *Cultivating the Mind of Love,* under my pillow: "You have only to allow yourself to be there, to touch deeply each thing you encounter, to walk mindfully and to help others with the whole of your being." Fine. That's very helpful.

I wrote in my journal, "A community that successfully practiced loving-kindness would be boring, and one that tries unsuccessfully to practice it is merely tormenting."

Then, as I sauntered about, tired and pissed as usual, but not particularly pissed, this happened:

I went to dinner and sat with a woman I like a lot, a tiny Vietnamese-German nurse named Chee, whose dharma name means "radiance of the source." A true naming: she has one of those lighted spirits, kindled from some inner tinderbox. She is a woman who struggles a lot with heaviness of mood and seems to have little capacity to see her own brightness, but she is a delight to me. Well, we chewed on our little dinner and I got up to serve myself some more veggies. Thich N'hat Hanh came through the kitchen. I was aware of him, though not especially interested. In fact, I had kept my back to him. He stopped to greet Chee, who was leaving the next day. They bowed to each other and then Thay put his arms around her and embraced her long and gently.

The wave of love hit me like a percussive force, as though the gas stove had quietly exploded. I burst into tears. Love itself entered my cramped and constricted being, with something, I guess, of the voltage Christian mystics in ecstasy record. My bones seemed to melt, jell, and finally harden again. If I had felt sick, I would have said I was healed. I was healed of what I didn't know I was sick of.

After a minute, I sat down at the table with a plop. Across from me Chee picked up her chopsticks and looked with sympathy at my brimming eyes. "You must be homesick," she said.

"I must be."

Armor

THIS MORNING WAS ANOTHER (and our last) day of relaxed practice, so instead of heading for the zendo at 6:30 A.M., I went for a long walk up and down the drifty misted hills, watching with a proprietary air the sun rise. It rises late and with no subtlety here in the Duras region because we are at such a high elevation. Salamanders come up to the road only at this time of day and often die there. They are rubbery black, their backs lined with yellow dominoes like something designed for a child.

One day while I was lurking moodily in the woods, I saw a monk come by on the road. It was the new head of practice at the upper hamlet, a young Vietnamese man of about thirty with an exceptionally peaceful smile and way about him. He bent over the body of one of these dead salamanders, unaware that anyone was observing him. He looked so stricken, and in his look was something of that spirit of infinite compassion that overwhelmed me last night in the dining room.

Humility is sometimes merely the knowledge that something is going on that you are too spiritually opaque to get.

But I don't think I will ever be able to enter in to the level of respect for animal creation practiced in Southeast Asian Buddhism, though I could refrain from eating meat as a rational fast. Certain aspects of religious culture, deeply felt, are irrational or perhaps suprarational. The Vietnamese at Plum Village regard the slightest infringement of animal rights with the horror I would reserve for an act of child abuse. If I comb one of the dogs for fleas and ticks, for example, I must carefully preserve each insect's life. Recently, working in the garden, I managed to assault two precepts at once by suggesting to the sister in charge that we lure the slugs off the lettuce with little tins of beer. She was somewhat willing to let the slugs get drunk, but when she discovered my goal was to drown them, she became agitated and scolded me.

After breakfast I helped Lydia—another American woman in the lay community—translate a poem of Thay's. He had written in the margin a number of English concepts that roughly approximated each multilayered Vietnamese word. Our job was to fit the intentions together with some eye for beauty and euphony. Lydia had already done this perfectly well with no help from me, so we simply pondered in a companionable way the connotations of "cardinal" versus "red bird," or something on that order. Thay needs a good editor. He is a careful and precise scholar, a good poet, and a flexible, passionate thinker, but little of this comes across in his English work. Like many Asian speakers, he reaches for too many intensifiers, using "wonderful," for example, more often than Lawrence Welk. As usual, count on me for a critical opinion.

Later, I took a long walk into the neighboring village of Loubes-Bernac to buy stamps, getting caught in a rainstorm on the way. I sheltered on the porch of an uninhabited farmhouse with a long view of its neighboring valley, hills laid out in the ancient, orderly way of land farmed since prehistoric times.

And later in the day, I got to go on a car ride, jumping into the back seat with the alacrity of Shep, my dog back home. We drove into the neighboring village of St. Foy, an unimaginable psychic distance, to put my departing roommate on the train. I was able to hitch a ride, both to say good-bye and to visit Mr. Cash Machine for my forty-two hundred francs. Also, I bought some prized moleskin for a sore foot. Life is elemental at Plum Village. A cough drop, a tangerine, a stamp are gifts of love taken out of someone's non-renewable horde.

"Why don't you buy what you need in the village and keep it in your room?" my family asks when I call home and whine about hunger and scarcity. The epicerie in Loubes-Bernac carries almost nothing useful to the Buddhist path—a little meat and cheese. It would be unacceptable, anyway, to keep any food in one's room that was not offered to the whole community, and it would invite mice as well.

The encounter I had with Thay on Sunday has changed my inner weather, maybe my DNA. I feel less guarded and more accepting of life here. Still, I do not apologize for my armor, which keeps me from entering in to the more cultic aspects of life at Plum Village. When Thay asks us to have unquestioning confidence in our teacher, for example, I consider the prospect with horror. But I want to take in what is useful, leave aside what is not, and respect practices that I have no intention of bringing home.

Regular Practice

"REGULAR PRACTICE" has begun, and there is a new focus and energy abroad. We begin before dawn with sitting meditation, then continue with chanting sutras. The Vietnamese sing in an eerie, highly ornamented chant punctuated by drumbeats in dialog with the great zendo bell, mindfully rung. We English speakers, by contrast, racket through a brusque spoken translation. When I can get my hands on a text, I try to chant in Vietnamese. The words are relatively easy to follow even if I have no idea what I'm saying; like Gregorian chant, a lot of the meaning is in the sound. I think that if I could get the music in my blood and bones, maybe some day, while stacking the woodpile, I would figure out this "form is emptiness and emptiness is form" business.

Then breakfast: hot muesli, hot applesauce, hot milk, bread and cheese, yogurt. A good foundation for the morning's work, newly inscribed on the community board. This morning, mine was to be "flowers garden." Annika, one of the German speakers, a strong young woman whom I admire for her quiet and practical nature, led me to a bed she wanted cleared for roses. It's choked with weeds and rampant blackberry vines. Gardening here means putting your spade into something like a bucket of moist potter's clay, and potter's clay is what this earth has been since Neanderthal times. The local farmers cut it with hay and manure. Now I look at Annika's work, her abundant November roses, with profound respect.

Plum Village is different from those California workshops where you go to be "nurtured" and pumped up. Thomas Merton's final words were something, half in jest, about "every monk for himself." This phrase has rung in my mind lately. No one here asks you what you do back in the world or what your family is like. There is none of that social chitchat to make connection. Maybe the community is so oriented to the present moment that such information becomes irrelevant. Maybe they are in hospitality fatigue. Maybe I have offended in some way. Maybe I should quit worrying about it and relish anonymity. Once or twice I have volunteered that, back in the world, I take care of sheep: it's been necessary to convey this in response to questions about what kind of work I know how to do. And that's why I find myself in the garden, up to my ears in sod.

Being no kind of spiritual health spa, Plum Village takes you into your illusions pretty quickly. There is no place to hide: not in identity, not in your past record, not in social chitchat, and not even in books.

Here in the garden, however, I manage to begin spinning fantasies, which chase themselves through my mind like the animals in my morning meditation space. *I hope Annika will come by and notice how hard I'm working. Maybe Thay will come and write a poem about my labor.* . . . I am proud of the pile of weeds I've pulled and decline to dump them in case someone should come by and admire my output.

After awhile, however, this mental posturing gives way to mere endurance of the physical labor. Each thrust of the fork pulls up about five pounds of clay, which has to be cleaned off before another thrust is possible. I clean it with a trowel, then scrape the trowel. Then my analytical process, that great hamster wheel in my head, begins to spin: is this task logical? Wouldn't it be better to put off turning this bed until the ground is a little drier?

I decided to cart off my trophy weeds, then realized that each root system had transported more clay mud into the basket than I could now lift and carry. I had to dump half and make another trip. Almost two hours into the task I had cleared about five feet of garden, a poor job of work by Minnesota gardening standards. Now I hoped that nobody would come along. At this point Thay materialized by my side. I bolted to my feet and bowed. He bowed back and made no comment about my labor or lack of labor. Probably he had worked as hard before breakfast.

He left and I leaned on my fork. I realized I was precisely at the end of my strength. Perhaps that realization showed a tiny bit of spiritual progress. At least I am now mindful enough to recognize when I am tired and hungry. Back home I can often work well past my tolerance level, bashing away at some garden task until I am sick of it and it is sick of me, and I will not be able to drag my rheumaticky body back until enough time has elapsed for all progress to be lost.

A bell rang to tell the workers that we were within ten minutes of quitting, plenty of time to clean boots and tools. By this time, like Winnie the Pooh, I was longing for a Little Something. It was not to be. Instead, we went up the road for a long walking meditation. No complaint. Since Hilda's course of instruction I have found this a wise and centering exercise. I fell into step behind Sister Angela, who has an elegant London debutante walk. I like to walk behind the people I admire—or even the people I don't like—as an exercise in understanding. How we put our feet down is *personal*.

Then lunch! My stomach burned with hunger like a pot in the kiln. We had clear soup delicately flavored with anise, beans with cilantro, gingered squash, potatoes (no butter or salt), heaps of fresh salad with chives and yogurt, and side dishes of brown and white rice (a constant). We all piled our plates to overflowing, except for Sister Angela, who sat with a bowl of clear soup in her beautiful translucent fingers. "But I do not work," Sister Angela smiled. She had spent the morning translating the manuscript of some sixth-century Chinese master.

My new roommate has arrived and I was drawn to her as to a warm hearth. Her name is Mira, and she is a vegetarian cook from Madison, Wisconsin. After lunch, we took a long walk into Loubes-Bernac—the long way around, past a medieval chateau—to buy stamps, exchange biographical tidbits, enjoy silence. Mira proved to be one of those rare people with whom silence is as warm and companionable as a chat.

We came home to find afternoon dharma talk had been canceled. A blessing in my view. It's not that I don't get a lot out of them; rather, it's as though I'm carrying a full jug of dharma talk on my head at the moment and, if one more drop falls in, the whole thing will slop onto the ground. In the freed-up time, I treated myself to a hot shower, one of the great sensory luxuries of Plum Village. Mail brought two letters from home.

Instead of evening meditation, we had a long ceremony to "forgive ourselves for any transgressions in the past week and resolve to start anew." The formality of a ceremony is (for me) defined by how many times you have to get to your feet, touch your clasped hands to your forehead, and then prostrate yourself on the floor ("salamander position," I think of it). There were about twenty prostrations in this ceremony, each in reverence to the naming of a bodhisattva. There are certain traditionally named figures, like the bodhisattva of compassion, Avolakatishvara, patient listener, Manjushree, the ubiquitous Ananda, and so on. But (like the communion of saints in Catholic tradition) there are innumerable holy beings both living and dead whose gifts we invoke and honor. Since the ceremony was in Vietnamese, most of its implications were lost on me, and, besides, I am developing an antipathy to prostrations, which hurt.

Worse, the spectacle of a good convent schoolgirl flattening herself before a golden Buddha raises some primal Catholic issues:

I see myself standing in my green uniform at the knee of Sister Iraneus reciting the answer to the catechism question, "How does one sin against the first commandment of God?"

"Sister, one sins against the first commandment by consulting fortune-tellers, believing oracles, worshipping idols . . ." This was one of my favorite catechism answers because it raised in the imagination such an exotic swish of drapery, scent of musk, and flash of jewels. It posited, besides, an utterly unlikely source of contamination for a girl from the Roseville prairie: worship idols, indeed! I was sure I would never sin against the first commandment.

Never say never.

Sister Angela has told us English speakers that, although we might not understand the Vietnamese words, we should respond to the prostrations with an attitude of willingness: "Bodhisattva, I am here!"

But, to tell the truth, I rarely am.

Why?

THIS MORNING WE HAD only a half hour of sitting meditation,
then a round of prostrations and chanting of the Fourteen
Precepts in English with our typewriter Anglican chant; our singing
must be a trial for the Vietnamese, whose chant is so mysterious and
beautiful. Since last night's ceremony was in Vietnamese, this one
was in English, following some undisclosed rotation. The shorter
ceremonies occur in both tongues and sometimes in French as well.

I love the hour between morning meditation and breakfast,
time for a long walk and a long think on the recurring subject,
"Why am I doing this?"

Not to be happy, not to find inner peace. Thanks to grace, physi-
ology, and the enormous blessings my life has given me like a bag
lunch from God, how could I not be content and at peace? Besides,
from childhood on I have been attracted to the kind of principles
Thay lays before us as a source of happiness, chiefly the ability to live
in the present moment. This is no credit to me; it's an ability that
comes naturally to sheep, for example. But it does make you happy.
In my time, I have wallowed: in nature, flowers, dinner, children,
lovers, animal presence, music, dessert. As Thay says, the practice
of mindfulness is a sneaky way to have a rich life. If I wanted to be
more happy, I think it would be a piggy desire.

So why am I doing this? To be more clear about the ground of
peace, perhaps. To regard it steadily and without distraction. As
a kind of athletic training, perhaps. Surely with a hope to moving

some blocks within: to learn to be more loving and compassionate, less judgmental.

For the pleasure of stopping!

This morning I was aware of how heedlessly, in my time, I have wolfed food. Heedlessly, because I have always had that Little Something in my stomach. But here, hunger is a daily, hourly reality. There is plenty of food—and others with a different metabolism complain that they are putting on weight!—but for me the diet is about as filling as grass. How I look forward to being able to eat what I want. The pleasure of laying down an austere regime is not to be underestimated; this is one of the reasons I used to enjoy the rhythms of penance and feasting in the old Catholic calendar. During Lent in the novitiate, we had to fast even from music and bell ringing; we would waken every morning to a harsh wooden clapper, a knock on the heart. Then, Holy Saturday night, the bells returned in an ecstatic sheet of resonance. For maybe five minutes, it was possible to hear what had always been available for hearing, had we ears to hear. Then the veil dropped and ecstasy withdrew.

I am nosily interested, as well, in why others are doing this. Especially Sister Angela, one of Thay's first Western nuns, a woman about my age. With her shaven head and headmistress ways, precise, yet awkward if she is caught off-script, her shyness, her brilliance with languages, her austerity—why is she doing this? Sticking with such struggle and loneliness, like a nineteenth-century Methodist missionary penetrating China—why? I cannot imagine such a life.

For the ardent Catholic girl impelled to become a nun, there is so much more of a reward in the offing. The vulgar concepts of eternal life and privilege in heaven may attract some. But more purely, the great dialogue of love, the sense that one is "led and kept" of God, keeps one to the difficult tasks of Carmelite prayer or Franciscan social engagement. Buddhism, by contrast, promises nothing, gives nothing. One does not "love" Buddha; he is not subject to projections, though one may revere the transhistorical energy principle that is Buddha nature. And Buddha does not "love" us, prostrate ourselves as we may. I suppose Buddhism does promise one great gift: freedom from suffering, specifically the suffering caused by illusion. Buddhism promises to strip us of our false notions, false selves. To the extent we submit ourselves to this process, we become refined in compassion. Buddhism is a recipe for making oneself into an infinitely compassionate being, and we see evidence in the great teachers, like Thay, that the path is a true one. We even see evidence in our fellow monks and nuns. The pleasures of Buddhism are the pleasures of truth rather than the pleasures of feeling. Love does not flow from God into the monk and through the monk into creation. The monk is himself the energy center; he gives.

Some days the whole thing makes me shudder.

Rich Life

THAY SAYS IF YOU PLACE your hand on your heart and breathe with presence, you will know what you should and should not do to stay healthy. Sister Edith says that if you feel yourself becoming ill, you should "rest with acceptance of all that is." You should not use metaphors of "fighting it off," which rear up the spirit in a posture of violence. This is what I learned today by announcing that I was fighting off a cold.

Sometimes I feel that I am fighting off hepatitis B. One of the more difficult customs here is that of washing dishes in cold water. "The idea that dishes should be washed in hot water is only an idea," I say to myself, still shrinking from the task. This is especially ironic, considering that "doing dishes to do dishes" is one of Thay's central metaphors for daily practice. I fear I am doing dishes to get hepatitis.

But in fact, this is all the chatter of monkey mind. I have felt energetic, strong, and rested here. "I am unhappy to discover," I recently wrote to my son, "that eating your vegetables really is good for you."

Accepted or fought off, the sniffles disappear.

Today I had to gird up my loins for another Mindfulness Day. Most people look forward to these miniretreats; I merely endure them. Mindfulness Day means a long dharma talk, a very long formal (and cold) lunch with "pleasant conversation" encouraged after a long silence. I hate the pleasant conversation more than the cold food. As to the latter, I have mastered a sly new trick: putting my plate of hot food, the soup bowl acting as a little furnace under it, beneath my chair; then, taking my seat, I arch my cold, stockinged feet over the dish. This works well when we Westerners are side-lined to a row of chairs while the monks claim, in rigid order of hierarchy, their zafus. We pick up our dinner in the kitchen house, then process outdoors to the zendo, greatest to least. Even Thay, at the head, waits until the youngest child receives her plate and sits. ("The idea that food must be hot is only an idea.") These days there are many guests from the neighborhood attending, so it is quite a long procession.

Lunch today was unspectacular (being cooked by the monks rather than by the nuns): good lemony spinach soup, salad and rolls of tofu wrapped in—um, tofu wrap. But a great drama arose. One of the new monks from Vietnam had brought a huge box of delicious Italian candies and passed them around. I ate my meal without tasting it because my mind was on the sweet that sat bathed in light on the edge of my plate. Finally the moment arrived and I ate it in five tiny bites. I thought I had made a pretty mindful job of this bit of chocolate, but then I lifted my eyes to see one of the senior monks regarding his treat like a dropped leaf in a lotus pond. He smelled it, viewed it from all angles, then made sixteen bites of it. (I counted.) "Mindfulness is a sneaky way to live a rich life."

I also counted the number of candies one of the long-haired American men took when the box went round for seconds: *four.* He put them in his pocket. When the box reached me for seconds, it was empty. Grr, you swine.

Thay's dharma talks—attended by a wide variety of listeners from venerable ancient Vietnamese to scrappy young monks to casual visitors—tend to career suddenly from the abstract to the practical, which is where I get on board. Today, for example, there was an hour of nattering about nonself and soul, exegesis of Vietnamese and Sanskrit texts. Then a cut to the pragmatic:

"When we breathe, that is normal. When we practice, we bring mindfulness to breathing. Breathing is always breathing. Right mindfulness becomes one with breathing and gradually transformation occurs. When we breathe with mere recognition, quite naturally breathing becomes slower. When we dwell in sitting still, the quality of breathing is different, feels light. This is the joy of meditation. There is letting go and freedom in that. Thus we nourish ourselves. Body and mind calm down and we smile.

"We smile out of our inner calm and that takes the calmness deeper. The breath is a rest between past and future. We bring our mind home to our breath. Only our breath brings about oneness of mind and body. *Breathing in, I am aware of my whole body.* . . . We invite our breathing to embrace our whole body. This is the beginning of love, compassion, and understanding. Calm and harmony embrace our body. When five or ten minutes pass this way, my body is calm. This is mindfulness of body.

"Next we practice so that feelings become the object of practice. Peace helps us to do the work of healing. First we have put our body at peace, then we turn to our feelings. We feel joy because we see that the path is helping us. *Breathing in, I feel happy.* . . . We need these resources of calm and peace; only then can we recognize our unpleasant feelings. We embrace them. We do not blame or oppress our suffering. Embrace a feeling like a little child. Who is going to look after your unpleasant emotions if not you? We must not let the child be alone. Right mindfulness increases our resources. Our healing gets easier. That is the dharma, that mustard seed. Water it so it can grow. Embrace your suffering with your deep and calm breathing. You don't need to do anything else.

"Mindfulness does not force, does not invade. When we're sad, when we're angry, this is the way to practice: *I breathe in and know I'm sad / Breathing out, I smile with my sadness* . . .

"Don't judge, don't scold yourself. Just be with the feeling. When we have embraced our anger or our sadness in calm, we will begin to see its root. That is wisdom, and that is what liberates us from pain. Right mindfulness is presence, body/mind in the here and now. We can only recognize something when we are present, and then we can embrace. We make it calm when it is painful, but if it is already beautiful, we make it more beautiful: full moon, sunset. Stopping is essential to looking deeply."

A bunch of us straggled out of the dharma talk, like Jesus' disciples coming down from Mount Tabor, trying to get our notes straight. That is, those of us who are academically inclined went through this struggle. "Wasn't he going to define the soul?" Sister Edith demanded to know. "I lost him." Someone else tells her the opposite of what I understood Thay to have said about reincarnation and she writes it down. All of us hear through a scrim of our own questions, life issues, and impediments. As I try to "get it right" as dutifully as I can, I understand what a hash any record of a master's teaching is likely to be. And yet, the consequences seem important. In two hundred years, might a dutiful reincarnation of Sister Angela be trying to reconstruct Thay's teaching from my notes? People all over the world are doing very hard things— turning the other cheek, giving all they have to the poor, eating potatoes without salt—because some confused and yawning student took a note . . .

Moving Woods

WHEN I WAS EIGHTEEN, I entered a Catholic convent and stayed till I was twenty, at which point I "gave up." At least that construction was put on my exit by certain other members of the community and by my family. In those days, leaving a novitiate was not the popular gesture it became only five or ten years later. I suffered so from the allegation of "quitting" that I developed a manic ability to cling to choices well past hope of nurture. Like a certain hapless lamb I tended in October, I have lain by the side of too many dead ewes.

So I do not give up. I can't bear the nausea you feel when you realize you cannot go on, the dread that the very words "I cannot go on" might create their own reality, yet the inability to withdraw the words once spoken in the mind's abyss, the sense that a rope inside is inexorably unraveling and will snap . . .

Last spring in Wales I felt the lick of it. Robin and I were climbing a rock coast, just out of reach of the tide. We had stayed out too long, suddenly becoming aware of dark water flowing rapidly in. Robin was safe on a rock ledge and it was my job to get myself up there with him. I gave it two pulls and realized I had not strength in my body for a third. There was no way out but up. I was not afraid, I was merely nauseated by the inevitability of failure.

A crafty solution presented itself: I managed to wedge into a nearby chimney formation and ooch myself up with the strength of my legs. Robin advised against this, because his strength is in his biceps and triceps. Mine, though, is in my legs. When you are the sort who refuses to fail, you track your reserves of strength carefully. In most situations, now, I have the habit of conserving a little energy, a little awareness, a little caloric heat to carry me into whatever rock chimney presents itself, a way out. To resist that loosening feeling, that sick slide that defines one of the ways we die. I suppose I will have to die some day, but I hope to turn and take the step as if it were a judicious one, not with a scatter of pebbles under my desperate boot. That modest hope may be, of course, forlorn.

And in this spirit I enter my third week here.

My job today was posted as "moving woods," just like those guys in *Macbeth,* apparently. When I got to my workstation, it turned out that the task was actually to reorganize the woodpile. The Victnamese sisters make a team effort out of every task, which for me is often harder than doing it myself. I've always thought it an aspect of their friendly cohesiveness. Moving woods with them, I realized it's also because of their physical weakness. Most are physically frail, and I suppose have suffered chronic malnutrition.

Josef, the tall, thin, German engineer, has become my mentor, each of us visitors being assigned a "spiritual friend," now, to help us progress. I spent last night's session with him explaining my problems with cold and hunger. He was sympathetic. He, too, is always hungry. The nuns, he told me, subsist on the subtropical diet of Vietnam, low in protein. Any other alternative would be painfully dislocating for them. But they are often sick. Josef agrees, too, that it's not the easiest thing in the world to lower your body temperature twice a day with meditation, and then subsist on vegetables, no matter how attractively sauced.

At breakfast, I was piggy. Knowing I had a woods to move, I took a whole ladle of oatmeal, though I could see supplies running low. (I wanted two ladles—and did I mention that I hate oatmeal?) Newcomers are slipping into the community every day, mostly nuns returning from retreat direction around the world, but the cooks seem to make the same small amount of food. When it's gone it's gone, and the kitchen is locked between meals.

Most spiritual directors, I'm told, prescribe cold showers as a cure for what ails you. Josef, by contrast, advised me to spend time under the hot water tap. So far, I have stinted myself on shower time, imitating how careful the nuns are with all resources. "Get heated up any way you can," is Josef's advice. Today Josef fired up the big woodstoves, in kind response, perhaps, to my plaints. Or maybe it was just "time." Moving Birnam Wood to Dunsinane would be a small price to pay to get deliciously warm.

Annika wanted me to move the huge community woodpile from one end of the terrace to the other and methodically stack it according to the belief system of Minnesota. While I accomplished this meaningless Zen task, the nuns stood around and chattered in Vietnamese—about my competence, I imagined; but, later, one of them confided that I had dislocated their tofu operation.

Then, during our free afternoon, I took the three dogs for a long walk. Since I miss my sheep so much, these dogs are my special pleasure. Their short intestinal tracks do not subsist well on brown rice, so I am happy to assist them in varying their diet by taking them out to range the countryside. Out of my sight, I think they break into the traps, set all through the surrounding woods, by hunters who catch small animals and (I'm told) songbirds. I suspect the dogs turn over a few garbage cans as well when I'm not looking.

Benji, the terrier, has a bad limp. One of the sisters told me that he has broken his leg so many times chasing cars that they have stopped taking him to the vet. "He has bad habit energy around that leg," she told me. Habit energy is a Buddhist term for a way of acting, which can be good, bad, or neutral. When we repeatedly perform bad actions, like taking more than our share of chocolates, we create bad habit energy, a tendency to continue doing wrong. Meditating, by contrast, establishes a habit energy of calm and self-knowledge.

We are in a beautiful region of Aquitaine near the valley of the Dordogne. It was not easy to find that out, as nobody at the monastery knows or cares where they are in geographical terms. It's not that they are inattentive to nature; in fact, we spend a great deal of time stopping and looking in wordless contemplation at a plum branch or a maple leaf; it's part of the meditation practice. But nobody cares much in geopolitical or scientific terms to situate themselves. The region is characterized by precipitous hills covered in vineyards and little conscientious farms. The houses are all built of stone and have red-tiled roofs. It's hard to tell which ones were built fifty years ago and which two hundred. Sometimes you come upon the ruins of a house with a great bake oven half the size of the house—but most of these have burned down at some time and are choked with trash and nettles, and the relentless blackberry vines. Each farm has two or three huge milk cows and a bull, perhaps some sheep, and a flock of red chickens with the run of the road. They plow deeply here with small, old tractors. Could farming at home be made this simple?

A farmer next door is growing sunflowers, and they have grown two inches since I came, so the clay must indeed be full of life. The farmer often complains to me that his land "gives birth to stones." He was out there today throwing the stones around.

Further down the road, a farmer's dog came to yap at us. Soon the farmer followed and yelled at his dog. He was as eager as I to talk. The people from Plum Village are well liked. It is odd to see several monks or nuns in their habits, with Vietnamese straw hats inverted over their heads, strolling down the country road towards a French hunter, gun over his shoulder and dog at heel. The woods constantly ring with shots, and this is a great source of sorrow at Plum Village; so is the hunters' habit of chasing game across our property and shooting it on the other side. For my part, the sight of a goodly male physique swells the heart, whether or not he's carrying a rifle.

Oceans

I HAVE ALWAYS BEEN DRAWN to the image, although not to the reality, of religious austerity. This vision has involved a gothic window with a deep stone sill, me wearing an interesting long wool garment, beautifully tailored, my skin translucent with purity and my face full of kindness. Instead, here I am in my old slacks, my nose red, living the pure life with a malcontent and baleful outlook. I'm almost ready to settle down and practice seriously, as Thay recommends. "Don't waste time," is one of his repeated injunctions.

Bodhisattva, I am here! Mostly.

The dharma talk today began with another lesson in bell ringing. Then—

"The energy of right mindfulness helps us to be in touch with life, to see everything beautiful and nourishing in ourselves and creation, to choose good things to nourish us, to be present. If what we are present to is painful, we embrace and transform by discovering the things in the past that have caused pain. We see the basis of things, the basis of our suffering. Awakened understanding releases us from our suffering.

"The energy of right mindfulness is the energy of protection. *The dharma is my breathing. It guards my body and my mind....* Say this gatha to remind yourself that the body and mind can be destroyed by forces outside. We have to protect our person as a king protects his kingdom. In daily life, people without responsibility, careless people, can be invaded. The six entrances to the body—

eyes, ears, nose, tongue, body, and mind—can be invaded. At each entrance we need a guard: the force of right mindfulness; the capacity to recognize what is happening in the present moment. When someone is on guard, he has to have the capacity to recognize who is going and coming. Don't be an irresponsible king. Pain and suffering multiply in our territory. We escape through novels, cinema, car rides. Return to your home! Each moment I stand, sit, and lie down in mindfulness. When I speak and smile I am mindful.

"Buddha asks us to be mindful in our consuming. Of food, we ask, is it edible, is it nourishing, is it friend or invader? Eat deeply, know what you are eating and drinking. The capacity to recognize is right mindfulness. Sickness comes by mouth; therefore be clear. Food that makes us suffer we should recognize, guarding ourselves with right mindfulness. God or spirit does not help us, but rather we guard with right mindfulness. We are protected.

"*The eyes are a deep ocean, full of whirlpools and violent winds and monsters, but, holding my purpose in mindfulness, I am safe from the ocean of form.* . . . This is a text given by Buddha. The eyes let us see the blue sky, the white clouds, the sun rising, the smiles of those we love. Yet the eyes are a dangerous ocean. Being careful is a function of mindfulness.

"*The ears are a deep ocean.* . . . *I vow to hold the tiller of my boat so that I am not drowned in the ocean of sound.* . . . If we are not aware of sounds, they come into our mind and we can't escape. Songs, complaints, and self-pity are some of the sounds that invade us.

"The nose is also an ocean. Advertisers tell us that if you buy this soap or perfume, men will run after you. The names of these products make me laugh. *Samsara*—this is a circle of birth and death. *Poison. Scorpion. Je Reviens: I will come back.* But the girl in these ads is just like us. She has smell under the armpits. She wants to make herself into something not-she. These are hooks for innocent fish.

The senses are a deep ocean, full of whirlpools, violent winds, and monsters, but, holding my purpose in mindfulness; I am safe from the ocean of form . . .

"Mind is a deep, deep ocean . . . may I not drown in the ocean of objects of mind. . . . Waves of doubt. Suspicion of the person we love, Thay, the Buddha, the dharma. How much pain! We lose our territory. Doubt arises when we do not practice in right mindfulness. Practice with all your heart! When we are very stable, we can resolve sadness, anger, and fear. Without walking meditation, we cannot have enough stability to guard us. When seeds of doubt arise, accept and recognize them. That is stable practice.

"Anger is a dangerous wave. Somebody does something terrible and a great wave rises. You need to practice on little irritations, so that you can resist the great waves when they come. Practice and look deeply.

"There was a certain woman whose baby shit all over the living room. When our baby does that we just clean up, do we not? It took her three hours to clean. She repressed her anger. She knew it was wrong to beat her child, but she had no method available to her except classical repression. The next morning all was calm, or was it? The baby tipped over the sugar bowl. She beat the baby. She did not see sugar, she saw shit. Yesterday's anger broke out today.

"We are like that woman. We need to clean up shit in right mindfulness. Otherwise, the next day is just *retour de folie.*

"Desire is a wave on the ocean of mind. If we satisfy it today, it returns tomorrow. We lose our happiness. Longing to pass an exam, longing to be a leader, we lose our peace and the daily joys of listening to the birds, seeing the leaves. Mind is a huge ocean . . .

"In practice we learn what to let in and keep out. A conversation with a friend may be full of joy or it may make us not want to continue living. In the monastery, we do daily *kung fu:* this means practice, not martial art. We give the consciousness good food. Sit to nourish mind and body. Every moment of sitting should give us food.

"But suppose you are tired. Meditation makes us less tired. The breath becomes deep and slow. If we're tired, we must look after the body. When you're exhausted, just nourish yourself. In this condition you cannot look deeply. Nourish with the breath. Smile with your tiredness. In—feel better. Out—remove poisons. In—*deep*, out—*slow*. Recite the Refuge Chant.

"We have been given a sword to break up blocks of ignorance. We have been transmitted the sword of deep-looking. When we are alert and well we can use it; when we are tired it is enough to nourish ourselves. Anyway, we must always begin by nourishing ourselves.

"When we are truly clear, we say, 'How in former times did I enjoy this?' When someone asks us to eat meat, we feel instead compassion for all beings. We do not need God to protect us, our practice protects us."

After our session, my American friend from the upper hamlet walked us halfway home. "What did you think of that dharma talk?" he wanted to know.

"It's take-no-prisoners time," I said.

"It's like he's saying, *'Get serious, you guys, I'm not going to live forever.'*"

One of our academics is carefully recording in her notebook the words, "Clean up shit in right mindfulness." She pauses. "He did say that, didn't he?"

"He did." We're sure.

Failed Novice

LIVING AMONG ALL THESE thin Buddhist girls, I am taken back to certain peculiar struggles I had in the novitiate when I was eighteen. I say "peculiar" because they are not struggles that followed me home or have recurred in my life in anything like the same form. We novices worked very hard both physically and mentally and submitted our every "creaturely" want to rigid control. To be a good novice meant to be strong, hard-working, and focused. There was a perfectionist drive in this ferocious intent of the will, and it became a drug that first promised relief from pain—specifically the pain of inadequacy—and then became a pain on its own. The first stage was dominated by a feeling of "If I can do something terribly hard, perfectly, relentlessly, I will be OK. I will be able to put to rest this inner demon that cries, 'Succeed! Achieve! Be faultless!' I will feed it success."

And it works, this all-consuming willfulness, if success is measured by getting A's in college and perfect marks in novitiate behavior (except, perhaps, in the priceless areas of humor, nonchalance, grace, gratitude, and joy). But then the desire for control begins to feed on itself. Personality is effaced, one becomes a working machine. At least that is what happened to me. I would take on any task, pick up any burden, and do it on little food, sleep, or love; I denied myself the pleasures of poetry and art. I certainly did lose my ego, if that is one goal of religious practice; my awareness was wholly focused on a kind of white light in the mind. I existed like this for most of a year, almost without an intervening thought.

Behind my self-punishment was deep grief. A trusted friend had turned against me; another had left the novitiate; anyway, we weren't supposed to indulge ourselves in "particular friendships." If I found myself taking pleasure in the company of another novice, guilt assailed me. Yet I was a prey to sentimental longings—to spend hours walking the neighboring hills with Sister M, pouring out my overburdened heart to her motherly affection. To weep over Sister D's rendering of a Chopin ètude. It didn't have to be a particular friendship to snare me: color—the priests' vestment case with its handwoven purples and reds, embroidery floss, stained glass; worst of all, music.

These pleasures, in retrospect, seem both so rich and so innocent that I cannot imagine why they filled me with such quasi-sexual shame. I knew nothing whatever about "real" sex—I put the word in quotes because perhaps what I had discovered was an aspect of sensuality that may only exist in contemplative monasteries. I knew nothing, I will amend, about physical sex. Still, I had heard so many morbid sermons about what was in store for those who surrendered to unspeakable pleasures that *any* pleasure began to seem to me unspeakable. Any aesthetic or emotional frisson demanded its counterpoise of work and fasting and denial of access to the chapel in its better slants of light. We were all enmeshed in a cruel and foolish system; yet it was no one's fault—not mine nor the enlightened novice mistress's. There is an aberrant energy in religious psychology, both Western and Eastern, that hooks into our heavy bodies and makes us long for the state of pure spirit.

I guess this is why today I enjoy the company of ewes and rams, who do not even know that they will die, who chew their corn and like it.

Without knowing it, and without letting on, I was on a dangerous path back then. I have seen people follow it to death or crazi-
ness; I was saved by a flare-up of sanity. Sleeping somewhere behind
the glow of the white light was a healthy rational spirit that turned
itself on one day and said, "You've been here long enough."

An old novice mistress, whom I'll call Sister Anselm, was living
out her retirement with us. She had a reputation for being a bril-
liant scholar, but was feared for her cruel tongue lashings. Usually
she had little access to the novices beyond the classes she gave in
church history because the rules forbade fraternization between
nuns at different stages of formation. In the normal course of things,
no one but our own bright, kind novice mistress was supposed to
meddle with our instruction. But Sister Anselm had a way of lying
in wait for me. It was a species of favoritism. In fact, I admired her
so much that I often felt honored by her sadistic attacks. She had a
passion for detail and fact that ran counter to my sloppy love of the
broad sweep and its informing metaphor, and this difference in our
intellectual wiring brought me into frequent collision with her. I
studied for her exams with my usual grinding conscientiousness,
but she would always trip me up on a weird date or numerical obsession. Indeed, I needed the intellectual discipline she had to offer,
and many other habits of mind she inculcated as well: but she was
not one to offer a spoonful of honey with the Torah.

On one significant occasion, I had failed her test on the Psalms
because I had studied their content and neglected to quote them
by number. "Why did you not study the numbers?" she hissed at
me later. "Sister," I whispered, "the numbers didn't seem to me
important."

That brought on one of her epic rages. "How dare you decide
what's important—" she began, raging on through every aspect of
my personality and behavior. She had been watching me, she spat,

since I had the temerity to enter religious life, possessed by a demon of pride. Even in my postulant's tunic I had carried myself with arrogance, as though I thought I was somebody special. Now I had revealed myself as that most perverse and venomous specimen of religious culture, a *false mystic*. One who dared to judge what was important . . .

There had been scenes like that before, and a few would follow before I left the novitiate, but that was the pivotal one. She harangued me up until Grand Silence, and I remember leaving her in a kind of fugue state, going to evening prayer and then to the room in which I monitored four postulants. I put on my black dressing gown and wrapped the white nightcap about my head and started out for the tub rooms. I see that walk clearly because in some strange way I saw it from outside myself. My "self" was up around the ceiling somewhere, crouching like a gargoyle and watching that vexed girl walk down the long hall. I filled the tub and lay back in the hot water. With a slightly different karma, I might have drowned myself or gone screaming mad.

But instead, I got out of the tub clear in spirit. It was then about the first of October, and I had in mind to leave before Christmas. More importantly, I resolved to leave with dignity, as people nowadays plan to face death. I would insist on the right to speak about my decision to the other novices, to pack my own possessions, to say good-bye, and to depart by the front door. (Usually the "failed novice" slipped out during five o'clock prayer, and did so as soon as her decision was made, in order not to corrupt the others. They would pack her few things and mourn as I had packed and mourned for my friend.)

And with the help of the enlightened novice mistress, that's what I did. I knew I could not try harder, and I knew I was not a false mystic. What I was—though I did not know it then—was simply a person with good intuitive equipment and scarcely any brains at all in the conventional sense. No wonder I confused any onlooker with a decent education and habits of order.

That is one way to tell the story. Here is another: On the path of a sleepwalking girl rose a great spiritual teacher who yelled, over and over, "Wake up!" But the teacher's voice could not penetrate the girl's absorption. She stumbled on, bumping into a wall here, a wall there, and now a wall in the south of France.

But you see why I am suspicious of asceticism and self-denigration, and why, through that suspicion, I cast a jaded eye on some aspects of life at Plum Village. Thay's dharma talks sometimes reflect a deep current of warning against the world that seems life-denying to me. I look around at some of these frail nuns and wonder if they are committing a kind of self-murder, longing to float away from this agony of chilblains and lovelessness. Me, I would like to go to Bergerac and have a big cream tart . . .

But it is not my business, tempting though it seems, to judge others' motives and condition. Each of us has a different path to tread in the world. I need its mud on my feet, its cream tarts on my tongue. It has been hard for me to learn to love the world, and intuitively I know I must keep to that discipline.

My dear roommate and I sit on our mats and share recipes in reverent detail. And this is how I caramelize tofu . . . and I put a little apple juice in my pumpkin soup. . . . Mira shares her vegetarian gourmet magazines and I pore over the pictures, saying the names of Italian dishes like words of love, *budini di risi, condiglione* . . .

"The way through the world," writes Wallace Stevens, "is more difficult to find than the way beyond it."

Trancing a Rabbit

HAVING AT LEAST A LITTLE HOPE for the future of book arts—
that is, for the handheld, biodegradable, palpable *book*—I
am trying to imagine new incarnations for this one you're reading:
remaindered, shredded, returning as artists' newsprint or scandal-
monger's newsprint or animal bedding—these words and the
reader's marginal notes and grocery lists still shadowy among the
fibers. It has been through many shape shifts already. From inchoate
images, words migrate to the tongue, into terse journal entries, then
into expanded essays, revisions, and retakes. Friends write in the
margins, editors query. The writer's life itself inscribes a new layer
over the old text. Present experience alters the past and one must
rewrite, remember.

So it is that, several years after my adventures at Plum Village,
I return to this history, blue pencil in hand, and interrogate anew
the memory as well as the memory behind the memory. Thus any
page becomes palimpsest, new versions covering old narrative.

I know that old newsprint can be converted into animal bedding because these days I'm rotating through an apprenticeship
in wild animal rehabilitation; from this time and this perspective
I look back on my experience in the novitiate.

Let me tell you how to trance a rabbit (do I sound like Martha
Stewart?): Lay it close to your body, its four paws in the air, and
gently stroke its cheeks from nose to ears. If you have established
trust with your rabbit, this maneuver will induce a kind of deep

hypnosis in one or both of you. It's a good trick to know if you are house-training a domestic bunny, because they are subject to fits of hysteria when threatened by a dog or a vacuum cleaner or one of the inner visions of the abyss that plague these shy mammals. They have the ability to leap straight into the air and attempt to go in several directions at once; they shoot in circles around the room and throw the contents of their litter boxes. Trancing is a useful skill; we all need someone to practice it on us now and then.

However, I try to avoid all gestures of taming with the rabbit who's sharing my bedroom just now. He is a wild cottontail and I intend to repatriate him to his native habitat come spring. Tranced or not, wild rabbits live out their lives in a kind of edgy dream, always alert. In the five months I've observed this one, I've only once seen him blink his eyes, much less close them. For awhile I wondered if wild rabbits had eyelids. He closes them in security, I imagine, in the secret place he's made for himself behind a shelf of poetry books, lining a nest there with his handsome, hawk-colored fur. He has an open cage in my room where he deigns to take water, pellets, kale, carrots, arugula, and timothy grass, but rarely does he spend much time at home. Rather, I will come upon him behind my typewriter, in the wastebasket, at rest in the knitting.

Yoshi, as we call him, though that is not his name, was about the size of a golf ball when he came to me, the only survivor of a flooded litter. He was hairless and below the triage weight at the animal shelter, so, since they would have euthanized him, I decided to try to save him. (It was Sister Anselm, actually, in the course of a lecture on Francis of Assisi, who taught me how to do this, at least in the abstract.) He required stable temperatures and sugar water from an eyedropper every hour and a half around the clock. During the day, I carried him in a little pouch under my clothes. Huggers learned to ask, "Do you have an animal on your body at the moment?" At night he slept in a beer cooler with a heating pad under it. He gained weight and graduated to a doll-sized nursing bottle, became paper-trained (or at least trained me to put down copies of the *Chronicle of Higher Education* for him), and has now claimed his hermitage, where he sits by the hour in Zen-like stillness and chews on the books of poet Mary Oliver. The wildlife biologists with whom I've studied have inculcated in me an ethic of "rehabilitate and release" (indeed, it's illegal—and unwise—to keep a wild animal unless you have a license). I've tried not to make a pet of Yoshi, but to some extent he's tranced himself. Simply keeping him alive has compromised his wild nature, and he chooses now to climb into my lap if I'm sitting quietly. He hops around with every evidence of glee when I descend from my sleeping loft in the morning and fetch his rabbit snacks.

What a strange vision he has of reality, how different his life from that of cottontails outside—yet it is his life, the only one he knows. I am thinking about the rabbit worldview because I am pondering the collective hallucination that held us in place back in my novitiate. What kept us faithful day after day, negotiating the rigid hierarchy, the repression of every natural instinct, the discipline of appetite, the rising at dawn, the enforced conformity of dress and behavior, the austere and incommunicable delight?

One Candlemas Day I saw myself, saw the whole line of us, reflected in a corridor window, as though from outside. We had gotten up in the middle of the night, eerily singing, and processed through the dark corridors to chapel, carrying lighted candles. It was January in the world's calendar, and a few cars passed below us in the driving snow. Where were the drivers going at 3 A.M.? To the hospital, the airport, to assignations and intrigues? What dream were they in, and who had tranced them? I saw us, for the moment, through the eyes outside, saw the unsteady mysterious light.

On Good Friday, while the altar was being stripped of every shred of fabric and lace, we would cry out polyphonally in Greek:

Agios o theos! Agios ischyros! Agios athanatos, eleison imas! Holy death-
less one, have mercy on us. Thinking about it makes me want to go
and lie down, for how could we presume? We were babies in the
cosmos, rank amateurs, skidding up to touch the heart of reality,
naming it Mercy, and getting away unscathed. Then we would stroll
off to meals, learn medieval sewing techniques, so useful in the modern world—here, let me smock that for you—learn chemistry, how
to get candle wax out of wool, watercolor technique, modal music,
elocution, table manners, cooking. We'd make great wives, we assured each other, and most of us eventually did. We got the giggles
in church, played stupid practical jokes, got over our childhoods,
and loved each other, despite outbreaks of virulent malice.

The quality of friendship that can be cultivated in a confined
space with no television and limited opportunities to converse is essentially *artistic*. For me, shy and inclined to leap into the air and
fling myself in several directions at once, the novitiate represented
two-and-a-half years of taming. By the age of eighteen, I had
learned to make my way through life with a kind of intellectual intensity that masked emotional stasis. But the novitiate—despite so
many prohibitions against intimacy—was a school for loving. From
edgy outsider, I gradually moved into the experience of community.
I don't mean, as pious romantics may suppose, that we novices
smiled at each other all day and cooed out girlish sentiment. Quite
the contrary. Moving lockstep from morning prayer to lights out, we
learned to tolerate the eccentric and difficult members of the group.
Truthfulness became habitual—at least to the extent we knew the
truth—in an environment where every word and action was flung
out like a flag for all to see. In a way, the novitiate spoiled me for
relationships outside, because I'm always misunderstanding how
much reality people can bear who haven't lived a few years in a
cloister, or perhaps Vietnam.

Of course, we could be cruel, defensive, silly, and vicious as we

unwillingly surrendered the supports and addictions of life outside. In this laboratory, raw human nature became relatively trans-
parent to the dullest of us. Each one, ground in the same press, was
getting different lessons to be sure, one to soften, another to grow a
thicker skin. I learned a number of useful things in my novitiate:
time management, for example, as well as a variety of rude and
blasphemous expletives. But above all, I learned to let myself be
tamed to love.

Three young women, in particular, Sharon, Marcy, and Judith,
tranced me with steady affection. The order we belonged to, which
followed a Jesuit rule, was famous for its intellectual discipline and
methodical training for ministry, all of which did me a great deal of
good. But these three young women were on a different and better
path. They followed a rule centered on art, kindness, and contemplation; its liturgy was a peculiar form of manic one-on-one basket-
ball. They took me in, washed up from my dumb perfectionist
misadventures, and taught me to shoot hoops. I came from a family
where no one touched much—this is Minnesota—but they were
strokers and handholders. Maybe they had gotten together and
hatched a plot to rescue me—they were witty and subtle enough
to do that. Or maybe, by good fortune, I just happened into the
spillover of their loving natures. They let me be a fourth in their
subversive conspiracy of warmth. They let me into their family.
That I knew anything at all about loving my own children, or
could manifest to some surprised ten-year-old a casual jump shot,
is thanks to them.

Every vocation, marriage, household, and job site exists in a
fragile web of preconceptions and agreements about the nature of
things. If I call it a dream or hallucination, it is not to denigrate the
state or those who share it. It's the life we have. We may think it
essential that our foundational beliefs be true—I've certainly de-
fended the most bizarre constructions in order, unconsciously, to

protect the web I was swinging in. But in fact it is the nature of most dreams to unravel; usually a shocking cruelty or an insult to rationality pulls the first string. Then you are in for it. All the issues of human freedom and integrity come into play, all frailty and venality. What to do? Stay in the violated nest, clinging to shreds? Rebuild on a better plan? Go into freefall and land who knows where? I prefer the second alternative, but inevitably choose the third, or default to it.

Soon Yoshi will return to the wild. He will go to a transitional shelter to be "desocialized." He will be introduced to other wild animals in a controlled setting. Time will dim the memory of his hot water bottle, poetry, his winter kale. No doubt the dangers and pleasures of his new life will distract him from the visions that come to him in odd moments.

Empty

I DON'T TRANCE WELL ANYMORE, which is why the vagaries of life at Plum Village annoy me more than they enchant. When I got to breakfast this morning, falling in toward the end of the line, *everything was gone*. All I got was a bowl of hot milk and two small pieces of bread. I nearly began to cry, especially as I had to sit across the table from a large American who had two ladles of hot cereal in her bowl. Thay teaches that when you feel a strong emotion, you should breathe it in and smile in welcome. Anger, in particular, is a part of us. Think of it as a little sister who is straying and needs our love . . .

"Breathing in, I know I feel angry and deprived, breathing out I smile and cradle my anger like a little sister . . ." Rather desperately, I abandoned myself to the gatha. With no warning, the veil lifted and I was taken away from Plum Village, away from breakfast, and into some landscape of desolation and horror. Suddenly, the hunger was not mine, but that of a starving, enraged Vietnamese child — and yet, *the child was me as well*. I sat in my chair, which at the moment was not my chair, blinking. I hate these sudden teleportations. It's hard enough to keep up a conversation without careening in and out of multiple realities. I was tempted to click my heels together and think of Kansas.

Coming back to the table, I probed for feelings of guilt. Not so much guilt as awakening. This is how things *are:* empty bellies and full bellies. I have taken too little care of this.

And I still want a cream tart.

Full

IT CAN BE EMBARRASSING to have your prayers granted, your
selfish wishes fulfilled: muesli and hot milk with raisins and
applesauce, croissants, crepes with strawberry jam, crème fraiche,
two kinds of cheese, crackers, and real tea. This morning the
hungry child was well fed. Presiding over this cornucopia of
blessing, the loving abundant hands of Hilda. The occasion: a precepts transmission. Today I and a beautiful young girl from New
Zealand went through the elaborate ceremony that binds us to
the precepts of Plum Village forever. With chants and prostrations
too numerous to recall, with friendly pokes in the ribs from one of
the nuns ("Now you stand!"), we received our new dharma names
and affirmed our intentions: to protect all life, to share time, money,
and resources, to behave responsibly in sexual relationships, to use
loving speech, to eliminate the toxins of alcohol, drugs, junk food,
and degenerate culture from our lives.

From the beginning of my stay, I have pondered the problem of
"taking the precepts." My first roommate took them only eight or
nine days into her stay because she had been living so much in accord
with them already that she felt no reason not to. But I had to struggle
with many aspects of the wording and intention. It helped when
Josef explained that the precepts represent habits of the spirit, rather
than injunctions. Next I had to write out my "vows and aspirations,"
a required paragraph about how I intended to live my life. My first
roommate had written about "self-actualization," I think, a worthy

project but too abstract a goal for my barnyard mind. I thought and thought. What was I called to do? What was my deepest leading? How should I spend the second half of my life?

It was kind of like inviting a bunch of fairies to your christening. Now's your chance; what do you want to achieve in the spiritual realm? Several weeks of musing led me to the notion that on the whole I could commit to an open heart and greater compassion for all beings, that I would like to transcend my judgmental nature.

Then a perverse inner voice rose up in my mind and said, "Listen, Mary Rose, maybe God wants you to be the unsentimental, judgmental, and snappish bitch you are. Maybe *you'd* like to be more lovable and kind and get invited to the better parties, but God must have made you a certain way for a purpose." After that, I couldn't come up with any vows or aspirations that didn't seem tainted with self-interest, fret and revise though I might.

What broke up this ice jam was that encounter with Thay in the dining room. In a transforming shot, my aspirations came to me in dead practical terms: "In my work as a shepherd, I resolve to be calm and present to my sheep and accurate in observation of their hooves and eyes, wool and breath, so that they may not suffer. I aspire to make my farm a refuge for all beings, a place where people can work, get hungry, be fed, and feel the deep peace of animal creation, the completeness we long for."

Sister Angela gave me an inspired dharma name: "Tending of the Source." I love its gerundive ambiguity! I love its image of a fresh spring rising out of sand flats; Robin once led me to such a place in the Wisconsin woods. I love its humility and honoring of plain work. I have no idea what it means!

I did not pass this happy day in idleness. Mira and I were assigned to cooking duties in the kitchen. Sister Thoai N'ghiem, our job captain, took me aside and told me seriously, "I rely on you and Mira. You are both so steady and reliable." My heart

swelled as much with her praise as with my new name; both serve
to heal the part of me which someone had called "false mystic."
And even as I rejoice, I see my illusions slide in, the panting need
to be perceived as a good worker. At least now I am able to see
them as illusions.

The nuns smile at me now and call me "sister." It is as though I
have passed some test I didn't know I was taking. The community
values its precepts, I guess, and the unity of mind they represent. I
have been taken into that unity; I have chosen to enter it. I have been
received.

Soon an assignment interrupted our progress toward lunch:
"Sister Ani is sick; will you make a tray for her? You must be *tending of the source.*" I composed Sister Ani's tray like a painting, her
tangerine a flower.

The kitchen lit by Mira's calm spirit, we cooked up a squash
soup with apples, black-eyed peas, and greens.

I had no expectation that this would be a happy day. I have never
been one to anticipate a sunny wedding or a birthday party; the best
days come without expectation, according to the dour tenets of
Minnesota, and they had best be unremarkable days like the one
Emily chooses to relive in *Our Town.* And yet, the day I made my
first religious profession thirty-some years ago, was quite a good
day, and so was this one.

The writer Maxine Hong Kingston is staying with us for a week,
so we had a BBC crew filming our precepts transmission ceremony.
She has been working with a group of Vietnam vets, writing about
their war experiences in the context of Buddhist practice. It's been
odd to trip down the stairs at 6:30 A.M. and come upon a BBC
camerawoman frantically applying makeup in the shower room.
Maxine told me that one of the crew, used to covering war, riot, and
turmoil, has reported feeling "never so disoriented as at Plum
Village." That made me feel better about my own adjustment

problems. Maxine is a tiny, gentle person with gray braids whose books I love, so why not love her as well? I'm happy she is my dharma sister.

Yesterday we had a big celebration to open the three-month retreat, and about six new Americans have arrived. Since the precepts transmission, I'm feeling tranquil and big with vision: I think a lot about the farm I want to live on, a place where people can come to write and pray and create in the peace of animal life. I feel that Plum Village is giving me what I need to know to build community with people of different backgrounds and degrees of engagement. It presents, as well, a religious practice that is accessible even if you don't believe in God or honor Buddha, if your motivation is merely to become more calm and centered and to share silence with your community. And yet the practice takes you deep.

At the beginning of this year I had no idea why I felt led to light out into the unfamiliar territory of sheep farming and Buddhist practice. Now a vision is beginning to form in my mind.

Stop

Thay's dharma talk today continued to explore "The Living Tradition of Buddhist Meditation."

"Above all we need to *stop*. We need to stop our wandering. Why? Each of us has a homeland, ancestors, parents, roots. Opportunities for happiness, peace, and joy, but instead we wander. When we leave home we meet suffering, danger, and death. We may betray our roots. Alphonse Daudet wrote a story about this, about a certain Monsieur Seguin and his goat. M. Seguin wanted his goat to be happy, but the goat was sad and kept running away. 'Don't leave the garden,' M. Seguin told his goat. He had to tie him up and shut the door, but he forgot to shut the window. The goat escaped into the forest. M. Seguin went into his field and shouted to the goat to come home. But by then the goat had been eaten by wild dogs. The dogs had made a barking noise. The goat had heard both the barking and the cry of M. Seguin calling him home. He chose the barking.

"In all of us there is a goat like that. We have the seed of a hungry ghost inside. Sometimes we are standing in our last opportunity to return home and don't know it. We move toward the barking. Sometimes for even a very small reason, a butterfly, a small mistake. When you've made a small mistake, don't weep anymore, go home.

"There have been a thousand years of running away. Elder sister must bring her younger sister home. The wind pushes us to be a wandering spirit and, if we look, we see that our life in the past is like a dream, and when we wake up we want to return home.

"It is like this: A student, tired and hungry, was returning from exams and collapsed at the home of an old man. The old man said, 'I will make you millet soup and you lie down.' The student fell asleep and dreamed he had passed his exams with distinction and that the king had given him a princess to be his wife. He became a mandarin, but then invaders came and he was told to lead the troops. Being a poor strategist, he lost the battle and disgraced himself. Deep in dreaming, he shouted out in terror. The old man touched him and woke him and when he awoke he saw that he was lying in the house of a spiritual master. 'Get up and have soup with me,' said the old man. In enough time to make soup, the student had been through so much!

"What am I following? What am I chasing after? A butterfly? A hare? All these things take us away from home. A spiritual master wakes us up and says, return to your home.

"We are 'drifting and sinking.' We are going around in circles like a wheel. In your heart, you're going round and round. This word, *wheel, huan,* also means 'to sink, drown.' When we come into the meditation hall we say, 'Coming into the meditation hall I see my true self and all drifting and sinking ends.' Meditation is a way of putting an end to drifting and sinking. Our daily life is filled with drifting and sinking, even if we wear monks' robes. Doing walking meditation, which should be free and joyful, we may be drifting and sinking. Sitting in meditation, we may be drifting and sinking.

Breathing in, I know that I am breathing in.
Breathing out, I am growing calm.

"Yet we drown at any moment. Our roots, our ancestors are calling us home. M. Seguin used his trumpet to call his goat, but the goat would not come. Buddha is our parent; he loves us like a mother, but if the child runs away, the love has no effect. If the child remembers, a miracle happens. The Buddha loves living beings as a mother loves her child. If the heart remembers the Buddha, then there will be a meeting in present and future. Running away has become a habit, but when we practice, we recognize the habit. It is as though we are chased by a spirit. We eat as if our house were on fire, sit as if on coals. We learn the habit of agitation. *Stopping* means to recognize unhealthy habit energies.

"In Plum Village, practice stopping when you walk. When you have a need to go somewhere, do walking meditation *as though you've stopped.* Whenever you need to go somewhere, go in the spirit of walking meditation. The habit energy of running away is so strong. We run away twenty-three hours a day—one hour of formal walking meditation is not enough to counteract it. Twenty-three hours of running! One hour of walking is not enough. *All* walking must be walking meditation.

"This is how to walk. Breathing in, I step with my left foot: *arrived.* Breathing out, I step with my right foot: *home.* You can walk quickly: *arrived arrived arrived / home home home.* Open the door to our true home. All it takes is mindful breathing. Even one step takes you home.

"But our unwholesome habit energies push us along. Smile to that: the force of forgetfulness, no-mindfulness. We have to recognize the force of forgetfulness. *Arrived home. Arrived home. Here here here / now now now.* Our practice is to realize returning. When we walk, we return home. It's the most important practice. Also cooking and eating.

"Learn to combine breathing and steps. If you need to go fast you can. The in-breath is simply measured by the number of steps you have to take. Just don't say you have arrived if you are drifting and sinking! That's like counting someone else's money. Give up the past and the future. Life-Buddha-mother-father: all are here and now. Everything is here. Pay attention to your breath. Perhaps, if you are a beginner, the outbreath may be longer than the in-breath. *Arrived arrived / home home home.* Be aware of what your lungs want. After practice, our breathing becomes more and more deep and slow. But the practice must be of the heart, not of the form. Return home with every step.

"From time to time, we stop and see the fields of our home, the bird, the leaf, our homeland. Dwell peacefully. Do not lose the bird, the sky.

"If you have legs, you can do walking meditation. Let's imagine an astronaut who goes to the moon and is stranded. He can't return to earth and has little oxygen left. In the last moments of life, what will the astronaut think about? Remember the earth. With eyes of right mindfulness we can see wonderful things. The astronaut longs to return to earth. Other desires are old ash. He wants merely to take peaceful steps on earth. That is enlightenment. Do we have the capacity to take light steps, free steps, nourishing heart, mind, and body, untying the knots? Get down to the practice. It's not hard. Peace and joy are in every moment. Paris is four hours on the TGV, but you can return home in one breath. We cannot maintain stability without nourishing our breathing. Mindful breathing holds us in our native land."

❧

I seem to be taking longer and longer notes on the dharma talks. I think this is because I am more capable of taking it in. The first week all I caught was "Return to the island of the self." And I hope I do justice to the talks in transcribing them, trying merely to straighten out a sentence that's trailed off or hitch together some frayed grammar. Thay speaks slowly, so it's not hard to get the words, and he repeats a lot. Still, as a teacher, I've observed how often my students write down the exact opposite of what I say. It's easier to get it one hundred eighty degrees wrong rather than just a little off. And of course, I can't reproduce his graceful diagrams, pictograms, and excursions into technical Buddhism.

As I take my notes, I gain insight into how to read the scriptures of any spiritual master: did Jesus' disciples sometimes write down exactly the opposite of what he said? And as I mull things over, I study the process of my own ongoing conversions. "Heart speaks to heart." If wisdom resonates in my heart's core, I try to take it in. If it baffles me, or puts me off, I let it sit awhile. Have I got it precisely reversed? Is it simply not meant for me? Or is it a "hard saying" that I will have to carry, a koan to be resolved in the deep inner recesses of the mind? In any case, there's little sense in swallowing what I do not recognize as food.

Today I felt out of sorts. After a few hours of conversation with Maxine and the men with her, I wanted to follow them back into the world, like M. Seguin's goat. I don't, on the whole, share Thay's distrust—as it seems to me—of the world.

Just before leaving for Plum Village, I spent a few days among fundamentalist Christians in rural Wisconsin. I was fascinated by the ways they've evolved for keeping out the world. They have fundamentalist Christian videos, fundamentalist Christian poetry, and fundamentalist Christian novels, for example. The stories usually revolve around someone's temptations to consult a fortune-teller or have an affair, and how the Christian ultimately made the right choice. Even to the little written reminders hung up everywhere ("God is not mocked," or whatever it be), I can find parallels to Plum Village.

We had similar practices in the novitiate, too. The bell, for example, used to ring once an hour to remind us of the presence of God; Thay's clocks chime every fifteen minutes, for us to go inward and say, "Heart, mind, and spirit in perfect unity. I send my soul along with the sound of this bell . . ."

Plum Village shares certain customs with fundamentalist communities, but that does not mean it is intrinsically similar. The differences, at least, are as important as the similarities: guilt and judgment are notably not in the equation, for example. I guess if you take a set of principles seriously, you find ways to, as it were, set them as a seal upon your heart and door. I know that when I go home, I will be in the market for a chiming clock. I cannot return to my heart for more than a few seconds every hour, on the average. And I want to. I do.

Still, I perceive the world to be negotiable territory: choose the good, stay out of the sand traps. Be mindful, breathe, but don't be extreme. It's well to remember that, once again, this is monastic practice, and what we carry back to the world ought not to be the *pure* practice of Plum Village.

I think I'm the only one who has these quibbles, so I get a little lonely and tend to keep my mouth shut. I study, above all, to see whether or not people are happy, for this seems to me a good test of religious practice. I've paid my dues to unhappy novitiates. Some of the nuns do not seem happy.

But what do I know about these women and why they are here, or what it would be like for them some place else? This may be the one spot on earth where a certain kind of unhappy woman can live the most sane and balanced life available to her. There are other signs, besides joy, of the indwelling spirit: patience, courage, integrity.

Surrender Again

PLUM VILLAGE, as I've said, is not a retreat center in the American sense. It's more like a mountain climbing expedition where the attitude is, "I'll tie myself to you, but try not to dangle unnecessarily because we're all going to be really busy on this mountain." We're now in the three-month Rains Retreat, a traditional period of extremely serious practice. More people are coming and going, including more Americans. In no way can we depend on our promised two-to-a-room, or even that we can stay in the rooms assigned. In a few weeks, most of the present community will be moved to new (reputedly shabbier) quarters to make way for Christmas guests, usually American couples.

I can't help but speculate as to how my first roommate would have fared in the community as it is now constituted, fiercely focused and struggling. One of the young women who has just arrived is both generous and demanding. She is beginning to be shunned a little. As another retreatant put it, "She's needy and I want to help her but not to the point where she invades the space I need to do my inner work."

I met a newcomer yesterday who spent some time in a Zen community. He told me, "How you do this is how you do everything." He told me, "Surrender."

How I do this is with a lot of analysis and bitching. I have no intention of surrendering to anything illogical. When I surrender it will probably be later, after I've gone home and thought about it. Next year maybe.

Dharma Rap Session

SINCE THE RETREAT HAS BEGUN, we've started a new form of group spiritual guidance called dharma discussion. It's quite fruitful. Essentially we sit together on our circle of zafus and talk about issues related to our practice. Andre, a delightful Frenchman of about my age, said at the first discussion that he was lonely and needed to have more intimate conversation. "Let us," he pleaded in his labored English, "put our *tripes* on the table."

After that, I put out a few of my tripes. I told about my initial reaction to the community. I said that, on the one hand, every community has to protect the privacy and integrity of community practice, not encouraging retreatants to wallow in the problems they might have brought along; but on the other hand, might it not be possible to practice hospitality in a way that makes people feel more welcome?

People seemed to take my critique with good grace, though one of the permanent community members simply said, "It's not that kind of place." Amazingly, I have grown quite comfortable with the kind of place it is. You certainly aren't called to pretend hospitality when you don't feel it. And it's a relief to escape from social identity, no one caring who you are back home, how many children you have, etc. Or at least, caring little.

In yesterday's dharma discussion, Sergei, a seven-foot-tall young Russian teenager who can barely speak English, managed to blare in ferocious tones, "Sister Angela!!! Have you had success in practicing anger?"

Silence. We all breathe in, breathe out. Sister Angela inclines her thin body toward Sergei and utters the word *no*.

Silence. We breathe in, breathe out. Sister Angela inclines again: "That is why I remain here."

Community

THERE ARE SO MANY new people in the group now that I can
barely keep track of the names. I watch their process of assimilation with interest. I'm always trying to figure out how people
can live together without tearing each other to pieces like cats tossed
into a burlap bag. But that is not the most appropriate inquiry at
Plum Village. "Community" is not a concept people seem to think
about—though this may change as more Americans come for the
retreat and the American obsession with "processing" kicks in. I'm
sorry I will not be here to see that. Still, I feel I am taking away some
valuable ideas about living with other people. It helps to have some
transcendent discipline to focus on, some reason for all to be gathered together that calls each beyond his or her own problems and
"woundedness." Here, it's the practice that calls, the nonnegotiable
time on the zafu.

Last week was pretty easy and mellow. I was warm and free
of aches. My roommate and I get on like two contented dogs who
amuse each other, exchange a few daily barks, and then flop on the
floor to dream about food. Then suddenly, irritation broke out all
over. It began when Mira loaned me the pruning shears she had
borrowed from Annika so that I could cut some bobbins for my
knitting. As I walked past the zendo, shears in hand, one of the sisters set upon me. "Where you get scissors?" I explained that Mira
had them from Annika. The sister said they were hers and she
needed them for flower arranging. I bowed and smiled and said

I had to return them to Mira. Within five minutes, two other young Vietnamese women were at my door, demanding the scissors. All of the participants in this fracas were women who had never talked to me before, and who had certainly never appeared on the second floor of the dorm. Nor had I ever seen such a degree of emotion among the nuns. Fortunately, Mira came in just then and I gave her the shears. She gave them to one of the young women, not without misgivings. What would Annika say? When you live in a situation where there is a lot of communal property, some people become inordinately possessive of, in particular, the tools of their trade, be it kitchen utensils or mud boots. *Inordinately* is not the precise word. Some people take care of tools and some people don't, and communities contain 50 percent of each type. Even Josef showed some upset the other day at the woodpile when he discovered the chain saw dull as a dinner knife. I sympathized.

But the dynamics of the argument are less important than how the parties are to be reconciled. Curiously, no apologies will be exchanged, I know that much. Last week, I asked for some rice to feed the dogs—my assigned task—and a young sister snapped, under pressure to get dinner on the table, "Get out of my way!" Later I apologized, because I come from Minnesota where, when someone bumps into you, both say "I'm sorry!" a ritual three times. Another sister told me, "We don't say 'sorry.' If someone offends you, that's to practice."

It seems to me that at Plum Village we often live in the chill that exists when manners are absent, or, worse, not agreed upon among the different cultures present. Josef tells me that we offend the Vietnamese constantly and they us, but we have no way to bridge the gap. And perhaps no necessity to, because offense is "to practice."

A friend of mine who works in the prison system in America says that the cardinal rule of prisons is "do your own time." That's true of Plum Village as well. Mira has told me how difficult she finds the newcomers who spill out stories of their wounds and their need to heal. We ponder whether they're trying to get others "to do their time." But what would be an appropriate and compassionate response?

Josef and I focused our consultation (again) tonight on these issues of "practicing anger."

"It's not even anger," I told him. "It's irritation. Irascibility. Someone pushes my buttons, makes unfair demands, and I get all testy inside."

"The important thing to remember, again, is that they're your buttons, not the buttons of reality," Josef reminds me. "Someone else does not have these same buttons. Therefore, your irritation is based merely on an idea of how things should be. A relative idea. You are producing the feeling with the underlying perception skewing your judgment. You have to get at the underlying idea."

"How do I do that?"

"It's very delicate and intelligent work. You have to wait. When I'm angry, I find at the roots of it some old hurt, some pride, some mistaken idea. That is the important aspect of practice. That is the transforming element."

All my life I've been dominated and motivated by the sentence "It's not fair!" This was a great rallying cry in my family and in the working-class socialist milieu where I had my political birth. The people I admired, like Meridel LeSueur and Pete Seeger and Dan Berrigan, were people who transformed personal affront into social agenda, who fought for things to be different. "But some things," I told Josef, "are objectively unfair."

Josef always smiles at me with great, lively kindness. I think he loves to sit on his zafu, "upright like a human being," and rant about philosophical positions. "The objective standard of fairness is only an idea!" he brings out with enormous pleasure. "Behind anger is always an idea. Here is what you have to understand: it is possible to change bad things in society without an adrenaline kick to motivate you. That is the fundamental thing Thay is doing."

"How do I change things without anger?"

"You observe that something is wrong and you gently put it right. It is as though you peer at a flower arrangement and reach out to adjust a branch." Josef smiled and leaned across the low table between our zafus to touch an imaginary flower. "With no more emotion than *that*."

Very interesting, very helpful. Very hard.

"You must try to learn a simple, open approach to reality, with no preconceptions."

"That's a big order. I'm full of preconceptions." I cast my mind back over the whole history of my nature, nurture, and graduate training. This is a real puzzle to me: how to take in useful information and to enter into the cultural conversation wisely—and yet hold ideas lightly, a juggler's golden balls. I don't rely on anger much to motivate my small contributions to social change, but I do rely on commitment and a certain intensity. The intensity, for sure, breaks my peace.

"The opposite of a simple, open approach to reality," Josef was going on, "is a consciousness dominated by old traumas. Thay calls these 'seeds' in the mind. When they are watered, by events or by our own encouragement, they grow into big trees in the mind. Each seed of anger or lust or greed is lovingly reinforced. Stop this process. We can only reverse these negative patterns by watching the feelings arise and not watering them. Don't believe in them. Don't get sucked into the drama."

I reflected that contemporary psychology tries to teach the difference between healthy and unhealthy internal conversation. You can tell yourself you are stupid, or too wounded to carry on, and this belief becomes your reality.

"Yes," Josef agreed. "We have to bring our minds into a

condition where we see the roots of behavior. Let me explain to you two Sanskrit concepts: *samata* and *vipassana*. Only with calm mind, *samata,* can we get *vipassana,* insight. It's nice to be calm, but the real purpose of meditation is to obtain wisdom. If we are practicing irritation, here is how we do it in the practical order: when I am irritated, I make a note. Perhaps I am in the kitchen and too busy to stop and meditate. But we have to acknowledge it. Always acknowledge the feeling. Then come back to it in meditation. Do the deep looking then. We are not doing walking meditation just to walk around and get rid of anger, we are trying to get at the roots. 'Breathing in I feel my irritation. Breathing in I see the roots of my anger . . .' It is a very deep practice."

Work

I NEED TO WORK HARD, if only to stay in shape for shepherding
back home, and I like to think I'm helpful to the community.
Lately, though, it's become clear to me that much of the work we
do is less community business than cosmic test. I imagine Thay
lurking around the fringes counting our respiration rate rather
than the number of logs we carry. For my part, having established
my credentials as Queen of the Woodpile and carefully bossed its
stacking and aerating, left notes all over it in numerous languages
about which wood is dry, which to take first, etc.—I, the Queen of
the Woodpile, have seen my management demolished at whim by
some tiny sister who decides the wood must all be moved elsewhere
in order to provide a space for her to squat on the floor and make
tofu. This makes me bubble with inward laughter.

My favorite absurd job this week was clearing land for the lotus
pool. The lotus pool is, just now, a huge dirt-filled basin the size of
a soccer field south of the plum orchard. At first glance, I thought
it was a watering system for livestock, or maybe even a swimming
pool. But no, Thay has a vision of lotuses blooming there. Our job
was to carry rocks out of the basin. Some twenty monks appeared
from the upper hamlet, and we all set to work bucket brigading
stones out of the hole. It was a great team effort and hugely amusing, though all of us knew that the slightest frost heave would fling
up another thousand stones, half an abandoned farmstead, and the
corpse of a Neanderthal hunter. We breathed and enjoyed each

other, despite a severe injunction from Sister Angela: "Work meditation is not to be used for chatter and exchanging histories."

I see some of my own earlier quandaries mirrored in those of the newcomers, particularly in a tall Norwegian who gets as impatient as I used to do with chain saw massacres at the woodpile and inefficient task management. Work, where both of us come from, has a goal in sight. We are not used to the idea of merely being *present*. "Working meditation," however, is relaxing, freeing, and gives the dullest task potential spiritual energy. (Still, I can hear my grandfather's voice demanding, "Well, are we going to do this job-a-work or are we going to have some kind of tea ceremony?")

Don't ask. Yesterday, my task was to find, wipe, and dry ninety leaves, red-gold and green, oak, maple, and, I dunno, maybe a few hemlock needles, to be put under each cookie at—the tea ceremony. At first I thought this a comical job; then I began to be as intrigued as I might be at an Impressionist gallery by the brush work on each leaf. By the time I had arranged my ninety leaves, I was disappointed to find the work over.

It must be time for me to go home. I'm getting too good at living here.

Formal lunch today was unusually formal. You are supposed to chew each morsel thirty to fifty times. Halfway through a long chew, I turned to Sister Edith and said, "Breathing in, I know that I am exquisitely bored." Eating slowly is of course more amusing if you have some of Sister Thoai N'ghiem's fried eggplant in your mouth than if you have a hunk of dehydrated tofu or (as I recently did) a majorly hot pepper. In general, I find it more productive to be present to happy moments than to painful ones.

We had another dharma discussion this week at the upper hamlet. I was asked to speak because I am leaving soon. I raised an issue that has been plaguing me but which I find hard to articulate: why is it that negativity has so much power, while the positive energy I am putting out (I hope) in my meditation practice seems so puny and ineffectual? For example, when something has gone wrong in the barn and a couple of folks are angry and kicking the sheep around, whatever little energy of calm I carry into the situation seems a match in the wind. It just doesn't affect the environment at all. I raise this humble example because not much is at stake in it. We're not negotiating a peace treaty in the Balkans or anything. Yet it seems to be a microcosm of moral quandary.

I say I find this issue hard to articulate, and I did not make my meaning clear at the dharma discussion. People immediately wafted off into The Problem of Evil. That's amusing to debate on the philosophical level, but my own problem is more down-home. I've been practicing meditation for some thirty years and I haven't the strength to affect the most unpracticed anger in another person. Or so it seems. Anger seems *naturally* strong; meditation practice grows at the rate of stalagmites. Is this fair?

I suppose one might say that it's easy to make a lot of noise banging with a drumstick on a coffee can, hard to play the violin. Most people in modern times prefer the cultural equivalent of banging on coffee cans. The only reason, nowadays, that I play the violin, badly as I play it, is that it changes *me*. I get Bach into my blood and bone, even if I never play well enough to make another human being happy. So I should meditate to change me, not the barn.

Perhaps, too, I confuse spiritual strength with competence. Dream on if you think you can manage sheep with spiritual strength; you have to know the job. In most areas of my life, I'm still the sorcerer's madcap apprentice.

Though, by damn, I know how to pile wood.

Lightning

THIS WAS TO BE MY LAST dharma talk, and I was hoping for lightning to flash across the sky of my invincible ignorance and jolt me all the way to Bordeaux. But no. Today's was one of the very technical dharma talks, mostly directed at the Vietnamese monks and nuns, that explored in excruciating detail some point of lineage. Sister Angela conscientiously translated the Vietnamese and I conscientiously wrote down the ideograms and foreign words. Finally Thay began to talk about koans, although his branch of Mahayana Buddhism does not do much with this practice.

"Koans are buried deep in the unconscious, watered carefully like flowers. They do not respond to intellectual reasoning. Mind has not enough power to break the koan. It should not be answered, but absorbed and waited for in right mindfulness until it explodes and wakens again in the conscious mind as a flower. *What did you look like before your mother gave you birth?*

"You cannot break this koan with your mind. Mind is like a train on rails; it has to go in a certain direction. Koans remove the rails. Most work happens in an underground storehouse that mind can only fertilize like a good gardener. It is not the object of dharma discussion, but of burying, watering, caring for. We trip on a stone and suddenly we understand.

"At Plum Village, our basic koan is *What are you doing?* The answer is *Breathing and smiling.* Often I ask a student, *What are you doing?* Often the student responds, *Cutting carrots.* I say, *Good luck.*

Now, you don't need luck to cut a carrot, but you need luck if you are going to get your practice back on track."

As Thay began to talk about arcane matters of lineage, I must confess I fell asleep. I woke with a start as I heard him say, "In this tradition we are taught that when we are sleepy, we should bring attention to our nostrils. And when we are agitated, we allow right mindfulness to descend to a point just below the navel. When we breathe in, lungs expand and push down the diaphragm, a curtain that divides the chest cavity from the abdominal cavity. When you sit or lie and your breath becomes long and slow, just enjoy it. Peace in body or mind. Love your body and transform it in peace and joy. When eating, sit with your back straight. Put your bowl in front of you and practice breathing. Be present for yourself and the sangha. Practice for elder sister is practice for younger sister. If we have stability in practice, our presence is beautiful for the sangha. Don't put anything in your mouth that isn't clear to you. Say its name: carrot. An ambassador of earth and sky. Eat food, not worries, not regrets. Don't chew the cud of anxiety. I only have to eat mindfully to be worthy. How can I eat so that stability, stopping, and freedom are there to nourish everyone?

"A certain student came from California. She cried every meal. She ate tears. It took her a month to see. Her head was drowned in regret, shame, suffering. The sanghagaya was patient. She wanted to be with Thay, not anyone else. But without the sangha, Thay is not there.

"Walking meditation should nourish and look deeply and help us to surrender, as well as sitting meditation. And when the time of this retreat comes to an end, I will have nothing more to say than that."

꩜

The time of retreat is almost at an end for me.

For my graduation exercise from Plum Village I've been given another difficult roommate. And I'm sure she is writing the same line home about me. We just don't hit it off. To look at it first from the newcomer's point of view, Mira and I have become a pretty tight unit. We have our ways of doing things, and we like each other a lot. I'd hate to have to break in as a third in this tiny room. But—here speaks Minnesota—if I had to do so, I'd be quiet about it, figure out the culture of the room, the unwritten rules, grovel a little. This woman, by contrast, has taken a lot of assertiveness training.

Her first night was not a happy one. We could hear her tossing around in the dark. Finally, she set a huge lantern by her head (two feet from mine) and began to read. Dozing, I leapt awake in panic. After about an hour of trying to calm my heartbeat I told her (which meant breaking Noble Silence) that I tend to have panic attacks at night and it's hard for me to sleep with so much light and action in the room. She took her torch to the opposite end of the bed and read under the covers. Fine, I went to sleep.

Today she came at me fiercely with one of those speeches beginning, "I have needs . . . ," a phrase that always sets my teeth on edge. It seems she hadn't been able to sleep at all, raging about being exiled under the covers. Her need was to have the light on at night.

This seemed to me stunningly unfair. "People sleep in the dark," I snapped. "Everybody knows that."

She came back at me with the language of conflict resolution seminars, which always makes me see red. "I want to hear from you that you value my pain, and then we can negotiate. I don't want to be told what your rules are."

I snapped that I didn't care to play New Age language games. The fact was, of course, that I did *not* value her pain. At this point we were practically spitting at each other.

Getting into fights with people is not uncharacteristic of me, and this is not the first time I have found myself spitting bullets in some pacific environment, a Quaker retreat, a classroom, a dinner party. It's very shaming. I have a terrible temper, and when I complain that my meditation practice has advanced little in thirty years, perhaps I should simply acknowledge that it's kept me out of a maximum security lockup so far.

Mira, looking on, was no help. She is so easygoing that she merely stretched herself out like a cat and drawled that she could easily sleep with the light on. Or, I should say, Mira was a great help, because she reminded me that, once again, I was making an absolute out of something that's relative.

It was a classic face-off: our new roommate asserting the hard face of "I need," me cruelly trying to convince her that her need was irrelevant.

Something happened, though. In fact, it had begun to happen the previous night, as I lay awake listening to her stalk around. Deep compassion had come over me and a feeling of connection between her insomnia and my own fearfulness. And at some point in our argument, this spirit of compassion rose and took possession of my anger.

Several years ago, my friend Peter Crysdale and I took a long and arduous summer car trip along Rehoboth Beach with two fighting children in the car and no reservation for the night. At one point, we stopped the car, hot and furious with each other, and in the next moment fell suddenly, unaccountably, into deep peace. I think of that moment in Rehoboth as one of my few experiences of grace, free and unmerited.

Similarly, some wing brushed over the lunch table at Plum Village. Compassion got the better of us. Suddenly we both became eager to compromise. "What I really need is another hour to settle down, read, and write letters. After that I can turn the light out," she said.

"OK. What I really need is just to know the light won't stay on forever. Nights are a tender time for me, psychically."

"For me, too." That was the crux of the issue. We had both blundered onto each other's nonnegotiable terrain of panic. And we managed to blunder off.

"So . . . ," I said to Josef, a few hours later. "The idea that people should sleep in the dark is just an idea."

He threw back his head and laughed. "You always carry things too far."

At each of our sessions Josef and I have gone a little deeper into issues of practicing meditation through anger, annoyance, and the distresses of community life. This may seem a rather petty and superficial inquiry compared to the great questions of contemplative prayer, but frankly I wish John of the Cross and Teresa had a little more to say on such humble subjects.

In my time at Plum Village, each of my characteristic areas of annoyance has been probed. The universe is such an efficient school if only we could see it that way, instead of fidgeting through the lessons that appear daily, tailored to the individual needs of the student. We pay hundreds of dollars in tuition at workshops to change our lives, when, instead, we could simply stay home and practice. We behave spiritually as I sometimes do in the gym: taking the elevator to the third floor in order to use the stair-climbing machine.

Certain predictable problems recur in my spiritual life—though I can predict them, they always surprise me: I become irritated easily, I make harsh judgments about other people, I let myself be invaded by assertive personalities, I love my comfort, I suffer from fear in the night, I hide when I'm suffering, and I expect to be an outsider. Each of these problem areas was probed on a daily rotation at Plum Village. The education was, as we say in the barn, "hands-on."

Susan, a lovely woman who came into the community during my
last two weeks, made an excellent point about this process one day
when we were having a chat on the end of my bed mat. She said, "I
came here with the idea that I wanted to become more flexible and
more tolerant, but I expected this to happen through a sudden flash
of insight. Instead," both of us threw back our heads and laughed,
"we have roommates."

Seldom do I look on daily inconveniences as opportunities to
become a more flexible and tolerant person. I try to get rid of the
inconvenience, the burr in the sock. I take an aspirin, or go to a
conflict resolution workshop, hide out with a book, get a divorce.

In our last conference I confessed to Josef what a ferocious spat
I had had with our new roommate and asked him how I might have
handled it better. "Sometimes you have to forgive yourself for anger
or depression or negativity. They are the price of knowing what
we feel. Knowing what we feel is the basis of compassion."

Some people think that Buddhism teaches us to detach from feelings. Not true. Thay's practice is always based on knowing what we
feel, which is one of the most reassuring things about it. Much of my
training, in conflict resolution, in Quaker practice, and in Catholic
pedagogy, has failed to tell me what to do with negative feelings.
Or probably they told me, and I was unable to get it. So typically I
work through a fit of anger by explaining carefully to myself why
I shouldn't be angry, cutting the feeling into bite-size pieces and eating it. Two hours later I scream at someone who cuts me off in traffic. My dad was this way, too. We used to hate to go to restaurants
with my gentle dad, who never lost his temper around the house
or at work, but was death on waitresses.

At the same time, those "get it all out" schools of anger management don't appeal to me either. "What do you think about
those therapists who have you beating on pillows and so on?" I
asked Josef.

"I think that may help you to know you are angry, if you don't," he replied. "And it's very important to know you are angry. But it doesn't do anything with the root cause. For that, you need a very strong practice."

I think of Sister Angela, who shivered in this place for seven years before any other English speakers arrived, with no one "to share my despair" as she said one day at dharma discussion, laughing a little too dismissively at her own pain.

The problem is not the feeling, but what we do with the feeling that makes trouble—be it break a plate, a heart, or a head, erode the stomach lining, reach for a drink. "Stay with your feelings," Josef told me, "but *stop*. Don't attack. Don't react until you can ask the other person what she means or feels."

One of my Quaker friends—a woman who, like me, has quite a struggle with anger—once told me about sitting in Quaker meeting across from a man she assumed to be an emissary from the National Rifle Association. He wore a shirt that read "Support Your Right to Bear Arms." The proclamation made her furious. She stewed all through meeting, building up quite a stomachache, by her own admission. Later, in the fellowship hall, she discovered that she had misread the man's shirt, which proclaimed instead the comic takeoff, "Support Your Right to Arm Bears."

So much of our anger is based on this kind of misunderstanding. It's our interpretations and constructions that cause so much pain in our own gut and in the outer world where we act out our misapprehensions. Popular culture is no help, because it frames issues in ways that teach us to feel offended at our victimization over one thing and another. But it's hard to play the victim at Plum Village because this is a community whose members have transcended horrors. A social activist during the Vietnam War, Thich N'hat Hanh has always opened himself with particular clarity and compassion to survivors of war. "There was a war veteran here," Josef told me, "so wounded in spirit he couldn't participate in community life. He lived in the woods with wires strung around his tent to warn him of any approach. When an airplane went over he would throw himself on the ground in fear. The monks told him patiently, 'You are not your past.' After a long time he recovered, and now he is one of our most respected retreat leaders."

I know that many of the nuns and monks suffered unspeakably in Vietnam, from every sort of physical and sexual assault, starvation, deprivation, and worst of all the loss and dislocation of family. Their bodies are scored with the wounds of war and poverty. Still, there is none of that "processing" that obsesses American communities. How impatient they must get with us, our "needs," our stories of "abuse."

"I was sexually abused on my last job," a young American woman told me recently.

"Did you report it to the police?" I asked.

"Well, I mean, I was passed over for a promotion."

In my experience, there are two kinds of difficult people in community: those who are deeply troubled in some way that makes them screw up every encounter, task, and friendship, and those who are pseudo-troubled and want to take up the community's time telling their hard-luck stories. The deeply troubled often get shunned, their presence so challenging that people simply avoid them. The mere whiners—these folks will turn any group of four into a support group for their issues, and, when the group has collapsed in exhaustion, move on to another and happily tell their story again. They operate in the same way with ministers, teachers, helpers of all kinds.

"How, then, does Plum Village handle difficult people?" I asked Josef.

"You need a sangha with a strong practice to carry anyone who isn't able to do it. The *practice* has to be inviolate, and it takes about fifteen strong practioners to handle one troubled person."

I have heard this ratio mentioned before. Thay sometimes takes in deeply troubled souls—or they simply arrive—and fifteen is the number of people he thinks necessary to absorb them and lead them to understand that "they are not their past." After a long time.

Strong practice. Strong practice. An individual, "sitting for the world," as Thay puts it, and a group sitting to support each other. This is not a quick fix. . . . You have to get cold and hungry, or sick, or lonely, or furious to develop a strong practice. That's why I'm glad nothing at Plum Village was the least bit easier for me than it was: because it made my practice a tiny bit stronger.

"What do you think of assertive feminists?" I asked slyly. Josef is a very masculine man, in the sense of being logical, tool making, problem solving, etc., so I can imagine that he attracts quite a lot of negative energy just by existing in the lower hamlet.

He confessed that this rejection sometimes occurs. "Some women are being taught to say *I* very loudly, and this blocks mutual understanding."

A Scotsman I know raises border collies, and for years I have wanted to buy one of his puppies, but he is so irascible and short-tempered that one must approach him cautiously on the subject of collies or any other thing. One day, with the greatest mildness I called him up and squeaked, "John, do you think you will have any puppies to sell this spring?"

There was an exasperated silence and then John's burr cut out at me, "The bitch will no' whelp because you want a puppy, lass."

"That's what I have to tell myself, sometimes," I told Josef, "when I'm getting assertive: 'the bitch will no' whelp because you want a puppy, lass!'"

Josef laughed at this, and agreed. "It's just what I want to say sometimes."

Josef wound up our conference with the suggestion that I spend some time every evening reviewing my day. "See it like a video without judging. Review what you've felt. Start backwards, from most recent events and wind up at the morning. It will give you distance and a little clarity. Befriend yourself. Insight means to *see*."

Excess

AND THEN I LEFT Plum Village. When the appointed day came, all of France was shut down in a labor strike. "Mary is leaving today, whether the trains are running or not," Rosa announced at breakfast. She knew me well. We shared hugs and addresses, work gloves, work pants, instructions on woodpile management— and then I hitched into Bergerac with a woman who was taking some clothes to the Red Cross. I was happy to be going, and sad, too. Each woman I left behind among the new retreatants was a little short story I wouldn't be able to read, and I longed to know how each one's time would go and what would happen.

Those first few hours in Bergerac were almost hallucinatory. Sensory deprivation had sharpened my hearing and sight. A few notes of opera, a piece of camembert, a cup of espresso would halt me in my tracks, almost unable to attend or swallow, so intense was my delight. I was glad I could be alone for twenty-four hours, because my new state was too tender to bear human encounter. I needed to eat a little and then retire to my hotel for a rest, drink a little tea, and turn my chair to the wall.

I have two dear old friends living in France, Joe Guerinot and Richard Strobridge, who came to pick me up the next day. How utterly peculiar that after a time of physical austerity and spiritual richness, I should be vaulted into blessed excess and *more* spiritual richness. Joe is a painstaking gourmet cook and Stro a magnificent artist. Stro has made it his task in life to decorate the little church

in their hometown every Sunday. Colorful, fanciful, and passionate, his images succeed each other Sunday after Sunday, and then
he tears them down. Their beautiful seventeenth-century farm is
full of Joe's family antiques. I looked at every beautiful thing like
a child recalled from coma. Their daily kindnesses made me weep,
their meals put ten pounds back on my frame. "Love calls us to the
things of this world," Augustine wrote.

PART THREE

I Saw a River Rise

Apprentice Shepherd

I T'S BECOME NATURAL to me to define myself—should anyone
care to ask—as an apprentice shepherd. There are other parts
to my identity, but this one sums up the state of the organism at
present. My work (by which I mean the duties of being who I am)
has taken me all over the country this year and plopped me, red-
eyed and blinking in the customs lines of several foreign countries.
Wherever I go, people ask, "What do you do?" And I respond, "I
take care of sheep."

Most people have had some kind of experience with farming,
so this turns out to be a good neutral subject—sheep, nature, manual work. It leads to interesting and useful conversations. It's so
different from saying, "I teach English," which used to be my answer to that question, and will be again in a few months. When
I say, "I teach English," people apologize for their bad grammar
and then clam up. When dentists introduce themselves, do folks, I
wonder, apologize for not flossing? Two other categories of people
I'm acquainted with seldom confess to their occupations: psychiatrists and nuns. Psychiatrists find it brings conversations to a halt,
as the interlocutor begins to censor himself for images of pine trees
and cigars. Nuns find they have to endure hours of complaint
about the trauma induced by Sister Mary Paperweight in fourth
grade.

Most job titles, after all, simply announce status. If you say, "I'm
an attorney" or "I'm a physician," people scuttle around and fight

to carry your luggage. But an apprentice shepherd has a humble vantage point from which to view the passing flow. A woman I admire, who could as well have claimed the status of "poet," wrote, "I'm nobody." If you're nobody, or an apprentice shepherd, you can sit there in your veil of skin and be at home, you can hunch on your backpack and talk to the porter or the woman who cleans toilets or the schizophrenic man hanging out on the floor next to you. Sing if you want to. Draw pictures; pray out loud. Take full advantage of your status as "common laborer." That's how a French customs official recorded me. I was so pleased. I felt elemental, an old bleached bone. "When we let go of all we're clinging to," says Meister Eckhart, "then God begins to be."

Flying into London, I reflected on what I ought to "bring home," to use Josef's phrase. I had already reneged on one of the precepts, for how could I disdain a crackling roast of rabbit prepared by Stro's loving hands? It occurred to me that if I did 50 percent of what I had learned in the monastery, I'd be living a significantly saner life. If I did much more than 50 percent, I'd be inventing a new form of eccentricity. This contrasts directly with the practice of my friends Lee and Luke who came back from Plum Village, installed a bronze bell in their living room, and began to create their sangha. They expect visitors to bow their heads every time the clock chimes, as they do, and say the gatha.

Such a classical observance would not be appropriate for me, and why not? There you have the whole mystery of personality. Luke is the sort who can sweep everything along in front of his genial temperament. And I am not.

Home

I GOT HOME IN TIME for Christmas, or at least my body made it. My spirit remained in the transcontinental void. I was confused about how to be. It felt like bits and pieces of my personality were floating all over the rooms I inhabited, and I didn't know what rope to pull on to find "mother," "lover," "friend," "cook," "Christian," "Buddhist," etc. My inner committee had expanded by about four new entities. My house seemed disgustingly cluttered. I wanted to put my mattress on the floor. I wanted Vietnamese food. The idea of cooking a ham for Christmas was nauseating, but when I announced that there would be squash soup and homemade bread and cookies for December 25, it confounded the family. "Cool," however, said my children. "Unacceptable!" declared my hospitable sister, who supplemented the austere board with her own treats.

I think I am still taking it all in. The desire to get rid of furniture and put the mattress on the floor has resolved itself into a deep, patient cleaning. I'm only emerging from the back of the furnace room at present. A huge stack of stuff has gone to Goodwill. We have at least three different vegetables at every meal and often (to the delight of my Japanese housemate) we eat with chopsticks. I'm in the market for a chiming clock. I try to avoid meat, to the extent it's compatible with hospitality and graciousness.

"Meditate on the feelings of starvation you felt at Plum Village," one of my friends has advised. "You will find there the green shoots of your new life." But I don't know what that will mean. I'm just patiently cleaning the furnace room.

Cleaning

SLIDING INTO THE DANGEROUS hypothesis of connection, "Say nothing!" I learned early on. Don't bother to mention ecstasy, trance, vision: the normal terrain of childhood. Yet extra worlds slip by us, interpenetrate maybe; we drift together in a web thrown out in the cosmos by unknowable fishermen.

If this were not so, our human world would contradict the data of all the microcosmic systems we are able to apprehend. Are we so different from the paramecium? Why should the world(s) end with us? Does the amoeba, trying to get the hang of rainbows, fish snouts, a finger in the pond, wonder as well? Clearly, he *should,* we might tell him, we, the fishers bent over his universe.

But, "Don't even tell your dreams at the breakfast table!" people tell us. Thus we are broken of childhood.

I was five years old, dazed to discover that I existed as some kind of consciousness covered in personal flesh. Covered yet flowing, dispersed among grasses, tiger lilies, animals; stunned in a disc of light, on the hillside above my grandparents' cottage. When the light faded, I ran bellowing into the house. "Grandma! I'm alive! I live inside this body! I could be in some other body but I'm not!"

My grandmother gave me a long look as though searching for signs of fever. "What other body could you be in?"

Yesterday, Haney's cows had gotten loose and careened down that same hill. Clinging to the water pump in the side yard, I'd barely escaped their hooves, interrogated up close the wild rolling eyes. "A cow! I could be in the skin of a cow!"

My grandmother cupped her hands around my face. "Listen, Mary Rose, don't allow yourself to think about things like that." She handed me a broom. "Now I want you to go and give the outhouse a good sweeping."

Whenever in my youth I edged toward mystical intuition of any sort and dared to express it, somebody made me clean a bathroom. In the convent, I got this charge so often that the other novices nicknamed me "Sister Mary John." My long apprenticeship to the practical has grown out of this training, and on the whole it's done me good, acquainted me with the heavens of earth.

When my own children, however, reported the moments of transcendence that come unprayed, unbidden to the young, it became our custom to light a candle. It doesn't seem to have made them peculiar. As adults, they are capable of tracking their stocks and bonds as well as the movements of heavenly spheres without much dislocation. They live in a bigger pond than I could be permitted.

So I was not surprised when few people, except my children, had any inclination to light a candle for my experience when I came home from Plum Village. People work hard and can't disarrange their lives to take in a traveler's tales or deconstruct a stranger veiled in familiar skin.

So I stitched together an acceptable identity, pinned it on like Peter Pan's shadow, and went back to work in the barn.

"Hi, Mary."

"Hi, Ben."

"How was it?"

"Cool. What's up?"

"You could clean that shit out of the lambing pens."

"OK."

"Did you get my Frisian bull semen?"

"Sorry."

"S'OK."

May all beings be at peace. May all beings be brought to enlighten-ment. May all beings transcend desire. . . . Thus I had prayed every day in a freezing zendo west of the Pyrenees. How could any of it be compatible with life on an American farm? I couldn't imagine.

When You Talk to Angels

I<small>T'S HELPFUL TO COME</small> again to your own religion after you have filtered it through some radically different sets of belief. "Beliefs," in fact, are what then come into question. When you hang out for awhile in Buddhism, Sufism, or whatever, you notice that religious phenomena remain constant, although the metaphors around the phenomena change. The beliefs that tether these blimps of metaphor to earth—they change, but events, across the landscape of world religion, are similar. Something happens. We name it, according to our cultural understanding, but that is not its *name*. We name *angel, demon, grace, redemptive suffering* because we have to invent some counter, some token, to represent our experience and pass it on. Then we construct a hypothetical framework to contain what happened, to position it within the shifting watery world of other things we know.

I saw an angel once, down at the Catholic Worker Center. I had led a group of students to this shelter for homeless people as part of a course I was teaching on peace and justice issues in urban life. Three or four of us had been eating lunch with a group of men who used the center as a kind of dayroom while spending the rest of their lives under bridges, atop sidewalk grates, and in the caves by the Mississippi. One man at our table was garrulous and argumentative, regaling everyone with fantasies and incoherent tales. Another, though, seemed completely dissociated, hunched over his plate with a hat shielding his eyes, out of it. Most homeless people, of course, represent the tribe of abandoned mentally ill, and you can't always be sure to what extent they are tracking any diversion the education and social work establishment has cooked up for their edification. All religious traditions treat wanderers with respect, however; such a one may be a saint or deva, sadhu or buddha-on-a-mission. As a Catholic child, I learned that St. Joseph often goes about—who knows why, for he was a good workingman—disguised as a bum. All mendicants were referred to in our novitiate as "josephs." If the beggar was drunk, the nuns told me, he could be presumed to be St. Patrick.

So it was that, at the end of lunch at the homeless center, we thanked our companions for sharing a meal and parted with friendly words. The hunched man, who had seemed so out of it, stumbled away to dump his paper plates and I thought, "Why follow him? He's crazy and won't understand a farewell. On the other hand, maybe something will get through. . . ." So I went after the man and touched him lightly on the arm. "Thank you for eating with us. I hope you have a good afternoon."

The man slowly turned around, his face visible to me for the first time. He straightened up out of the long black coat he was wearing and looked at me. I fell back two feet. I think I put my hands over my face. In retrospect, I can see why such visitors begin interspecies communication with the words *Fear not*—because his face was full of light and energy radiated from him that seemed about to push me over. This was not one of those kindly, peaceful angels domesticated in recent years by purveyors of New Age goods. The feeling—or communication, if such it was—I got from him was, "Excuse me, but I'm busy keeping this whole boiling room from exploding into outer space. Thank you for your interest. We'll get back to you. . . ." Maybe after the Rapture.

I sat down. Later I thought that this must be the phenomenon which those who encounter it call "angel," *deva*. But that fell short, by a lot, of its name.

If I call this a religious experience, I mean simply that it involves a phenomenon accounted for within the structures of religious inquiry and not so well-delineated elsewhere. It may be a phenomenon best addressed by physics, for all I know, only physics hasn't gotten around to claiming it yet. Both the naming and the categorizing must be tentative, especially because contemporary culture invests words like "angel" with more drama than they warrant. In the spiritual economy, compassion is significant, surrender is significant, forgiveness is a very big deal; angels, by contrast, are nothing special.

When you have a religious experience, the next person you meet on the road is important. A certain kind of psychiatrist may categorize what happened as a psychotic episode. A fundamentalist Christian may try to frame it for you as an occasion to submit to a very limited schema of interpretation and rules. Maybe it's best to meet no one at all, or someone whose car has broken down and needs help changing a tire.

Barn Ecology

WE LIVE ON THIS FRAGILE earth by a slight series of adjustments necessary for life to thrive, and minor alterations in barn ecology have major effects on the health and well-being of animals. Last year about twenty ewes aborted at the beginning of the January lambing; pigeons nesting in the eaves had dropped a small amount of dung into the feed bunks, causing an outbreak of psittacosis. This year those same animals have acquired immunity to psittacosis, though we remain at war with the pigeon community.

Our winter lambs are being born with a variety of anomalies—thick amniotic sacs, an imperforate anus, a cleft palate—"monstrous births" that would send farmers of old into trances of terror: Are demons abroad in the land? Witches? Our own explanations are scarcely more rational most of the time. We blame global warming, pesticides, pig farmers, and politicians. Fortunately, not all the little shifts in barn ecology move us toward a tragic view of life. A little yeast added to the feed, for example, is promoting record lamb growth.

Maybe I need a little yeast in *my* feed. We humans run about the same weight as sheep; "things"—though not necessarily pigeon shit and yeast—must affect us to the same degree as it affects them. This careful nurturing of animal welfare makes me aware of what we do to ourselves. As Robin and I watch our old, but hearty, dogs tear around, we wonder if we should start feeding ourselves Science Diet.

It's been twenty below zero for quite a long time. One of the guys in the dairy barn told me that a cow dropped a cow plop on the tail of another heifer, who was lying down at the time. The plop froze instantly, pinning the second cow to the ground until somebody chopped her free with an ax. He swears this story is true. It may be.

Yesterday we lost a ewe, smothered in the middle of a circle of sheep huddling against the cold.

Kids in my neighborhood have been making a game of throwing a glass of water into the air and watching showers of crystal fall down.

We lost triplet lambs this morning about 5 A.M.—the one hour in the barn when no one is likely to be checking. We are there all day, and we check as well in shifts at ten, midnight, and 2 A.M. Usually ewes can lamb on their own, but this time around we have lambs smothering in those amniotic sacs as thick as freezer bags. "Old ewes," the vet says (or witchcraft?). We've had two C-sections, one yielding healthy twins and a triplet who died soon after birth. These unexplainable losses make us uneasy, savages sitting around trying to read the entrails of our beasts.

Literally, yesterday, we were doing just that: we posted the dead triplet in the lambing barn on the back of an old shed door. We needed to see if it had breathed and suckled or died before birth. Ben slit it open with a scalpel. I've never dissected anything before, not even the junior high fetal pig. None of the schools I went to took science seriously enough for that. So I was surprised to see the shiny technicolor organs stowed away as in an efficient sewing kit. Stomach contents good, nothing apparently amiss.

"Ben, you should have on your surgical gloves."

"Yes, Ma."

This class was hard on the new students. Docking tails, then a postmortem. If it's a class with lots of women, I'm more attentive

to the possibility of students crashing to the floor in a faint, but in
reality this is a sexist assumption. Our new students are unusually
competent and questioning, many coming from farms of their own.

"How can you justify docking a lamb that's going to be slaugh-
tered at twenty weeks?" Paul wants to know.

"You wouldn't have to if you knew for certain he'd never get
scours, but if he does, and his tail gets dirty, you'll have sheep maggot problems." Scours is a common animal diarrhea; Ben can describe sheep maggot problems in breathtaking detail, but, deep in
the sewing kit, he doesn't bother.

"In Britain they have a law about leaving enough tail to cover
the anus," I say. "What's our rationale for not doing that? Would it
help the prolapsing problem?"

"We feel it gives problems with breeding," Ben responds. "If
there are any hard balls of dung back there, it hurts the ram's penis."

There is a sheep show coming up on the weekend, so Lucy and
I will be on duty in Ben's absence. It also means we had a long job
of washing and currycombing our best animals. Last summer, Ben
was so embarrassed about the sign I painted for our booth at the
state fair that he never hung it up. Artistic it may (or may not) have
been, but from the standpoint of breed conformation it would have
put us to shame. With six months more experience, I laugh at its im-
perfections. My ram didn't look "stylish." It had a "feminine" breast.
It's amazing how you see the details of a thing when it involves your
world of stewardship and concern, though of course the rest of the
world doesn't care. I suppose one kind of knowledge is best defined
as a deeper and deeper insight into the details of a thing.

The Best Way to Work with Lucy

Lucy: Let's milk off that ewe with the big teats and tube her lamb.

Mary: OK, sure. . . . You know, some guys might back 'er up in the corner and hold her there while the other worked the lamb at the teat.

[They toss some hay around.]

Lucy: Mary, back that ewe up in a corner while I work her lamb at the teats.

I've discovered that the best way to work with Lucy is to follow her orders and never contradict her directly, which makes sense because she knows more than I do, especially about science. But she tends to prefer dramatic interventions and fast athletic solutions. Some of these are necessary in production farming. But I, for my part, do not like to intubate lambs if I can avoid it. The procedure is essential if lambs have no sucking reflex or if for some reason you can't get colostrum—the mother's first milk—into them. Without this substance a lamb has no immunity and will almost certainly die. But intubation is essentially traumatic and, while interfering with the mucosal lining in a lamb's throat, it introduces bacteria. What's seductive about procedures like intubation is that they tend to be quantifiable. You know how many ounces of milk you have gotten through a tube, but it's harder to tell how well a lamb is suckling on its own.

We have a fridge full of dead lambs at present. They lie in there like a heap of Goodwill toys.

Yesterday, Sunday, I stopped by the barn on my way to the Quaker meetinghouse. Lucy was picking up the dead lamb she had been intubating. A ewe was running around with an afterbirth trailing out of her. The dogs were snapping at her heels, trying to eat the afterbirth. Normal chaos.

I took off my skirt and sweater, got into my filthy snowmobile suit and boots and worked for several hours instead of going to meeting. Two sets of twins had been born in the early hours of morning, one set dead. We fostered one live twin at the bereaved ewe, who accepted her well, and kept the other with her mother, a ewe with teats so gigantic the lamb couldn't figure out what to do with them. They are the size of inflated rubber glove fingers (if you happen to go around inflating your rubber gloves).

Maybe it boils down to what a person's good at, these issues of intervention. Efficiency and economies of scale also enter in. Anna, in England, used to say that women who had borne children had a natural instinct for raising sheep. This may be true. I know how to get human babies to nurse: engage the turning or rooting reflex by tickling the baby's mouth at the corner; tickle top and bottom lip to get it to open. When it's open, slide in the nipple. That's how I work with lambs and their mothers. It's a patient and quiet business, much more time-consuming than intubation. But I love to sit in the dim warm barn with a lamb on my knees bringing it on to nurse. At such times, there's nothing I'd rather be doing. I wouldn't say I missed meeting.

Farm work provides for me a space that the spirit can sink into and repair its frayed ends. I'm told that the musculature of the physical body sustains little tears and insults as we go about our daily work, and that we need deep sleep to repair damaged tissue. In stage-four sleep, the brain secretes a growth hormone that, in turn, nudges the liver to produce an insulin-like substance that goes to work easing the microinjuries of every day. A busy cycle of internal healing operates while we're unconscious. I'm convinced that the spirit, too, needs deep rest to reduce its habitual overdrive— rest that, in the mercy of creation, used to be woven into the daily fabric of chores. Vigils in the lambing barn, stacks of dishes to wash, a garden to weed—I smile to myself when I hear my children and young coworkers rail against this repetitive work. It takes half a life to realize that these unsung, secret, rhythmic occupations are creation's gift to our species.

The more such tasks are mechanized, of course, the less we sink into deep stage-four peace. I write this in longhand, overlooking my garden of native plants, and the motion of pen on lined tablet harms neither my soul nor my carpel tunnels. By contrast, the first time I plugged myself into word processing equipment, it cost me a night's sleep, my mind unwillingly rewired for words limned in artificial light. After awhile my fingers demanded a choice be- tween playing the violin and tapping at a computer keyboard. No contest there, though the neighbors might have preferred a dif- ferent decision.

But, on the whole, what resilient animals we are (unlike sheep). We learn to survive these insults to the psyche. I'm no Luddite (well, not much of a Luddite); these words will be eaten by a computer eventually. But not too soon! Not too soon!

Balance. An Amish farmer told me once that his people keep their farming simple not because they are quaint reactionaries, but because they like to control the pace of change and keep modern devices at a distance from the intimate spaces of home. Slower change means that the old always have something to share with the young, and lots of easy tasks are available to the infirm and to children. Family ties are rewoven daily in this simple system. A production farmer atop his huge tractor, by contrast, might as well be in a downtown office, so inaccessible is he to his family and to nature.

You often see Amish homes with a telephone at the crossroads, four families sharing useful access to the "English" world. "People say this is hypocritical," my Amish friend told me, "but you see, it's not that we exclude gadgets, it's that we want to be careful about how close we let them get."

Traditional farming, by its nature, allows space to rest, if only because heavy manual work forces you to lean on a shovel now and then and stare into space, or because lambs take awhile to get born. Farmers make good companions because their spirits are rooted in these stillnesses. I've mentioned my friend, Conor, the dairy farmer, and his calm, listening way; I never understood it till I helped out with milking at 5 A.M. This man runs about twenty-five cows with a cozy inefficient parlor. I watched him attach the milk machines on a steady, slow rotation, holding the lines to his cheek to keep track of when the temperature changed as milk ceased to flow. There it was—that inward look you see on the faces of really good therapists and confessors. It put me in mind, at that moment, of two other heroes of mine, Dan and Philip Berrigan, distant cousins on my grandmother's side, who came out of Minnesota farm families into lives of priesthood, social action, and leadership in the peace movement. I could easily connect that morning discipline, not so different from prayer, to what these men went on to do.

Better than prayer, maybe, because it's unmistakably grounded in the real. You are washing udders, relentlessly cleaning. While you are going through this patient meticulous barnyard pavane, the cows raise their tails and shit on you.

It's hard to keep prayer rooted in the world, perhaps because we think God is somewhere else, somewhere *up,* and we are most likely to turn to God when things smell bad and there is too much crap on the floor. Our prayer or meditation has often a quality of "Get me out of here!"

If God is up there, airless in space, I can't get interested—living is so dear. Nobody is going to have an easy time dragging me out of this world, and even being buried in it for all time, no trumpet to wake me up, seems preferable to joining forces with a disembodied spirit. I've felt this way since childhood. The nuns told us about a place of natural happiness, called Limbo, where good people who happened to miss being baptized spend eternity. "Everything is just like earth, only there is no starving or murder. But you don't get to see God," the nuns told us.

"Can I get an option here?" I wanted to know. "Can I take early decision?" For years I was vexed with my parents for having had me baptized.

Inside and Outside

THE EWE WAS LYING on her side in the pen, breathing the quiet death of animals. Behind her, loops of intestine flowered from a prolapsed vagina.

"Go help those students shear the rams!" Ben ordered me.

"Can't I stay with you?" I said, like a little kid sent out on a phony errand.

"Lori doesn't want any students around."

"I'm not exactly a student!" Not exactly.

"Go get some towels, a 3 cc syringe, and the intubation set." This did not sound like a phony mission, so I trotted off down the longbarn.

Bounding into the kitchen I almost bashed Lori, the small-ruminant vet, a tiny woman with a star tattooed on her left temple, trailed by two vet-meds in their beige jumpsuits. One was Kristin, a beautiful six-foot-tall woman with thick blonde braids, the other a gentle African American man who looked about sixteen.

"Lori, I can't find a 3 cc syringe on the place."

"Just bring that 1 cc. Where are the scalpels kept?"

Good question. Maybe in Ben's overalls pocket.

"Mary, bring some towels and give me a hand." Lori frisked out and I charged after her, past the shearing students and even Beth, Ben's best helper, who had gotten stuck demonstrating ultrasound techniques to another bunch who had to be kept out of the action.

"Have you got a rifle?" Lori asks Ben.

"Just birdshot."

"OK, we'll give her the euthanasia fluid and then we'll cut for the lambs."

Lori's scalpel barely glides over the side of the perishing ewe. It amazes me how thin our scrim of flesh is, and how different what lies beneath from what's outside, an unimaginable world within the world, wet, bright, and pulsing with urgency. Astronomers gaze into the rhythmic expansions and contractions of space, cell biologists count millions teeming on a slide of pond water, Lord Krishna in the *Gita* proclaims himself "Lord of the Field." Caul within caul: where does the field conclude?

Something like a long, wet black sock falls into my towel, the unborn lamb. Instinctively I wrap it and then swivel my fingers in its mouth, pulling out mucus. "Joshua, show her how to take it by the feet," calls Lori, pulling another lamb from its dead mother.

Joshua, the African American student, swings my lamb by its back hooves. Another wet sock drops in my lap. I have to resist my urge to suck at its mouth, not the safest practice for the shepherd, though most of us would give in to the instinct.

Ben is now slapping the lamb Joshua has passed to him. He's not getting any response. But mine gulps air as I swing it. Lori takes the first lamb and intubates it. "Feel for a third," Lori tells Kristin. Efficient and respectful, we work in silence. Kristin is rummaging in the dead ewe's body as though in a tub of purlescent laundry.

"She was a good ewe," Ben says.

"She was a good ewe," Lori repeats responsorily a few minutes later. Then, more fiercely, "She was too fat. Did you see that fat on her? Reduce their protein by half a pound. I haven't seen one of these for twenty years."

The lambs' eyes are sealed shut. Even the one that gulped air is simply too premature to live. Still, Lori keeps trying to resuscitate them. The silky bodies steam in the freezing barn air. Their skulls are flat and angular like arrowheads. Then they are still, toys. I cover them with towels. *Listen, Ananda, form is emptiness and emptiness is form . . .*

"Mary," says Ben wearily, "go milk off the ewe with the big teats and intubate that buck ram."

"It's been nursing pretty well."

"Goddam, would you intubate it, please?" He's furious about the death of the ewe.

"Can't I bottle him?"

"Whatever."

Back in the lambing barn, I sit down in a pile of shit and squeeze the big glove-finger teats. Nothing.

Ben stomps in and gives me a ferocious look.

"She won't let down for me."

"That's because you're too gentle." Ben's big hands take over. Milk streaks into my Happy Hamburger plastic cup.

"OK, I get it."

The milk flows. I fill the nursing bottle.

"Not that goddam bottle," says Ben. "This goddam bottle. That one has a tear in the nipple. You'll drown her."

I pin the ewe in a corner of her jug, sit with the lamb in my lap, and go through my tickling routine. The lamb sucks greedily.

"Not that goddam buck lamb, Mary. *This* goddamn buck lamb." He points into the middle of six animals. "Isn't that buck lamb nursing OK?"

"This one over-here-down-there? He's not so bad. I couldn't figure out why you wanted me to tube *him.*" The buck is the better for a little extra help, though. I prod him to his feet. He staggers, too weak to reach the teats. But his mother is a good ewe and nudges and positions him.

"OK," Ben nods. "Now work with that little shit lying on the floor behind the water that's trying to die on me." Ben stomps out wearing a small cloud of fury on his head.

We have positioned a ewe whose babies died in the big pen where she can act as a feeding station, relieving some of the thin ewes with twins and triplets. She's tied in a wood halter, patient as an old cow, but my best moves get no milk from her. I prop a fence around her and bring in the tiny foundling. I line up the bottle with the lamb's mouth and tickle top and bottom lips, holding her on my lap. She opens and I gently slide the bottle in. She begins to suck greedily. My stomach lets go a cramp of anxiety. When she has a good tummy full, I move her up to the ewe. Standing next to the bottling baby has engaged the mom's let-down reflex and her milk squirts as I squeeze. I position the lamb, tickle her lip, and slide in the teat. She sucks competently as I hold the udder in place. After another fill, I let her down on the ground where she completes the whole survival circuit: stand on your own four feet, find the teat, suck on it. She takes her milk greedily. Oh, good work, Mary. I lean for comfort against the ewe's flank, breathing deeply her smell of dung, lanolin, urea: life.

Ben strides in and snickers, "Mother Mary, Queen of Lactation." After eating a pizza and a half in the kitchen, he is in a better mood.

I leave the barn to change clothes. The mercury has gone up to forty. It's back to dickies and light boots. No more dirty encumbering snowmobile suits. At the moment, my favorite gray overall is stiff with shit, lanolin, blood, tattoo paint, puss. It could stand by itself. I don't put it to the test. Hank arrives and starts keening over his dead ewe. "What do we have?" he winds up. The eternal farmer's plaint. "We don't even have the meat."

"We know how to cut a terminal C-section," I console him, heading out.

"Where do you think you're going?" Hank wants to know.

I have a dinner date, hireling shepherd that I am.

Ben will be at work till bedtime just cleaning up the mess.

I drive my car a few blocks, then park by the roadside. What's happening to me? When an animal's alive, I work hard. When it dies, I chuck it in the fridge and go dancing.

I have to stop and sit, let my consciousness fall asleep a moment so that the barn can fill my spirit with its images, so that I cannot deny them.

Hallucinating

T HE ANIMAL LET OUT four shrill cries, each one with a rest
between, four notes, while I prayed in horror, "Let it die!"

When an hour had passed, I could open the wood stove door
and see what kind of animal had met such a terrible end. I found
the shriveled carcass of a squirrel.

The knot of horror rode with me to the barn. I blamed myself,
for I had not been attentive. I had heard a scrambling in the chimney as I laid the fire, but had not taken the time to let it register in
my mind. I had not been *present*.

I drove up to the barn, parked, and went to work.

As I came into the freezing longbarn, I gave a jump as Ben's big
buck ram aimed the tractor at me and gunned the motor —

No, no. Hallucinating. Or rather not precisely hallucinating, but
feeling the mind slip its lead strings and try to make sense of whatever absurd data has been presented by the eyes. I reset my mind to
try to process the crazy information one more time: I see a stiff, dead
lamb, sitting on a tractor seat. Our big, healthy, twenty-pound buck
lamb, Ben's favorite. Is this a cruel joke? Ben was so proud of this
huge, thriving animal. It's like coming on the scene of a bizarre
murder.

Slowly my mind tries to frame an account. I imagine Ben coming upon his favorite, unaccountably dead. He must have carried
him around for awhile, from the lambing barn into the longbarn.
He must have been in an altered state. We don't prop up dead

lambs for a joke. He must have *placed* him there on the tractor seat, the only cold surface off the ground.

Ben stamps in. "Mary, if you were a man, I'd wrestle you. I just need to beat on something." Failing this option, he wearily gives the day's orders. "Go bottle that white Dorset twin, the smallest."

Ten minutes later I have to bang on the shower door where Ben is running water and yell, "It didn't make it!"

"What?"

"It's dead."

I carried the Dorset around for awhile, then propped it next to the buck lamb.

Freezing

WE HAVE A NEW GROUP of students in the barn learning
about lamb processing—docking tails, castrating, lactation,
and so on. Plus, we had to run in twenty more pregnant ewes and
crotch them out. In the midst of this confusion, three students from
environmental science showed up to rig us in monitoring devices
designed to measure how badly we were poisoning ourselves with
grain dust, fungus, and pesticides. While we were busy crotching
and docking, the wandering environmental science students
watched a ewe have triplets without bothering to alert us. The miracle of life. I guess they are used to watching nature shows on TV.
One was born dead (mummified), one died in the amniotic sac
(this one we could have saved, had we known), and one survived
to douse me to the skin with amniotic fluid and meconium.

I don't mind reeking of sheep; I like their smell. Sheep eat a
good vegetarian diet and their warm dark odor comforts me, like
the smell of humus and compost. I exclude from my catalog of ruminant aromatherapy the stink of necrotic tissue and the sharp
ammonia scent of urine. We in the sheep barn are snooty about the
smell of hogs, and never willingly go near the pig barn, but pig farmers take exception to our disgust. They profess to like the smell of the
smart animals in which they take such pride. So it goes.

As we were busy processing lambs, a graduate student ran in
a couple of rams to get a sperm count. We hiked an estrus ewe up
on the fit stand and let each ram mount her a couple of times while

pulling him off at the critical moment. The object was to get him to ejaculate into a vessel called an artificial vagina. Each ram did his job.

Then I was off to the unheated longbarn to bed pens. Out of my overalls, into my snowmobile suit: even so, by the time I got over to Robin's house an hour or so later, I had reached the convulsive stage of shivering after which it is impossible to get warm.

I had gone to Robin's to pursue a little argument we were having, but ten minutes into it I had to say, "Excuse me, but I just have to stop and get into a tub of hot water." While I was in there, he made supper and after that it seemed pointless to fight. It's no fun to argue with a stinky, frozen, hungry woman.

We got the postmortem report on Ben's big beautiful ram lamb, the one last seen driving the tractor. He died of a twisted aboma-sum—one of the sheep's four stomachs. That's nothing we could have prevented or cured (short of surgery, had we known), which makes us feel a little better and less like wrestling each other. I guess we're just having a run of bad luck, rather than suffering some un-derlying disease process or curse: here, a thick amniotic sac, there a fat ewe prolapsing, now a twist in the gut.

What You Know

A LTHOUGH NO PLACE on earth is safe, we need to believe the
barn is safe. Of course we're conscious of avoiding the fork-
lift or falling into the grinder, getting stabbed by hoof trimmers
or stomped by a three-hundred-pound stud ram—yet we feel an-
chored here, "heefted" as Scottish shepherds say, their word for the
sheep's instinct not to stray from home. The barn demands above
all that precious combination of attention and relaxation. We have
to drop our outside cares and hunker down to the simple—or sometimes complicated—gestures of animal husbandry.

But at the moment our sense of security is compromised. The
environmental science students' investigation has made us all wary
of contamination. Sheep death is, at best, mysterious: they are fragile animals. We have had a number of unexplained fatalities in our
flock. Then there is the vulnerability of the shepherd. We are all
down with bad upper respiratory infections and have a compulsive
tendency to consult our new chart listing the strains of fungus and
bacteria found in our barn.

Walking through a shopping mall recently, I was drawn into a
friendly debate with three young women from PETA (People for
the Ethical Treatment of Animals) who had set up a display. Not
only were they vegetarians, but these young women believed it
wrong to "objectify" animals in any way, using their wool or milk
or butter. I asked them how they might respond to the idea that
sheep, if they were not used for domestic purposes, would long ago

have become extinct—this was a favorite argument of my English shepherd friend, Anna.

One young woman, named Grace, replied that in the world culture she envisions, humankind would become so compassionate that we would all live harmoniously with other species and keep sheep for their own sweet sakes, as we now preserve endangered species.

"I think that people are more willing to change if they are confronted with moderate alternatives: for example, we might talk about more humane methods of docking and castrating, dairy as opposed to meat production, support for the small family farm," I suggested.

"But any young farmer could and should switch over from animal agriculture to growing soybeans," said Grace with a limpid smile.

"But that's a little like asking a displaced marketing executive to try nursing," I said. Besides, shepherds love sheep, though it's impossible for people of a certain mentality to comprehend loving a life that you will take eventually. Killing has an integral part in one coherent and responsible approach to nature. It happens not to be the one I prefer, certainly not the one I learned at Plum Village, but I speak from a privileged position: I have other ways to make my living.

I explained to the young women how, for a woman in traditional culture, efficient management of sheep and goats might mean the difference between graceful survival and death or prostitution. The PETA students again replied that such women could be set productively to soybean cultivation.

I wanted to shriek, "Child! You cannot raise soybeans in Iran or the mountains of Greece!" But I merely went on my way. Her mindset fascinates me. How can one be so fixated on certain facts, so dismissive of others? I would like to understand her better, to hear what brought her to this uncompromising position.

It is very puzzling and interesting to meet people, especially intelligent ones, who seem unperturbed by any clash between the vision that they see in their minds and the world as it actually exists. I sensed it would be useless to point out to Grace that we do *not* preserve endangered species very well, or to try to sort through her conditional tenses: how can she make an argument about the real world based on the physics of an imagined utopia where people are loving and compassionate?

It's one thing to say, "I choose not to eat meat or wear leather, because I wish to hasten the day when we will all evolve into a (presumably) better species." In fact, I think such a witness is essential to social change. But it's quite another to try to force other people to alter their ways in homage to your vision. To me, this is an obvious and crucial distinction.

Afterwards, I went back to the barn to pick up any messages the student observers might have left after their night checks. Ben came in, as a young man's panicky voice issued from the recording machine: "The sheep are OK but the dogs are bleeding from their penises!"

Ben, being Ben, merely said, "He's observing, as he should." Another bystander convulsed with laughter: how could anyone live with dogs for six weeks and not know they are female or grasp the concept of "heat"?

Easily, I thought. I'm the one who came upon a ram ejaculating and got ready to treat it for seizure.

It's Not Free

RIGHT AFTER MY CHAT with the PETA people, I came in to feed and found in residence three new Hampshire ewes from California. Ben told me that each one cost about two thousand five hundred dollars, each one genetically superior and in perfect conformation to breed standards. We intend to breed them to a three thousand-dollar ram. OK so far.

After implantation, we will flush out the embryos and implant them in less expensive ewes. Then we will rebreed our stars, beginning the process all over again. This is standard practice in the dairy industry (notice I do not say "in dairy *farming*"), though not so common in our sheep barn. After working here a year, it's the first I've heard about it.

I understand the economic issues. If we breed a star ewe nature's way three time in two years, we might get four or five lambs at best, three thousand dollars each, for a profit of from twelve thousand to fifteen thousand dollars in two years. And with each pregnancy, we'd run some risk to the ewe's life and fertility. In contrast, by flushing embryos, we'll breed her some ten times in two years, at a profit of forty-five thousand dollars. Who can quibble with that? The ewe will be, I suppose, healthier and live longer. Perhaps we are improving her quality of life.

I suspect that the serious farmer who doesn't engage in these practices falls out of competition. And sheep farming is a marginal operation: it costs eighty dollars to keep a ewe through the winter, and we get about the same amount for a lamb. That means we only make money on twins and triplets. At that rate, how can one afford to reject a modern technological solution? Yet the whole thing makes me deeply, metaphysically uneasy. It frightens me at the level I used to be frightened by the fairy tale about the goose that laid the golden eggs. She gives us her bounty; maybe we can make her give us a little more. Chilling. I operate from the premise that animals should be allowed to live their brief lives as comfortably and naturally as possible. Carrying babies to term, dangerous as it might be, seems a natural goal for ewes, if they can be said to have a goal.

How do I figure out what to think about this? I need to call dial-a-philosopher. On the one hand, a certain kind of animal rights advocate argues that animals cannot be used as a means to any human end. But in the Christian stewardship model espoused by most farmers I know, God gives us dominion over the beasts of the field, and they are subject to our decisions.

Both these alternatives make me nervous, but my own via media has no philosophical or theological underpinning. If anything, it's a sort of musical idea, or perhaps an aesthetic idea. I hear a choir of instruments, each sounding its note, the whole ensemble producing a balanced sound. I imagine a traditional farm, where farmers care for a few animals and the animals return their wool and milk and even meat. A certain harmony of parts exists.

Logical or illogical, I know when aesthetic balance has been disrupted. A certain level of mechanization disrupts it, a certain level of pesticide use, a certain kind of manipulation. Why? Perhaps not even because of what happens to the animals; it may be that their level of consciousness is not at issue here. Perhaps because of what happens to the *farmer*.

One day in a foreign land, I was bumbling around a dairy barn helping with chores and running on to the farmer about the big herds and milking machines in the United States. My companion stopped his work, astonished. "But how would a man know his own beasts?"

It's a struggle to maintain human scale, an environment in which man and woman can know their beasts, talk to their children, and at the end of the day have a good long stare across the top of a stall, as Ben and I did yesterday while bedding the lambs.

"It's so beautiful to me," Ben said, "though I suppose it's just an old brown field starting to green up. When I was young I couldn't see it..."

I turned to Ben as my substitute for dial-a-philosopher. "How often do we flush a prize ewe like that?"

"Maybe eight times a year. Shoot, with some ewes, more often. Depends on the ewe. But it's not free, Mary. You have to pay to bring her into estrus with a shot or a progesterone pessary. You have to pay for the semen, for the flushing, and to bring the recipient ewes into estrus. Then we'd probably get twenty lambs a year."

It makes me happy to know that some economic principles will contrive to defeat the factory farmer. "Where this works," Ben goes on, "is in your beef herd. When you buy a ten thousand-dollar beef cow and build a herd around her genetics."

"Clone her, you mean?" They're doing that in Scotland, to public outcry.

"Essentially. Confidentially, Mary, those California ewes aren't worth shit. I wouldn't give three hundred dollars for one of 'em. That guy that bought 'em, he just gets excited at auctions."

Nothing to Do

WE WERE ALL TOO TIRED to do any work today. Ben gets as weary and arthritic as I, though he's only twenty-one. That's farming for you.

I rounded up three big lambs gone running around the long-barn like three little maids from school, and then I came and put my feet up in the kitchen.

"I haven't seen those overalls for awhile," said Ben. I had on my favorite warm-weather dickies as opposed to my snowmobile suit, and under it my pink silk long underwear. I can't stand that big suit another minute, though it is still freezing and icy and snowy. These are the days all Minnesotans wish their ancestors had kept going south.

So we stayed inside and had a couple of Cokes. "Ben," I start in, "those PETA women said what if we give the lambs a local anesthetic before docking and castrating?"

"Anesthesia is always a risk, even local. I'd have to give it in the spinal column. Am I gonna dock them or paralyze them? Besides, their brains aren't developed enough to feel pain. They don't call them pea brains for nothing. Especially if you dock and castrate before they're ten days old. Those PETA people have sure got under your skin."

"I just want to tell them the truth." I mistrust, for starters, the information of anyone who argues that animals can't feel pain. That piece of "science" has been footnoted by every abuser of the weak since Vlad the Impaler. "Maybe," I venture, "that's why God lets *us* suffer. 'Their brains,' he tells himself, 'aren't developed enough to feel—'"

Ben snorts at my theology. "You better talk to someone who knows more than I do." In his worst moods, Ben dismisses all animal rights activists as "doctors' wives with nothing to do." He's not in his worst mood today, just his tiredest.

To sum up the lambing season: we got thirty-six lambs from twenty-four ewes, with a survival rate of 1.5. About average. It's that .5 where a shepherd's margin of economic survival lies.

It is clear, I hope, how much I respect and cherish Ben—and not only Ben, but the world that produced such a steady and conscientious man: his parents and the small Minnesota farm that formed them all. It grieves me to contemplate the future of family farms like his. What lies ahead for the independent farmer, in an industry dominated by conveyor belts, twenty-four-hour production, the cruelties of the factory mindset? The sight of chicken wrapped up at the grocery store makes me queasy when I think of the filth and agony in which fowl are raised, and their processing workers exploited and endangered. I've seen cow barns where disconsolate heifers lie chained in their own excrement and never see daylight. But the evil is not done only to dumb beasts. It is done to humankind. Barns like that will not produce men like Ben.

But the women from PETA have, I think, stationed themselves too far out along the moral continuum. Surely it is possible to define a moderate position between exploitative factory production and visions of soybeans as impractical as visions of sugarplums. I say this because I want to preserve the endangered species of *Ben*.

I received my dharma name, Tending of the Source, at Plum Village only after a long interior struggle with the Buddhist principle of protecting all life. Would it be possible for me, in conscience, to take this precept for my own? The most benevolent wool or

sheep-dairy farmer must get rid of ram lambs; only a few genetically superior males can be held for stud. Castration is essential to
control populations, and tail docking to health. Shepherding involves daily violence.

As a little boy of four or five, my philosophical son happened to
hear a street preacher ranting on the streets of our city: "Why did
God give us life?" Jude tugged on my hand. "What I want to know,"
he said, "is why God gave us death?"

This question is unavoidable in the Manichean barn. Why are
things this way, and since they are, how does one live wisely and
kindly? It's tempting to just walk away on feet that tolerate no
leather: no meat, no milk, no compromise. But if we do this, we
leave farming to the cruelest applications of agribusiness and
subvert the sane and ancient alternatives of families like Ben's.

After much discussion, I had learned that the precepts of
Engaged Buddhism taught at Plum Village are compatible with
moral evolution. "They are pillars of wisdom," Josef had said. "You
cannot break a Buddhist precept,"—those injunctions about truthfulness, nonharming, etc.—"as you can break a Judeo-Christian
commandment." Once a week the sangha examines its conscience:
"Brothers and sisters, have you tried to live your life in light of this
precept?" How each one answers will depend on the issues of his
life, what path, what barn.

What Language Does God Speak?

BEN IS A LIBERAL in the conservative branch of the Lutheran church he grew up in, while most of his relatives, he's told me, remain on the right-wing side. As I've gotten to know Ben and have talked to him a bit about my theological studies and pastoral sideline, our conversations have become more concerned with religious questions.

"Some people in my family say it's wrong to talk to atheists and people who don't believe what I do," Ben says, as we push the feed cart into the longbarn, "but I say that's how we grow."

"Well," I respond, "there's always a larger idea of God to get hold of. You aren't going to outrun the thing, if you know what I mean."

"They're afraid I'll lose my faith."

What you might lose, I think, is your *idea*. But, as Buddha tells us, people with ideas only go around bothering each other. I don't say this out loud because there is a rule to barn conversations that they should contain only about ten sentences, five for you and five for me. Then you have to be quiet for awhile and let it sink in, throw some hay around. It's rather like a Quaker meeting.

When I speak in Christian terms or in Buddhist terms, I'm simply selecting, for the moment, a dialect. Christian words, for me, represent the comforting vocabulary of the place I came from, hometown voices, saying more than the language itself can convey about how welcome and safe I am, what the expectations are, and where to find food. Buddhist words come from another dialect, from the people over the mountain. I've become pretty fluent in Buddhist; it helps me to see my home country differently, but it will never be speech I can feel completely at home in.

This point about religious language is a delicate one, and I am making it conscientiously to myself as I retrieve bits and pieces of shearing equipment from the shower room and wherever else the last worker has laid them down. I know that in Ben's fundamentalist community, holy words have a direct one-to-one relationship with holy things. To tamper with a formula is to risk muddling the truth. Words, to me, stand for more fluid and intangible realities, so I don't lean on them too hard. But respect for Ben calls me to tread carefully in the vicinity of his dearest hopes.

When I first learned to read and began devouring history books, I came upon this astonishing sentence: "What we call a *bay,* the Norsemen called a *vik.*" This sentence cast my world into turmoil, because I had never heard another language spoken—or at least had not recognized it as *other.* Indeed, like most Catholic children, I had learned to sing in Latin as early as I sang in English, but I thought the foreign words to be mere scat, like "Mairsey dotes and dosey dotes." When we went to Benediction, we sang about the rather incomprehensible adventures of two little girls—so I thought—named Janey Torey and Janey Toquay. But this sentence about the Norsemen shattered my concept of reality. "Which is it?" I demanded of my grandfather, looking out at the *bay* or *vik* on which our cabin stood. "Who's right?" I was confident he'd take our side against the Scandinavians.

My grandfather was a philosophical man, though uneducated, and he began to pull at his hair. He grasped the problem at once in its full existential horror. He began to yell for my grandmother, as though I'd stumbled into a nest of wasps. "Rose! Rose!"

My grandmother scurried out in her apron, grabbed the book,

and ran her finger under the horrible sentence. "Which is it?" I cried again.

She never had any trouble setting me straight. "It's a bay. Those Norsemen are long dead."

Thus I was able to pass many more years in serenity and knew no more linguistic confusion until I began to study Greek and encountered twenty-four letters instead of twenty-six. Worse, the Greek alphabet represented slightly different sounds, sounds we did not make in our language. The idea that human beings might make different sounds unsettled me; I told my mother about it. She at first disbelieved me, and then attempted to explain it away as a printing error. If all human babies are made to roughly the same pattern, surely they must make the same sounds.

"Well, if it's a symbol, to hell with it," Flannery O'Connor said, speaking of the Eucharist, but perhaps she was joking. She was a woman who certainly respected the symbolic nature of language. When I teach poetry, I usually encounter a class of students who can recognize a metaphor and distinguish it from a simile, but who have given little thought to what, intrinsically, a metaphor is and what its existence implies: namely, that there are things going on that we can't precisely *name*. "It's from the Greek *metaphero,* to *carry over,*" I tell the students. "Think of it as a bridge."

Thomas Merton used to say that it's hard to live the spiritual life with the spiritual equipment of a poet. You see a bridge, where others see the rock of ages. You'd better learn to keep your mouth shut. Throw some hay around. The Sufi mystic, Jelalludin Rumi, wrote:

> Out beyond ideas of wrongdoing and rightdoing,
>   there is a field. I'll meet you there.

> When the soul lies down in that grass,
>   the world is too full to talk about.
> Ideas, language, even the phrase *each other*
>   doesn't make any sense.

I heard some fine preaching recently by a conservative evangelical who was trying to help his congregation sort out what in the Bible they had to take at face value and what they could leave alone. There had been some infighting in the church about a male youth minister with long hair or some similar trespass. The minister preached a good sermon about how we have to take into account the culture out of which scriptures come. He was kind and funny. "When they say, 'Don't look on the wine when it's red,' they mean, 'Stick to chablis.'" He said that women didn't have to cover their heads in church, and he found solid reasons for them to preach, but eventually he rounded up the usual tempting subjects for exclusion: fornicators, homosexuals.

Jesus, who'd have dinner with anybody, near as I can tell, would have gotten off this train a few stops earlier, but I stayed it through, and then went out for pancakes with my friends.

"I think I'm more of a fundamentalist than he is. I take it *all* seriously, but seriously as *metaphor*. 'Veil your head in church'—well, maybe this means something about the secretness of the soul, the anima, the reverence we should have . . ." I babbled to the woman whose church we had visited.

"If it's a metaphor," she said, "the hell with it."

Hard Metaphors and Soft Facts

I T'S INTERESTING TO ASK people what they mean by words like *spirit, soul,* and even *God*—in fact, for me, these are about the only conversations worth having. My philosophical training was dominated by the empiricism of thinkers like A. J. Ayer, and what searing, wonderful discipline it was. I would spend my days in college brooding over Ayer's systematic abolition of metaphysics, then come home and find my grandmother on her knees happily conversing with her dead relatives. The need for a young person to choose one or another perspective becomes pressing, rather like the pressures of bilingualism I read about in books like Richard Rodriguez's *Hunger of Memory;* to speak one language means to live in a world of affection, touch, food, and soft flannel next to the skin, while to speak another brings mastery, respect, and exotic power. Earnest young people may feel a responsibility to seek truth rather than comfort. If it can be demonstrated that only matters subject to sense verification can be "real"—as A. J. Ayer taught—then the heresy that one is guided by the loving presence of a dead mother or an angel guardian has to be rooted out by any person of conscience.

But I had the good fortune to be a literature as well as a philosophy student—at one time I was majoring in both disciplines while trying desperately to keep up my music—and this crazy juggling saved my sanity. Reading a play like *King Lear,* one gets a different take on British Empiricism—for here is a man demanding tangible proof of what's by nature intangible, a daughter's love. Thus he sets himself up for a tragic outcome. Blaise Pascal became the patron saint of my bumbling philosophical inquiry, so French, so mathematical on the one hand, so intuitive on the other: believing the heart to be an instrument of inquiry. Often so vulgar (the famous wager) and sometimes so tragically wrong (Port Royal). A spirit with whom I could identify, in all the contradictions of my inner world.

A young friend who recently finished her M.A. in theology said to me recently, "I'm so pleased with my education. Finally I can do a real analysis. I can offer an elegant proof."

I remember the headiness of that feeling, and, indeed, the purity of heart that goes with it, but for my part I say, "I've finally learned *not* to compose an elegant proof. People with ideas go around bothering each other."

It was Peter, my spiritual companion, who finally cured me of my overly rational approach. I would call him up in the middle of the night, ranting Wittgenstein, and he would say, "There are many threads you can pick up in life and follow where they lead. Some lead to lightness and hope and others to despair." He read me William Blake:

> I give you the end of a golden string,
> Only wind it into a ball:
> It will lead you in at Heaven's gate
> Built in Jerusalem's wall.

"Do you get it?"

"Um. Sure."

Another time he put it this way: "Analysis is like jumping into a swimming pool full of baby rabbits."

"Does William Blake say that?"

"No, it's in Deuteronomy."

Religious ideas—and every idea apprehended by the heart—are metaphoric. But human beings want to turn soft metaphors into hard facts, the better to control them. Thus grace, for the parochial schoolchild, became a mysterious reviving liquid, like Gatorade, flowing through a spigot controlled by priests. Thus the soul is imaged as a milk bottle, carried within, pure and pasteurized, or contaminated by lies to Mom. In the discipline of philosophy, the process of turning soft metaphors into hard facts is called reification. When you reify something, you turn what is fluid and conceptual into something with body and mass. When I read the passionate dialogs of Luther and Erasmus on grace versus free will, it seems to me that each man has converted a fluid metaphor into a large intrusive object: how can a gigantic refrigerator like "grace" inhabit the same kitchen as "free will," shaped (for Erasmus) something like a stove? Surely one must crush the other. But if we imagine grace as a dancer, free will her partner, they can waltz through the narrowest passage. Grace and free will, for philosophers, cannot logically coexist, but anyone who has ever watched a parent help a toddler learn to walk knows that both qualities must hover: Baby, you must do this on your own feet, but my hands are an inch from your body. I may let you fall, but I'll not let you hit your head on the coffee table.

And so, what do we mean by "spirit"? This is a question I like to ask. I do not know, myself, but I know its absence, which I discovered when our cat, Naoise, left his body in the laundry basket and departed for urgent business elsewhere.

Weather Shifts

As SPRING KEEPS TRYING to establish a hold, Ben grows more and more exhausted from the intensity of lambing, not to mention his schoolwork, home life, and three weekly visits to church. He gives me more heavy work to do, which makes me enormously proud: hauling fifty-pound bales of grass hay and alfalfa hay down from the top of the barn onto the hay cart and out to feed. Proud and tired. He rattles off instructions: ". . . three chunks in each of the first six bunks, grass on the west side, alfalfa on the east. Half 'a bale to those ewes. The cows—"

"Ben, wait, I have to write it down. My brain's not working today." Even so, I gave the Simmental cattle hay in their corn feeder and corn in their hay feeder. I sigh as I watch the big tongues patiently try to extract corn through the interstices of a metal bunk. Finally, with great difficulty, I tip the heavy metal feeder over and dump the corn onto the ground for them. Corn mixed with mud does not pique their vast indifferent fancy. Then I haul the hay out of the corn feeder and put it in the hay feeder. The cows follow me like huge dogs, my knee-high boots sucking in the mud. It's great to see (feel, hear, and sometimes taste) mud. The snow is finally gone. I gave the cows another half pail of corn to be sure.

Now the alfalfa hay. I'm proud that I can finally distinguish grass hay from alfalfa hay and both from straw and know the use of each. Usually. I squint into the barn. It all suddenly looks the same. Some of the bales have been tossed together. I sort it out, but then where is my hay knife? I spend an hour looking. We cannot afford to misplace that indispensable tool—but it's merely fallen off its hook and gotten kicked under a bale. That reminds me: *plug in the fridge,* which we've unplugged to use the electric clippers. Left to thaw, lamb carcasses would make a grisly scene.

Back at it, alfalfa to the east. But someone has mixed the bunks labeled east and west respectively on the left and right of the barn. Did Ben mean *real* east or the bunk *marked* east? Nine and ten have been reversed; did he mean real nine or the bunk *marked* nine?

It's hot today. Last week we were in snowmobile suits. Today, it's sixty degrees, prickly alfalfa hay stuck all over my body. Our pregnant ewes stand panting. Tomorrow they'll be shorn, and we can't let them into the pasture at present to cool because it looks like rain. It's no fun shearing a wet ewe.

Later, we "roughed out" some ewes for a judging class in the school of agriculture. This is a rather tedious kind of shearing in which you take off about an outer inch of wool and smooth her out as beautifully as a wooly sculpture for the judges. Washing and blow-drying are a final refinement—say, for the state fair—but we didn't have to go that far today.

Lazy Day

A LAZY DAY at MacDonald's farm. We took down some creeps—
the feeding bunks where lambs are kept separate from the
mature ewes—and stacked them behind the hay. The new lambs
are now weaned. We started them each on a dose of sulfa in their
water as a preventative against coccidia. Then we ate a lot of food
standing around talking about religion, marriage, and TV. The
conversations we have in the barn tend to go deeper than those I
used to have with my colleagues in the faculty lunchroom. How
to account for that? Lanzo del Vasto, who founded the Arche
communities in France, says that only in poor agricultural societies
do people really converse or pursue the best of the business of being
human.

People go into academic life (at least I did) because I was interested in serious human questions, but the level of abstraction we
bring to academic conversation often kills any hope of reference
back to life. We begin an academic inquiry with a quandary or
query from the real world, but then translate the predicament into
such a linguistic game that any reference to living, breathing animals
gets lost. Not all university teaching is so disembodied, but the conventions are hard to resist.

I am gently palpating a ewe's udder with my left hand as I shear
with my right, protecting her delicate tissues from my shears and
at the same time querying the state of her pregnancy. By now my

work is second nature; still, sometimes my hand recoils in a kind of independent tactile respect for the life in her.

We finished the day with a good long spell of petting Sally's puppies. Sally is Ben's old golden retriever, previously considered to be sterile. Then she got in with a cocker spaniel and presented us with two females and a male. They are sandy, wrinkled bags of fur, with tiny pads, noses, and claws. Eyes barely open. "Love calls us to the things of this world."

Haltering Up

M Y JOB FOR THE next two weeks will be "haltering up" ten lambs for a show and sale. That means tying them in halters every day (after catching them, of course, which takes an hour) and generally playing with them until they become tame enough to lead at the judging. After two hours of merry struggle, Ben said, "If they only knew they just have to stand still."

"That is so Zen."

After a few days, I have gotten good at haltering up. Ben calls me the head tamer. I'm so vain. I can catch the lambs pretty easily now. They seem to sense my confidence and give up. Much like children, they make a big fuss, but respond to rather little show of authority. Willingness to throw a flying tackle also helps.

The halter should draw under the lamb's chin, coming up through the loop on your left hand as you sit astride the lamb. Then you tie him short so that he has no space to butt his way through the fence or break his neck running to the end of the leash.

Then I spend quality time with each lamb. I draw it into my lap and hold it close, put my arm round it, and breathe with it. As it senses my body heat, I can feel it relax and become comfortable. Then I try to get it to lead by tugging at the halter just a little and putting my hand under its chin and easing forward. A little push on the tail does wonders. Meanwhile I coo "Co'lamb" and bleat softly if no one is around. I see the lamb perk up its ears at the bleat, no matter how ridiculous I feel. Animals respond to sounds in their own language, I've noticed over the years.

I never drag or hit them. They're coming along very well.

Lake

THAT PLACE WHERE I TUMBLED down the hill and squandered myself in ecstasy or vertigo across the available creation—that was in rural Wisconsin, at a cabin on a lake. My grandparents had cleared the land and built the little white house, green-trimmed, in a valley between two hills right next to the water. Grandma wanted to be able to hear the water purl at night, and in those days we had no indoor plumbing to nurse through freeze and thaw.

Now suburbs encroach on our anachronistic little house, which remains only one large room plus a sleeping porch. Several years ago we were required to demolish the outhouse, and now a whole precarious system has to be drained and shut down in the winter. Year-round dwellers crowd the shore, telecommuters and people who drive around in jeeps and vans. Their huge houses and hot tubs bulge to the edges of our property lines.

They remind me of a family whose children attended the same parochial school as my children did, and came next to us in the alphabet. For community events, we were all seated in the parish church in alphabetical order, and each family got the same number of tickets. Our family was usually late, however, and this whole neighboring family—dad, mom, and grandparents—were punctual and also overweight. By the time we O'Reilleys trooped in, the Big Family, as we came to call them, would be filling up their spaces and ours as well. They were immovable, so we would stand through graduations and scout deployments, lurking disconsolately in the aisle by our assigned seats. (I suppose they called us the Late Family.)

I feel surrounded, these days, by Big families. They drive jeeps and four-by-fours. They ride around the lake with ninety-horsepower motors whose wakes erode the shoreline. They fertilize their lawns to resemble a city park and pump phosphorus runoff into the water.

Robin and I are spending a week at the lake. We sit on the porch playing fiddle duets. A loon calls.

"It's funny, when I was growing up here we said this lake was too overpopulated to attract loons—there were about fifteen families and a couple of fourteen-horse Evinrudes."

"It was too busy for *those* loons," Robin answers.

"Huh?"

"The loons of your childhood. These loons have evolved. They now tolerate jet skis."

Will I be able to?

At night I lie on the sleeping porch and look at the constellations and think, my great-grandfather slept right here. Up on the hill is a Norway pine planted to celebrate my father's birth.

Now the neighbor comes out with his weed whacker, making an intolerable racket. And since he's a year-round resident, winter will bring snowmobiles and whatever new contrivances they invent to destroy the tiny delicate hairs on the whorls of inner space.

"A week at the lake": this is a Minnesota phrase denoting a retreat into mystery, indisposition, vacation, or retreat. It's our all-purpose excuse and explanation. We have no missing persons in this state, they're presumed to be "at the lake." People from outside may puzzle about it: "What lake? Where?" We don't even know how to process these questions, which interrupt our retreat into mist, otherness, wrensong, somewhere "up north."

This week the wrens can seldom be heard above the buzzing

and screaming from jet skis and high-tech water toys. When I was growing up (for this was a place I spent every summer till I left home), our nearest neighbor lived in a shack up the hill. But now a new family has covered the whole lot next door with House. In order to induce their children to savor country life, the parents have invested in satellite dishes, four speedboats of different kinds, a fleet of cars. There is some new thing called—and honestly I do not know what it is—an "off-road vehicle" that has been tearing through the woods behind our cabin. I picture it as something like the Star Wars tank toys my children used to play with. In the spring, I went back there and dug out the beheaded trilliums and other mashed ephemerals this new machine had done in and tried to re-root them on our land. Technically, I could be arrested for moving wildflowers.

In summary, I have spent a day at the lake in a rictus of fury at my new neighbors. Every time the blond twin sons roar off on matching jet skis I wish them, at least, the ruination of their blow-dried hair. With luck, they will "shear a pin." I hope the new motors are not immune to this disaster. In the old days of fourteen-horse Evinrudes, a sheared pin was our all-purpose explanation for fishermen not returning at suppertime.

Now the neighbors are spraying their land with herbicide and the haze drifts over our quarter acre. This is as much as I can stand, and I commence ranting and ruining the mood of my gentle companion, so slow to indignation, righteous or not.

"What if you were to consider these people to be your dearest spiritual teachers?" he suggests. "Anyway, how do you know it's herbicide? Maybe it's liquified organic compost."

That's enough to make me storm off into the woods. Thay would agree with Robin, of course; still, Thay never saw a jet ski. How could these obnoxious people be my spiritual teachers?

When you read some wisdom in a book, or assent to a dharma

talk, it seems so attractive and logical. If you are of an imaginative temperament, you are already *there,* a realized soul. It's like reading about a new diet or exercise program. Exercising merely the mind's eye makes you svelte.

But my spiritual self is not very shapely at the moment. Thay had to deal with the Vietcong and the Green Berets. I can't even deal with screaming water toys.

These mornings I've been reading a little from Brian Walker's translation of the *Hua Hu Ching,* outtakes (as it were) from the oral teachings of the Taoist master Lao-tzu. Pondering Robin's suggestion, I come upon this reflection:

> Do not imagine that an integral being has the
>   ambition of enlightening the unaware or raising
>   worldly people to the divine realm.
> To him, there is no self and no other, and hence no
>   one to be raised.
> His only concern is his own sincerity.

What humbling words. I have spent a Sabbath blackening my reality and my companion's mind with hostile words about my neighbor; my neighbor, by contrast, has spent a better day: entertaining his children and improving, according to his best guidance, a plot of ground.

One of my wacky friends used to have a cosmic theory that troubled me a lot at the time (1968). It represented a kind of scorched-earth quietism: everything, he believed, was exactly as it should be. Hitler was as he should be, for example, and as valuable to the cosmic puzzle as Gandhi. Thus, nothing should be resisted.

I never succumbed to his logic, if only because resistance is my major contribution to spiritual ecology. But it gives me plenty to think about. Any good idea, given free reign, creates disaster, I've noticed. So it's healthy in the spiritual ecosystem to have opposition and contrary forces balancing each other. My neighbor, for example, looks well-to-do, and perhaps his money will have the power to do some good. Surely this lake will work its own gentle transformation on him, on his blond twins, and on their investment plans.

And our little cabin, looking now so out of place in the developing suburb, speaks too. When people around the lake ask where I live, they often register pleased surprise at my answer. They comment on the peace and serenity of the tiny white house with green trim on its big stretch of conifers and oak — as we sometimes look out the car windows at Amish farms and wonder how people can live with so few toys. Of course, as they honor our cabin's simplicity, they contemplate how much better it would be if we would add another storey, a deck on the front. "Why don't you tear the cottage down?" they boldly say sometimes. "It's such a good lot."

I long for Americans to be converted to simpler lives, simpler structures, and preservation of open space. But how do deep, radical conversions come about? Not because some righteous neighbor scolds about herbicide, but because one feels the relentless gnawing of one's own soul. Because one is spoken to by a little house or a great blue heron, or by the offhand remark of a happy person at peace with herself. Some deep bell in the self reverberates to a bell struck outside. Anyone who comes to any level of ecological understanding has done so after a long internal process. I ruefully remember the days when my dad had one of the biggest motors on this lake, a scandal to many, though it was puny by today's standards. My sister and I did our share of tearing around on obnoxious water skis, and wearied the neighbors with our relentless efforts to teach a succession of cocker spaniels to surfboard.

Next day, Robin and I stop to visit an elderly woman friend in her little house on the "branch." She's a biologist who has spent her retirement years educating people about the lake ecosystem, the effects of lawn fertilizer on the water table, and so on. She's put in her time haranguing county officials and getting to board meetings at inconvenient times of night, but mostly she works with children. She'll jump into any running water, try her horny feet against any sharp bed of freshwater clams, to pull out some oozing creature for a crowd of preschoolers, then explain its role in the system — Hitler or Gandhi? — to the eager listeners. "Get the children," is her advice to me. "Don't worry the old people. They grew up within a different frame of reference. But teach the children."

And feed your own peace, she tells me without words; leave your neighbors alone.

Missing in Action

I SAW THE BOY RUN across the slope of my grandparents' property (as I still call it). "Tommy!" I thought, the boy who used to
go worm fishing day after day with his Grandpa Pat. But that boy
was killed thirty years ago in Vietnam, and Pat, too, is long dead.
So are my grandparents, though I still call the cabin theirs. The children running down the hill replace each other, and it is nothing to
the hill. In a tin box on a shelf in my grandmother's closet are the
letters written when her son, my Uncle Buddy, died, another boy
who cut through here some time before World War II; and under
them lie the letters of a cousin, written from a forward dressing
station at Ypres. He was a doctor and a musician, and he had managed to import his piano into the trench, so the letters tell us, along
with an amazing range of gourmet food. Perhaps I carry a reces-
sive gene for frivolity.

When a family lives on a place for a long time, individuals mean
less to themselves, they don't feel so new and special. I squint at the
lake and try to feel my life as evanescent as Tommy's, as the pianist's
under fire. It is not hard to do.

If Tommy and I had known each other as young adults, there
would have been friction. It made such a difference in the 1960s
whether you did or did not get inside that big war machine. Our
lives seemed very important to us in those days. We filled our skins
then, I tell you.

At about the time Tommy was getting killed, I came home

from two and a half years of quiet life in a cloister and took the job of music director in a parish church. Our novitiate chapel had been cold and resonant. The dark vault with its gold flecks seemed to gather silence like the heart of a bell, shifted but never driven out by the methodical inquiry of our Gregorian chant. Silence would slip back as the young nuns drifted out, black figure by black figure. One or two always stayed behind for private devotions and to watch the silence in its foglike descent.

Silence was our element, our opponent, our mentor. We were somewhat convinced that God lived in it. My only way of dealing with silence was, finally, music. "Musical notes exist to define rests, the shape of silences," my chant teacher told me. This lesson I began to generalize to everything. Words, spoken or printed, were boundaries around silence. Words, music, cochineal, make it possible to *see* silence. Of course, every Japanese schoolchild, struggling with a calligraphy brush, knows this.

Born prematurely out of the novitiate stillness, I found myself in a parish church. It had the architecture of a bowling alley and not a cubit of private space, a sheetrocked box painted baby pink and blue. Everything in it rustled: Easter hats, polyester ties, dynel jackets, mimeographed hymnbooks, satin vestments, lace surplices, and the very altar breads. My job at the front of this vibrating pink window on the infinite was to lead a small schola of choir dropouts. Catholics did not sing much in those days, but the Second Vatican Council had recently mandated vernacular liturgy and song. The schola's job was to introduce the rest of the church to the unwelcome new forms.

They weren't all that welcome to me, either. I had spent two years of daily study under one of the best chant teachers in the world, hoping to major in music and become a specialist in this arcane form. I was only beginning to enter into the infinite subtlety of Gregorian chant. It was—and remains—the only public prayer

I have ever been able to engage in without feeling like a phony and a jackass. But then, one day in 1965 or so, it was simply abolished. With a stroke of his pen, Pope John XXIII—who had such good ideas about other things—declared that liturgy would henceforth be in the vernacular language of the people. That was, effectively, the end of Latin chant.

Then all those monks and nuns who had devoted hours and hours a day to chanting began to sicken and fall into depressions, but nobody noticed for a long time. Maybe, as I can well believe, the music toned up their systems in some mysterious way. Or perhaps chant really was a language that God understood. Faced with numerous liturgical scholas shrieking away in the new vernacular hymns, Divinity may have covered its ears and withdrawn, leaving the monks to pine. We parish musicians, illiterate in anything written after the thirteenth century, stumbled around trying to score liturgies for guitar and bongo drums, trying to make sense of texts like "Eat his body! Drink his blood!"

It wasn't because the music got so bad that I quit going to Mass, but it certainly was the beginning of my doubts about papal infallibility. Besides, a gulf was widening between some of the hierarchy and those of us who were beginning to understand religion in terms of social justice and nonviolence. As a fifteen-year-old student in Guatemala, I had seen the puzzling alliance between illegitimate dictatorship and the Catholic church. As a teenager, that had shaken my faith. Now, as an adult, I couldn't understand why many pastors refused to write letters for young Catholics trying to establish conscientious objector status in the Vietnam War. The inner cities were burning; most of us radical schola members spent our evenings and weekends marching between polarized black and white neighborhoods, demanding integrated housing.

Then, one July 4, the pastor told us to sing "America, the Beautiful" as a recessional at the end of Mass. Obediently, we tuned up. Then, when we got to the verse about "Thine alabaster cities gleam / undimmed by human tears," I slammed my hymnal shut. My sister shut hers, too, and we tromped out the middle aisle, followed by the rest of the schola—all of us in love with the drama. That was our last gig in the pink church.

Now that I know a little about conflict resolution, I can say that this was not a good example of it. Obedience had been drilled into me, and, in fact, obedience (rooted in the verb "to listen") is central to a deep surrender of the spirit—but that isn't what used to be taught, or drilled, in parochial school. I wish that, instead of submitting to the pastor for so long that an explosion was bound to come, I had negotiated early and wisely, tried to understand what experiences had led him to his intransigent position. Fear and duty kept me in place: "What demon possessed me that I behaved so well?" as Thoreau put it. Maybe we could have reached a compromise— maybe we could all have held hands and sung "Kumbaya." Then again, maybe not.

Still I hung on to the church like grim death, hanging out mostly in house churches and university communities. I love the Catholic church with an emotion one can perhaps only feel about one's family religion. It was, above all, my dad's church, the church of Bing Crosby (their voices uncannily similar) singing "Faith of Our Fathers." It was, back in Ireland, the Troubles, and what the family had gone through with the Klan in Minnesota and the Orange in Canada. Most importantly, I could find God there, at least until 1972.

One day at one of the house churches, we sang a verse from "The Great Mandala," which had the chorus, "And I told him, 'Listen Father, I will never kill another. . . .'" Little did I know that my newborn son's eyes would be too weak ever to make the Air Force, but I began to sob. I had to, had to find a church that would consistently support a peace testimony. That's when I started to attend Quaker meeting.

Nowadays, feistier, I would have stayed in the church and made them deal with me. But I had been trained too well in submission instead of in obedience.

The Council of Nature

THE BEST BLACKBERRIES SIT in a moat of poison ivy. Each thing in nature—the Vedas teach—has its guardian spirit and I hope that I have mine, for I am deep in bear country at the moment. For years, the bears have not been a "problem" here at the cabin, though place names testify to their ubiquitous rambling: Black Bear Lane, Bear Island, and what almost ended the discussion, Bear Trap. Lately, however, the animals have been gathering deep in the woods and holding council, it seems: "We can't keep them out of our habitat," they say, "so we will have to lumber down and wing in and see if we can coexist." Indigenous tribes have almost always made this decision—at a certain point, it becomes the only one available—and it tends to go against their interests. For this moment, though, I relish the return of the loons, bear scat by the public road. Yesterday, floating around in our favorite swimming hole on the St. Croix, we watched twelve eagles ride the air currents over our heads.

I'm looking for blackberries here on the ridge where the trains used to run, and I still can't stop listening for the high ghost whistle. In my childhood this ridge was off-limits to kids and, of course, I came here whenever I knew the berries were beginning to ripen. It was a trial walking miles on bare feet along the hot rails. The tracks ran through dense pasture, brush, and woods. If the train came along, you'd have to ball yourself up and dive into a gorge full of bramble and poison ivy. How deep the gorge lay I didn't know, because I never had to jump. But my ears were always tuned to the whistle, my toes to a vibration in the track, and I crossed the higher isolated sections of trestle on quick brown feet.

More realistic was the fear of meeting a local dairyman once convicted of rape. One rapist in a county was more fearsome in those days than the hundred probably brushing elbows with me in my present life. Or Geordie might be about, the fearsome Retard, who helped out on the farms. The casual cruelty of our naming offends me to inscribe, but in those days the differently abled were presumed to be sexually warped and predatory.

Given all we feared in those days, it must have been tempting to tie a girl to the big lion feet of the oak table, teach her to dust each paw, each toenail, and stay inside. In fact, this dusting was my morning job, along with sweeping the outhouse, but after that I was free to run like a wild animal, commended to my guardian spirit at each morning's prayer.

The blackberries are fat and sweet and almost seedless this year. Most years they are small and seedy; even the bears leave them alone.

The tracks were taken out last month, and there is talk in town of running a bike trail along here. Everything changes, as Joseph Stalin used to say.

Yesterday I bought an old truck inner tube from a toothless man down the road who advertised "Tubes 4-Sale." The price was outrageous: five dollars. "I had 'a get 'em and patch 'em and blow 'em up," the old man told me in justification. "Yesterday a lawyer bought seven of 'em." Quit whining, Miss, these items are in high demand. Not too far away is a river where people raft down the rapids on tubes, tied to their beer. "Here," the old man points out the nice long air nozzle on the black rubber. "You can tie your cooler to that."

But I just want to float on the lake, smelling hot rubber and musing about a lawyer bargaining for inner tubes, a man in blue shirt and suspenders: "Hello, I'm an attorney. I'll take seven of those." The young boys next door, with their speed-lined jet skis, will no doubt envy me my new upscale water toy.

All the poison ivy hereabouts was started by Miss Gwen, a retired schoolteacher who lived up the hill from us and hated children. At least this was the tale told everywhere about the poor old recluse—or happy old recluse, she may have been. I can see why a schoolteacher would grow to hate children, but I cannot hold Miss Gwen responsible for this profusion of three-leafed vines. The cure for poison ivy, in my family, was to lather the child in brown soap and let dry. I never got this treatment, however, and believed myself to be immune from poison ivy. Now I know that such immunity is not possible: I have by some miracle simply not been sensitized yet. But as a child I won considerable status among the farm kids by rolling in beds of poison ivy on any dare. We children had, of course, been taught simply to avoid anything with three leaves, so I was probably rolling in hog peanut vine.

I knew that Miss Gwen kept a .22 propped against her mantle, but so did my grandfather and everyone else we knew. He'd sometimes lean out a window and shoot feral cats or rabbits. When rabbit appeared on the supper table it was called chicken to save the sensibilities of bunny worshipers. Once I got what was presented to me as a drumstick, found it suspiciously hinged, and ran screaming from the table. After that, my grandfather said, "You can't put one over on her. Don't even try."

In the summer I was sent to the country for months at a time to live with my grandparents. Usually the confinement of the city or the horrors of school had brought me down with pneumonia or something, and I would need fattening. Grandma would put twenty pounds on me and I grew tall and formidable from love.

As the only Catholic child for miles around, I had more free access to the homes of the surrounding Scandinavian farmers than they had to each other's because the Lutherans were always feuding over aspects of dogma. So I was well received, rather like the wandering minstrel, bringing news of the Johnson farm to the Ruuds and the Ruuds to the Iversons. This freedom had limits; one day, after visiting a family named Petersen, I came home with a note pinned to me that said, "Please teach this child not to mention religion or politics." My grandparents howled with laughter. What else was there to talk about? Some of those Scandinavian families, though, had been divided for years over various fine points of religion. Therefore, you could drive down the main street of town, and, in a place of seven hundred inhabitants (the joke ran), see signs for First, Second, Third, and Free Lutheran. There was also an Episcopalian church (though nobody belonged to it that we knew), a Catholic church with moody clerics all reassigned from somewhere more important, and various rowdy fundamentalist communities, who took up serpents, for all I know, or rolled in poison ivy.

Grieving

So are you moving to Wisconsin?" Ben wants to know when
I return. This seems to him, Minnesota boy, a frightening
alternative.

I've been given a new student to train, a very tough, macho young
man named Andy. I give him enough instruction every day to keep
him from hurting himself or an animal, then leave him at the far
end of the barn to work out his methods. After about half an hour,
I wander up and ask how he's doing. Then I show him how I do it
and we work out some methods that negotiate the difference between his body and mine. This is not how Ben trained me, but Ben
had a clearer idea than I of the various ways one might accomplish
a task and what might be the best approach. Depending on one's
age, sex, center of gravity, athletic prowess, etc., there are radically
different ways of managing sheep.

Last week I taught Andy to halter up and train lambs. This
morning Ben stormed into the kitchen. "Mary! I just found a
grown man out there with a lamb on his knee going 'Baa!' in its ear.
And I ask him, 'What the fuck?' and he says, 'Mary taught me.'"

"So how do *you* get them on a lead?"

"I kick the little shits."

This is not true. Ben does not think lambs are cute, and he does
not think sheep have souls, but he Cares About His Animals.

Affectionately: "Damn, you are ruining this barn, Mary." He
gave me a bottle of warm milk for our bottle lamb, a little crippled

ewe who's going to Lucy's as a pet. "Bottle her. Or did you want Andy to breast-feed it?"

The first of our new ewes, who's been lying around in the mud and off her feed, gave birth to twin lambs last night—a relief, because we were watching her for signs of pre-eclampsia.

I am going to Maine to be interim minister in a rural church, so I won't see the rest of the ewes deliver. It makes me sad. These twins may be my last lambs. I snivel over them for awhile till Ben says, "You can always visit."

"It won't be the same." I've felt valued here as an anonymous worker among workers—a worker with severe limitations, to be sure, but valued because I do my best. And I have my little place in the daily kitchen banter and repartee—there will not be much time for that in my new life.

Weights and Measures

Recently I got hold of a cookbook from Africa, printed on cheap paper, the weights and measures unfamiliar and a challenge to my recall of arithmetic. I make that admission about my math skills to explain why you could have found me, one day last week, standing by the stove irrationally chopping up my tenth onion. By then I had 1/16 of the ingredients for the Ethiopian stew in my biggest pot and the pot was full. I wound up making the dish in two huge stock vats—serves four, the recipe plainly said.

I called up my son, Jude, who, having spent his junior year in Ghana, loves Africa with all his heart. "Oh, that means four *families,*" he told me, "or maybe four villages."

I love this image of overflowing prodigal generosity. And I was thinking, too, about how labor-intensive—and woman-intensive—such cooking is. The stew took me all afternoon to make. The bread that went with it—strange, bubbly injera, of which the mystery ingredient is soda pop—created what looked like a toxic waste problem: baking soda bubbling away in club soda, bits stuck on the wall and the cat. That recipe, too, made more bread than my block could eat.

But my block would not want to eat it. My block is multiethnic, multinational, multigender-preferred, and we speak to each other as little as possible. Any of us would nod to Robert Frost's famous aphorism, "Good fences make good neighbors." One young man on the block, Saladin (Arab-Irish), put it this way: "I'm afraid if I say hello to my neighbor, I'll wind up cleaning his garage."

I'm brooding about these things over the injera because of the new ministry assignment Robin and I have been given: co-pastoring a small meeting community in rural Maine while the church searches for a full-time minister. Most traditional Quaker meetings, like ours in St. Paul, do not have a formal ministry. In the nineteenth century, however, several groups—like this little one in Maine—began a separate tradition, which includes the hiring of pastors. Robin is going to bring his music and I will be expected to preach on, for example, a text from the Acts of the Apostles which I am now reading with horror: "All who believed were together and had all things in common. They would sell their property and possessions and divide them among all according to each one's need." They broke bread together—Who did the cooking, I wonder?—and ate it "with exaltation and sincerity."

Things, however, did not stay so cuddly. By the fifth chapter of Acts we have the villains emerging, a couple named Ananias and Sapphira, who seem so like me and my neighbors that it's hard for me to judge them harshly. This pair sold a field, hoarded a little of the proceeds, and lied about it to Peter the Apostle. He caught them and, like a good TV cop, interrogated them separately. Separately they lied and separately they fell down dead. Vaporized, presumably, by the spirit.

The outcome: "And great fear came upon the whole church." Isn't that pathetic? First we have joyous, spontaneous feasting and generous sharing. Then we get hoarding, fear, and threats. Living generously, in a family or even with one other person, is a full-time test of the heart.

Doing ministry, I know I'm supposed to be on the apostle's side of this one. But I'm not. I would like the story better if, instead of trying to trap this couple in their lies, Peter had sat down with them and listened to their history and their fears: how they hoped that field would sustain them in their old age, how they didn't trust the Arab-Irish guy who wouldn't help them clean their garage. All the wounds and knowledge that keep us hanging on to our goods.

Every morning, I do a yoga posture *(paschimottanasana),* which images surrender. I try to stay in the asana and question each of my muscles and joints: is there more to let go of? When I think I'm done, there is always more. Some days, when my age and history are upon me, I can only go a little way. Surrender is inward and personal. No outsider can live in our bodies and minds and judge whether we are extending or holding back. I think the apostle is on the wrong track here.

I'm thinking as well of a Catholic priest who I once heard remark that the nuns who served his school "are like tubes of toothpaste—you can always squeeze them and get some more." I suppose the priest talked this way because he himself had been subject to a similar system from seminary days.

Infuriating. It's one of the cruelest things on earth, to take the beautiful inward struggle each one of us negotiates in our own time and make it subject to power, coercion, and fear. We suffer from that horribly, most of us, in our jobs, in corporate life, and, too often, in our families and churches. And in our own minds, because these cruel power structures have become internalized.

Dark and Ebbing Energy

I'M HAVING A DAY of Service to Others. No one was at the barn this morning when I arrived, and all the work had been done, presumably by elves and fairies, so I took off and visited an elderly woman who lives nearby. She spent the visit maligning her relatives and complaining about being abandoned. Then I went home to feed a malevolent black rabbit, thumping away on my deck. One of the young women bucketing through here lately left it behind. When I told Ben about the abandoned bunny at my house, he volunteered to take the creature off my hands. "Skin off like a prom dress," he said happily.

I lay out a perfect plate for the Japanese student who is now renting Jude's old room from me: three fresh apricots on a fan of mint, sugar peas tossed on the flame, cooled shrimp in a curry glaze, fresh blackberries in coconut milk. The cat, who is using me, yawns to his dish of star-shaped nibbles.

At the moment, I don't feel like taking care of anything, anybody, or any rabbit.

Love is an outgoing energy but nothing in our physics goes out all the time. Why is it so hard for us humans to understand that? To bear the dark withdrawing ebb, which is so prominent in me just now? Why do preachers promise *endless day?* Most things in the garden bend toward the light, even surly monkshood, but we can have too much of it. Seeking the dark arbor at the foot of the garden, I become bloodroot, hepatica. Here is hole full of silence breathing. Here is a dark well.

Tibetan Buddhism makes a point of attending to negative feelings—though I would be scolded, in that dispensation, for using the word *negative*. Feelings simply *are*. The goal is to feel your condition, then try to merge with all the people in the world who suffer that same condition, be it anger or depression or grief—or benevolence and joy. When you meditate that way, you break down the barriers that separate "good" (or merely lucky or strong-willed) people from those whose temperaments or karma drag them down. The Tibetan practice, I think, represents an attitude toward life that people of all religious traditions fall into who have been touched by radical grace. The Quaker abolitionist, John Woolman, whose journal I read and reread, had a remarkable ability to be present to feelings of every sort—first, his own; then, other people's. He could converse with a slaveholder on such common ground that the other man felt no separation, no unwelcoming righteousness. Freeing one's slaves, on that ground, becomes a simple fraternal act, rather than something one is shamed into or has to defend one's personality against.

This runs counter to lots of Christian pedagogy, in which we're taught to root out "bad" feelings like a pig in turnips. Fortunately, most of us aren't very good at this, or it would be a dull and priggish life.

Elf Patterning

ONE OF THE DICEY THINGS about teaching English or lamb haltering is that, in order to focus a student's attention, you have to hammer away at a few central principles which, to the conscientious learner, begin to have the force of law. But they are merely transitional truths, and when you see them start to harden in the learner's mind, you have to gently nudge him or her out of security and inculcate what is always the final lesson: there are, in fact, many ways to reach a goal—several of which are logically opposed to each other. Much of what we call "knowledge" is merely a temporary frame around chaos.

For all creation is "myth woven and elf-patterned," J. R. R. Tolkien said one day to his friend, C. S. Lewis. Tolkien was a Roman Catholic, struggling along like Thomas Merton with the shoddy spiritual equipment of the artist. Lewis was an atheist, then, trying hard to be an analytical empiricist, but A. N. Wilson, in his recent biography, attributes Lewis's conversion to his friend's chance remark about elf patterns. Makes sense to me. Religious people—and those who oppose them—often mistake the essential dreaminess of Christian story for hard-edged argument. It's a good thing Tolkien didn't pull out Thomas Aquinas's "Five Proofs for the Existence of God." One of my theology professors used to demonstrate that this "argument" works equally well for the existence of Santa Claus.

Tolkien believed that myth is truer than the dogmas derived from myth. When I think of the truth of myth, or of poetry, I imagine one of those revolving, many faceted balls of light that used to swing over high school proms. Refractions flash here and there, you cannot take it all in. One beam catches your attention, then another. To stop the motion or to focus on any single stream of light is to demolish the effect entirely. Thus Tolkien, coming upon the death of Balder in Norse mythology, was transfixed by a wild constellation of meaning, grasped not with the mind but with the whole being. Far too large, the meaning of myth, for limited minds to grasp.

If the woodwork is full of elves and fairies, how can you teach anything? Well, you can teach *that*.

Heading Out

SANCTIFICATION."

Ben breathed the word quietly as we were staring off into the north pasture, his hands busy mending a lamb harness.

In the small, conservative religious community where Ben worships, I believe this word resonates, as some words do, with a transcendent note. I say, "Excuse me?" but he does not repeat it. The word has been invoked, and its cognitive content is irrelevant.

"I'm going to look at a farm near New Prague tomorrow," I had begun. It's the third farm I've visited this month, always returning crestfallen. Each farm has been expensive, half under water, encroached on by suburbs, or all three.

"Boy, you're really serious."

"I know it's crazy." I begin to talk myself out of it. "An hour of commuting, then get home and feed the animals . . ."

That's when Ben whispered, "Sanctification."

"Excuse me?"

"If you can't breathe, see the stars, be quiet, what the hell?"

I hate the concept of hobby farming. I sigh as I drive past the five-acre parcels that extend our suburbs into what used to be deep country, each with its two hundred thousand-dollar house. Sod is laid down, fertilized, and nuked with pesticide, the dregs run off into the water table. Yet each of these settlers wanted stars, quiet, deer, etc. Americans—and I am one, of course—are driven by a mythic urge into the wilderness, each one Natty Bumppo, each one carrying the contamination of civilization with him. Everybody seems to want to live on the edge of a cornfield, forgetting that all the land around here was once cornfield and tomorrow the cornfield you look on will be tract housing or a strip mall. Then if you're rich enough, you move out, drive up farm prices, despoil more cornfields.

And before the cornfield was prairie, and before us, people who did not believe in owning land lived on it.

But all is not dark. There's a local developer, for example, pioneering the idea of "cluster housing." Instead of planting five houses on twenty-five acres, each with its five-acre parcel, he groups the houses together in a little community and keeps the rest in agriculture. Thus, residents satisfy their paradoxical need for community and wildness; farming goes on in their midst, their children see toil and slaughter, drought and plenitude. It's good for children to see these things.

"What do you want, Mary?" Ben wants to know.

When I began telling this story about my year at the barn, I did not know the answer to that question. Now I do, but I've never spoken my dream aloud and I'm so excited I begin to babble. "Forty acres in sustainable agriculture, and on that forty acres I want to build five little hermitages where people can come and stay . . ." And turn and live with the animals, as Walt Whitman recommended.

"I get it," says Ben, mulling it over. "A religious petting zoo."

Sheep May Safely Graze

A MACHARA.
Some people navigate by sight or kinesthetic impressions, others by the music of things. I'm one of the latter, and when I heard this beautiful Gaelic word, it sounded as much as it meant: soul friend.

For the last two years, I've been studying for certification in a graduate program in spiritual guidance. I've enjoyed rereading many of the classic spiritual texts that I studied as a young novice, and catching up, as well, on modern theology and spirituality, but I find the contemporary works, on the whole, disappointing. The readings seem to be composed from a circumscribed set of words like those on the lists issued to writers of children's books, words reprocessed over and over through each writer's theological cuisinart: grace, faith, call. Few of these words connect with daily life. Lovemaking does not enter in; the word *dog* does not appear; the writers cannot seem to distinguish one species of evergreen from another.

The readings make me feel, depending on my inner weather, sad, angry, stupid, or just disinvited. After so many years of feminist theology, I see few attempts in religious circles to unify the physical and spiritual. How I want to cry out against this relentless negation of life—negation once by commandment and caveat, negation now by silence, erasure. Even a Christian must admit God entered the world like a lover. Even a Buddhist breathes God to the beloved in self-abandonment and surrender.

In contrast to theology texts, the people who come to me for spiritual companionship talk of sexuality and birth, mercy and mothering. They say a lot about their pets and gardens.

The conclusion, therefore: I would rather talk to people about their spiritual experience than study theology.

Several years ago I read Catherine de Hueck Doherty's entrancing book *Poustinia,* which narrates her journey from Russia to America and her founding of a hermitage in New York. In Russia, every village lucky enough had its *staretz,* or hermit, who acted as a kind of spiritual director, hotelier, and antic wild (wo)man to the local populace. Antic wildwoman seemed a job description I could grow into, and the idea of creating a sanctuary for spiritual companioning was born.

Since Plum Village, the idea has grown. The variation I bring to Doherty's vision is that I want my poustinia to be a place of security for all beings. It's comforting and grounding for me to live with animals, so I assume that a few others share this disposition. I want to find a small farm and share it with other *amacharas,* those who speak and paint and make love and make music, those who bleat and low and bark.

May all beings, as Buddhists say, be at peace. At least on these acres.

Maine

WHEN YOU GET A LONG way from home, you can see where you've been.

I'm looking out the parsonage window at a sweep of meadow: in the midrange lies an abandoned garden popping a few clumps of daffodils; at the far end of the meadow the white pines begin at an old stone wall. The land dips and rises beyond the wall into the Quaker cemetery, one hundred and fifty years old. As I sit across from Robin at the breakfast table, I watch the gravestones, flung down the far hill like counters in an old-fashioned game; beyond, the pines begin again. The gravestones are weathered gray or black, but the tops are white with a lichen that reflects frostily, as though the dead lie in perpetual shafts of sun.

I say I watch the graves; one might prefer to say "see." But indeed, morning, noon, and until the light fails, whenever I sit at the kitchen table, I watch them. There is a woman buried there whose first name was Desire. The *Book of Revelations* says that each of us has a secret name, written on a white stone. I think Desire is my secret name. No wonder I have such a struggle with Buddhism. My mind goes back to that odd incident of reverse satori in the zendo: *I do not want to transcend my longing.*

"My love is my weight," Augustine wrote. "By it I am drawn wherever I must go."

I have known women, pastors' wives as it happens, who've hated the seventeen windows of this house, the isolation of its country site along with its paradoxical element of display: three times an hour some Ford pickup goes by and records what's doing at the parsonage. When we draw a blind or hang wash, when we sit on the porch to play our Swedish fiddle duets, the actions of the unmarried couple in the parsonage are being mulled over in the Brunswick five-and-dime or Captain Mike's.

I do not mind at all. "What do you write about?" "Myself." It's the nature of our kind to hang our wash on the line.

I watch the graves; I sit at the long meeting that goes on up there. "How do you stand the brutality of farming?" a friend asked me the other day, a friend who had spent his boyhood on a cattle farm.

"It reassures me," I responded. In cleaner occupations, like teaching or corporate finance, the brutality is hidden, but you know it's there. You'd *better* know it's there. I prefer the light and the darkness laid out like a country landscape. No subterfuge. Maybe I'm just poor at negotiating subtlety.

I like it here at the parsonage. When you tell people your job, you have to deal not only with your own sense of that job but also with other people's projections. I love teaching, but I never wanted to own its public image: no, I do not live to correct grammar. When I say, "I'm interim pastor of Durham Friends Meeting," I find that I can be comfortable in my own sense of the task and also in other people's vision of it.

It's strange that this is true, because one of the terrifying aspects of ministry is how it can imprison you within a false persona. Religion is hard enough to practice; religious culture tends to be impossibly stultifying. I guess I feel free here because I have no secrets from the people of Durham. My wash is out there.

This conservative community seems able to accept us, has indeed taken us to its heart, not because they all approve of our theology and life choices, but because they respect each individual's process of discernment. This is a fundamental Quaker tenet, and I, too, hang by it. I don't know if what I think and do is right; I try to stay open to new understanding. Robin goes so far as to say that two rough beasts are a positive asset to the parsonage. It signals, he tells me, that marginal people are welcome at the Quaker table. I suspect, however, that several people in this community simply didn't know what they were getting into with us. "Why, Mary," one elderly lady confided to me, "when we heard that you had a 'long-time companion,' we just thought you were an old crippled person."

Called to preach last Sunday, I spoke about the time after the resurrection when Jesus was always jumping out of bushes and surprising people with new ideas: to what extent will we let ourselves be surprised by ideas of love in fresh disguises? This week I'll be on to the Good Shepherd (how could he work in those clothes?). If I can't remain as pastor, maybe some farmer will take me on.

My Sunday sermon didn't score any points with one of the octagenarians in the congregation, but mostly she took exception to its brevity (I try not to speak any longer than fifteen minutes). "I do not like short preaching," she told me. "I lie awake long into the night and have enough silence, thank you."

Robin and I spend a lot of time walking in the woods with indomitable old women who give me hope for my later years. The woods erupt just now in lacy clusters of bluets (in common parlance, Quaker Ladies); each one looks like a veil dropped by a fleeing bride. In yesterday's woods, we also tramped past a bunk of tires, plastic sleds, an unbroken milkglass vase sitting on a rusty muffler, and a broken toilet. The botanist walking with us apologized. But again, I would use the word *reassuring*. The mess is laid out for all to see. We are made of that, I thought: plastic, old driers, first glances of each newborn, red lichen, photos put out by accident into the trash.

As well as an ocean, swollen with light.

The Religion of Natural Process

MINISTERS, LIKE NUNS and psychologists, attract their share of people who just want to taunt you about how immune they are from needing your services. Such a one came to me recently for spiritual companioning, after announcing that he had no religion at all and thought it was bunk, "except for the religion of natural process." I respect that religion, actually; it has some fine saints—Thomas Hardy, Dylan Thomas, Philip Larkin.

The man in question fetched up in the parsonage kitchen, however, because something had awakened the fear of death in him. Clearly, he was not practicing his religion of natural process well, for that faith, no less than Islam or Catholicism, demands the surrender of ego to some larger scene. The poet Mark Doty writes eloquently about his partner's death from AIDS, and how the process of decline gently stripped Wally of all that was not Everything, and how in that millrace he became *most himself.* Doty says that death is "the deepest moment in the world ... even if that self empties into no one, swift river hurrying into the tumble of rivers, out of individuality, into the great rushing whirlwind of currents."

Later he writes of scattering Wally's ashes in a tidal marsh, the dust swirling into currents of air and water, shards of bone visible among sea shells and sea wrack only a few days, then taken. How the ash blew back into his own face, how it eddied up, and how these days it seems to meet him every time he flies into Logan Airport.

Buddhism asks us to contemplate literally and frequently our own deaths, a salutary rather than a morbid practice. In the days when I sailed a lot, I learned to be at peace with the concept of burial at sea, my sinews gnawed through by fishes, bones dispersed in the rush of ocean. Earlier I had preferred Thomas Merton's account of how Trappists convey their dead, unembalmed and simply shrouded, to the earth: whatever returns us quickly to everything. I have, for my part, a reservation in the airspace above Alma, Wisconsin, the great flyway of the tundra swans.

But when I am not contemplating death like a good Buddhist, I am figuring out how to sink my fingernails into the dirt, never to be dislodged—*living is so dear.* The two interior dispositions, hanging on and letting go, form a paradoxical whole. People who work in nature, poised simultaneously in life and death, tend to live, on a daily basis, consciously. They are connected to an organic pattern in which life and death sing two-part harmony.

Religion: the word derives from the Latin *religio,* to connect. When I ask people—as I do in the spiritual autobiography classes I teach—to define what spirituality means to them, *connection* is the most common word that comes up. *Belonging* is another. Gretel Ehrlich, in *The Solace of Open Spaces,* makes a similar point in appreciating the "rare delicacy"—call it spiritual life—of Wyoming cowboys: "Because these men work with animals, not machines, or numbers, because they live outside in landscapes of torrential beauty, because they are confined to a place and a routine embellished with awesome variables, because calves die in the arms that pulled others into life, because they go to the mountains as if on a pilgrimage...." Her balanced sentences remind me of the litanies of my Catholic childhood.

Indeed, these cycles of eternal return are the ground of all litany. What happens in church, at best, mirrors what happens outside it.

Farmers live at least part-time in mystery and cannot help but be formed by it. When I converse with a Benedictine monk, I wonder whether his ancient gentleness has been formed by liturgy or by gardening. My Amish friend, Aaron, is a patient and good man, despite a catalog of cruel and moody "religious" views; "I know why the *Titanic* went down," he let me know when I related the movie plot to his unwilling ear. "It was full of the non-God-fearing." Despite this rigid theology, he always receives me with placidity and kindness, a temperament formed, no doubt, more by the daily struggle with a team of Clydesdales than by his church's teachings. I hope he prays over my Volvo, also loaded up with the non-God-fearing; it can't do any harm.

When I die, then, bury me, scatter me anywhere, excluding Logan Airport. I will be with you, recombinant, wanting to belong.

Hot

I GOT HOME FROM MAINE, went to the barn, and found Ben out of the action. He's on leave for July and August, and Beth has become the interim manager. I think it was quite a struggle for him to take time off, but he's worn out.

When I walked into the longbarn this morning, it was already ninety-five degrees in there, with a kind of furnace updraft near the steel doors on the northeast side. Beth, in her heavy overalls and steel-toed shoes, looked faint and shiny with sweat. She'd been left a job of shearing twenty-one rams, each at about a hundred and fifty pounds. Forty-five minutes later, I, too, was getting faint and shiny. It took that long to drag in the second fit stand and jury-rig the head clamp (missing a vital part), hook up the extension cord, and find the fuse, which immediately blew when we started our engines. The fit stand I was using to shear had no side guards, so it was chancy shearing one-handed as you gripped the ram to keep him from falling off and hanging himself in the head stand, which (thanks to our jury-rigged bolt) had no quick-release capacity. The stand would not jack up either, so I had to kneel to get at his belly. This puts you in the way of a hoof in the face. "Please, God," I prayed as I so often pray, "don't let me be killed by a sheep."

The rams have to be sheared or they will overheat and be sterile. Beth, like Ben before her, will overwork herself for the sake of the animals. So will I. But now the task has become almost impossible. If Ben had to make bricks from straw, Beth is being asked to make them from spaghetti. Our clippers are too dull to clip grass.

It's a lot like teaching school, a job I will have to go back to soon, if I want to save enough money to buy a farm.

July

I'M THE THIRD IN A LINE of poets to know this piece of wisdom and perhaps someday I will pass it on to my daughter, Julian, and she will be the fourth:

Hang on like grim death to the lamppost. When I heard this advice from my beloved postulant mistress, quoting her own beloved teacher, I blinked and said to myself (being young), "Is that all there is?"

It's not a poetic phrase and it doesn't even make metaphoric sense. Is death clinging to the lamppost? Or is one to cling *like* death—which by definition clings rather little?

Meaningless advice, perhaps. Yet many sutras and stories have had their moment, then fallen from my refrigerator magnets. This remains: hang on like grim death to the lamppost.

I mumbled it this morning as I watched a mourning cloak butterfly, awakened from gestation in the woodpile, cling to the face of a lily as the breeze tried to drag him off.

High nineties predicted today. The competent Beth has gotten us some helpers, so we are now four women shearing the testicles of twenty overheated rams, making lewd remarks and hogging the shower. Hank tore through and helped us rig up the fit stand, supporting its wheezing pneumatics with an overturned plastic feed bucket, as OSHA no doubt recommends. We inquire hopefully after our missing wing nut. A student, he says, has probably stolen it.

Hank says he is looking for a lamb to slaughter for the upcoming barn open house.

"Are you going to slaughter it as the high point of the day? Or marinate it beforehand?" I inquire.

Hank gives me a look that says, "Go back to the Planet Mongo."

"Are we going to dance around it wearing staghorns?" I pursue him.

When someone is looking for a lamb to slaughter, I clear out. I set up in a corner of the barn with a big Dorset on the stand and dreamily watch wool slide off the pink body till he wears fleece like a skirt. After the precision of show shearing, this is easy. Nora, the new helper, has sheared a cute topknot onto her ram. "Ben says I'm weird," Nora reports.

"Ben says I'm weird," each woman chimes in. "Ben's weird," we say in unison. Three little maids from school.

Sin and Grace

WHEN ONE HAS THE SLIGHTEST understanding of the bright, blinding, ruthless light of what we call God, felt the amoral wind that sweeps across holy places, one feels like one of those laboratory animals who, escaping the cage, wants nothing but to run back into it, certain of water and crunchy nutrients behind the bars. No wonder the early monastics prayed to stay out of "the eye of God." It didn't look like a comfortable place to be.

Peter and I have been talking about some of the great betrayals in our lives—the times we've tromped on love, sent back the letter, as it were, from kindness and connection. Is *sin* still a useful word for that? I wonder, both of us crying, again, on the phone. I think, for example, of one night in a freezing attic in the north of England. Robin and I, on our relentless budget, had opted for free lodging in an abandoned seventeenth-century Quaker meetinghouse. Stretched out on the floor, I tried not to sleep because I kept dreaming about a man putting a noose around his neck in the stairwell next to our attic. Robin, as the night wore on, got progressively sicker from eating bad fish. I crawled out of bed and down a stairway thick with ghosts to make him a cup of tea and fill a hot water bottle. I felt furious, begrudging, and abandoned. Why? I don't know. As Thay taught, simply feeling your feelings is deep practice: "Breathing in, I know I am afraid, breathing out, I feel the roots of my fear."

"Zero at the Bone—" Emily Dickinson said of fear. This was a condition of zero at the heart.

It sounds like a bad space to be in. It is and it isn't. To reach out and let this condition fill you so that you truly understand it and yourself is to come to a profounder understanding of the human condition, Sister Ani, the Tibetan nun at Plum Village, taught. And to do that, you have to be a little detached, like a gatekeeper at the sewage processing plant who watches the sludge flow in and out.

Someone I know once shocked me by screaming at her husband while he lay dying, "You're betraying me! You said you'd always take care of me, and now look at you!" This outburst troubled me at the time. For many years, until that night in the north of England, I had trouble understanding her feelings. But, as I shimmied down the dark loft stairs and made that cup of tea for Robin, I visited the place where that woman had been standing. The experience punched out some windows in my heart. Not only could I understand her. I *was* her.

It used to annoy me, as a Catholic schoolgirl, when good people would tell stories about their lives and call themselves "sinners," to say they could find common ground with the most hardened criminals. Augustine is a case in point, and Thérèse of Lisieux another. Here they were, living lives of prayer and service, while braying on about their sins. I thought they were showing off. But now I know that what the churches call "sanctity" is simply the end of a patient process of inner healing and smartening up. If you really know your feelings and do not hide from them, it's perfectly clear that not a blade of grass separates you from the most cruel and destructive behavior.

To know the truth of this condition is also to know the truth of its opposite. Traditional writers have characterized grace in imagery of flowing waters. Sacred Harp singers wail this text:

> Sweet rivers of redeeming love
> Lie just before mine eye.
> Had I the pinions of a dove,
> I'd to those rivers fly.

"As pants the heart for cooling streams . . ." Robin and I sing on these hot days until we have to go for a beer. Grace is the opposite of the condition of lovelessness, a dank tarn, dammed up and held in. To acknowledge that one is shut up with the spirits of black water is to release, in the same psychic wave, the bracing torrent of the opposite condition. All human ebb and flow mirrors this eternal action, though we prefer the flow to the ebb.

The cruelly hot weather makes me cross and stupid as though humidity were sapping vital fluid from my nerves. I've been jumpy, insomniac, and mean for five days. Then yesterday I went to Robin's and snapped at him for awhile till we decided to take a nap in front of the fan. We made love instead, slowly and carefully, and then fell into one of the four or five and surely the sweetest of the varieties of sleep. But it was less sleep than a long swim underwater, changing more than mood, to awaken in different skin. Later, at the kitchen table, we pulled out the red book and sang one of my favorite shape note songs:

> Beneath the sacred throne of God
> I saw a river rise . . .;
> The streams where peace and pard'ning blood
> Descended from the skies.

Leaving

O F COURSE, I'VE ALWAYS KNOWN that I would have to leave the barn some day—if only to go back and teach school—but it hurt to go in and tell Beth that the moment was at hand. Last week, while standing atop the fit stand shearing a ram's wool cap, my weak left leg went out from under me, and I almost sheared off Nora's pony tail. I can't trust my body anymore. Some kind of arthritic condition that worsened in Maine causes my legs to collapse, my fingers to suddenly lose their grip. With sorrow, I realize I can't handle the barn without Ben. He was strong enough and experienced enough to make up for my lapses and keep us all safe.

I'm sad but not devastated because I know I'll be able to handle twenty sheep of my own some day, if not two hundred belonging to the citizens of this state.

Beth said, "Don't feel bad. If they don't get me some help, I'm going to quit. I can't deal with this shit."

The legislature won't allocate enough money to the college to staff the barn and, consequently, all its systems have run down. Ben carried it on his back as long as he could, and Beth can't carry it four feet more. What a shame. A teaching farm right on the edge of a big city is an unusual resource. I know that we contribute to the ephemeral, much vaunted "quality of life" in a way that will only be reckoned when we are a ghost barn, ghost sheep, ghost shepherds.

Our poor rams look like Christmas critters, all starry with gold antiseptic spray where we've gashed them.

True and False Personae

D IANE ARBUS, FAMOUS for her photographs of "freaks," said, "Everybody has that thing where they need to look one way but they come out looking another way and that's what people observe. You see someone on the street and essentially what you notice about them is the flaw. . . . Our whole guise is like giving a sign to the world to think of us in a certain way but there's a point between what you want people to know about you and what you can't help people knowing about you."

That *freakpoint,* of course, was what Arbus tried to photograph. It's also the point that meditation practice brings to attention: the rift in the personality, the fault line. Many people try out meditation as a way of relaxing, then discover that sitting quietly brings up anxiety, buried anger, or mere sleepiness. One may flee a meditation practice that seems to stir up a nest of hornets. But to meditate well is not to enter an altered state of blissful repose: rather, it is simple observation of *what is.* That's why, in the long run, paradoxically, it's relaxing. It teaches us to sit quietly with fear or depression or elation or whatever inhabits from moment to moment the freakspace.

Focusing on spiritual things doesn't make you a good person. It's like focusing on, for example, music. You can play well or badly, misuse your gifts; show off; fail to practice; practice humbly, daily; be tried by a bad instrument; fail your teachers or honor them, transcend them or be brutalized by them; come into the world with innate gifts or not; be in tune, be out. I know a little boy who took flute lessons for years merely because he liked to carry the case around.

Zen teachers often use the image of "taking tea with the demons." Fear—to name merely one demon—grows huge as we flee from it, but, when we turn and face it, it shrinks. Running from fear is about as productive as running with your clothes on fire.

When I was eighteen or nineteen, I wrote down a sentence from the existentialist writer Romain Rolland: "The only heroism is to see reality as it is and love it." I'm still working on *seeing;* loving may be for another day. Breathing in, I feel the deep roots of my fear . . .

If you are like me, not subject to dramatic religious experiences, meditation like this does not call up a revelatory vision. Over time, though, it puts you in a condition of receptivity, so that insights, dreams, chance encounters begin to shape the contours of an answer.

Living in contemporary culture forces us to take on layers and layers of false personality. Mirrors are everywhere, and we learn to be always posing. We grow a kind of shell or carapace over the real person in order to go out and find jobs or mates. Not only are religious people not immune from this pressure, they are under *extra* compulsion to demonstrate a suave social manner, an exemplary marriage, a perpetual sweet-suffering-Jesus smile.

This process of growing a false skin is so universal and unavoidable that I think it must serve some developmental purpose. Fortunately, another natural process is also at work: at the same time as false persona grows, false persona erodes. The nature of the carapace is to dissolve and set the spirit free, over the course of a good long life. Meditation helps us to move with this natural process rather than against it. We have such a strong instinct to hold on to false identity. We spend so much money, after all, buying those clothes, that education.

I had a nightmare about this process recently. I'm getting ready to go back to the classroom, a major site of phony behavior for all parties concerned. The dream came to me after I had spent the day composing a list of courses I proposed to teach next year. In the dream I was in a stone house during an earthquake. In the room were two closed boxes, and somehow I knew that in one box was a living baby and in the other a doll. As the wall started to collapse, another presence materialized in the room, a man with a gray beard who looked rather like Pete Seeger, the folk singer. As the wall collapsed, Pete shouted, "Don't save the baby! Save the doll!"

I felt both agonizing fear and certainty about my course of action. I reached for the baby and cradled it. The wall crashed down on the doll.

As I escaped with the baby, however, the doll rose up from the rubble, became a kind of robotic, horror movie toy, furious and "possessed." She reached out for me and I woke up screaming.

This got my day off to a bad start, and I stalked around pondering what it might mean. Then in a moment of inattention, stepping over a puddle, I realized that the dream mirrors some painful, practical difficulties of choosing between true and false personae. I *know* the real baby from the doll, and I know where my true business lies. But lots of respectable authority figures—represented by Pete Seeger, for heaven's sake—yell at me to save the doll. And though I (barely) have enough sense to grab what's real, that crabby doll will make my nights hell. Meanwhile, the walls are caving in.

The next day, I retracted my proposed course schedule and composed some more imaginative choices. They would be, as it turned out, rejected by the scheduling committee.

Getting Dressed

I'M WASHING MY OVERALLS and packing them all away, getting out instead my respectable professor's woolens.

One of the introductory assignments I give my students is: write about some clothing in which you feel truly yourself. One winter that was, for me, a pair of faded red cotton leggings from Sweden, a torn plaid flannel shirt that came from the rag bag in the Quaker community I once lived in, and moccasins made in northern Minnesota by an old Ojibwa woman called Lydia, every bead a prayer. Winter that year brought us steady ice storms and weeks at thirty below. All that red flannel next to my skin seemed to radiate like true love. The soft age of the fabric helped; I can leave a new dress hanging till it's out of style. That crisp sizing puts me off. Drive a pickup over something a few times and I may put it on.

I used to wear my red leggings to school in winter, under a long gray cotton skirt, until one of my colleagues remarked, "Oh, isn't that cute. You're wearing long underwear."

There was enough of a smirk in her voice and enough shame in my psychology to make me feel a queasy, outsider's spasm. My students often tell me, "I want to be myself in my writing, but I also want to get an A." So do I. To be yourself is to court mockery. Being original is right next door to being a nut case. You have to negotiate a frightening passage to "be yourself." You have to empty your pockets at a few haunted tollbooths. Anything original looks strange because it *is* strange; it hasn't been done before.

God sides with the weird—whatever is "spare, strange," "fickle, freckled," writes Gerard Manley Hopkins—but humankind does not. Remember junior high? Our literary and social traditions pretend to value "the road not taken"—whenever I teach that tricky little poem of Frost's I get a bunch of student essays that boast about being on that very road. I want to write in the margin: "Why are you at this school, then? Why did you do my assignment? Why didn't you read the poem more carefully?" However much we pretend to value originality, face it, most of us would rather see the movie. It takes a sane and deeply healed community to nurture prophetic vision. Few of us grow up in such soul-making space, so the instinct to conform overwhelms our best ideas. We hear that singsong voice chanting, "Nah nah nah, you're wearing long underwear."

Oh, for the single eye of animal creation. Just as I go to sleep, just as I wake up, I see the calm gaze of wolf looking at me through curtains of shifting snow.

Forgiveness

A FRITTILARY — WHICH LOOKS like a baby monarch but has a bouncier, low-level flight pattern, different from the bigger butterfly's soaring habit, like the little Cessna my dad used to fly — alights on a purple coneflower. The orange center rods of the corolla, where the seed heads form, look vibrating and hot to me, like the element of a tiny grill. How does it look to frittilary, this dangerous landing strip? What a world of color he inhabits, so sensual a space. Similarly the honeybees, embayed for this moment in monarda. But do they *know,* in any useful sense, the trembling crimson ground their hairy little legs attend? Perhaps it takes rational intelligence to live in the present moment, despite all our human difficulty with doing so. The bee, perhaps, minds only the honey sacks on his thighs: fill, fill, fill is his imperative. Like a stock trader.

But maybe not. The creator's intelligence seems to supply the inducement of joy to every necessary evolutionary act. I hope the bee's pleasure, sunk in August, is deep as mine. May all things be brought to enlightenment. I read in an article by Tom Seeley of Cornell University that honeybees are being decimated by tracheal and varroa mites at the rate of a million colonies every two years.

The Sufis teach that in order to reach a new plane of understanding, you have to "pass" a specific number of experiences. One hundred? Five hundred thirty-eight? Who knows? Then, in some cosmic transaction, your visa gets stamped, and you move on. It's as good an explanation as any for how differently people live on this planet: some bound on hurting and damming up the flow of mercy, others prodigal as Francis of Assisi, throwing away all they own for joy. And most of us making our cautious way between, ignoring Hutus and Tutsis, indulging in the righteousness of the Left or the Right, getting and spending: believe me, I am right in there, belly up to the trough.

Still. If meditation teaches us to sit with the long threads of our darkness, it also, mercifully, fills us like a glass bowl with light (sometimes), gently as this frittilary touches down upon its heart's desire. Adrienne Rich has written that gentleness "invents more merciful instruments / to touch the wound beyond the wound."

One day last week when Robin and I were making love, something changed between us, as though a cloak slid off the soul. Something slipped on the breath: *forgiving* might have been the word. But not forgiveness of this individual man, who holds a fifteen-year unassailable record for *ahimsa,* not harming—though, believe me, he drops his socks on the floor like any other male, scratches the same eleven notes on his fiddle over and over while I'm, dammit, thinking, and so forth—but a broader forgiveness. Not something between us, but something laid on that bed by the ghosts before houses. The need to love someone well becomes like the skin's longing to close a wound, to stretch the length of a burn lake, of a blue-rimmed bullet hole. That wise, that single, that hard.

So let us say that was, in the Sufi dispensation, experience #304. But other times I just stand around yelling, as the old song goes, "O Zion! More love!" and not getting any response. For years at a time God does not answer the phone. Hello, Central? I'm still bitching.

Forgiveness, for example (it's on my mind), moves on some glacial scheme of its own.

"Never turn your back on a buck ram," says one of my experienced barn helpers. "They'll butt you to hell."

I suppose the slow pace of forgiveness, the tedious creep of skin

over laceration, maintains some cosmic economy I cannot comprehend. We're threaded into a pattern too vast for our own eyes, and
even a red ribbon of anger plays its part. Meanwhile, I shake my fist
at the Most High: look at all the anger I've taught my daughter, for
example. Surely that cannot be good for her. Would it spoil one of
your major plans, I sing out like Tevye, if I were to become a better
person?

The Most High responds: teach your daughter never to turn
her back on a buck ram.

Healing

M Y LEGS GO OUT from under me at odd moments, so I always hold onto the banister when I go up and down stairs. Therefore I can't imagine why I was not holding on, was unanchored in space and time, when a young woman named Nancy tumbled down on top of me. Nancy had been entrusted to my care by her mother, who told me, "She's had a little brain damage." Both of us were attending a Quaker conference on healing, designed for care givers and care receivers. Who was which? If we had known when we signed up, we didn't know anymore.

Back on another track in the world, I have been negotiating the price of a small farm. So much about it seems perfect: a ten-acre parcel within a reasonable commute to my day job, lovingly maintained by a young farm family ready to move to larger acreage. Our negotiations have been calm and respectful. Once I watched two Quakers buy and sell a little trailer. The playlet evolved something like this:

Tom: Nice trailer you've got there, Bill. Think of selling it?

Bill: Built her myself. I could let you have her for one hundred fifty dollars.

Tom: No, that's way too little. Look at all the work you put in. How about two hundred dollars?

Bill: One hundred seventy-five. That's my final offer.

I think someone at Harvard School of Business has called this a win-win solution, and my chats with the young farmer have gone just about as well. Still, he needs a little more than I can afford to pay, so the whole thing is making me fearful.

Fear is a perfect site on which to practice spiritual discipline. I am sitting these days on a ten-acre zafu listening to my nerves: *You don't have enough. You aren't strong enough to do this alone. Who do you think you are, anyway?* And so on.

I had been running this script over to myself only that morning, after a sleepless night worrying that my offer on the farm would not be accepted or, worse, accepted. As I was walking up the stairs behind Nancy, a Biblical text entered my mind with the kind of authority that leads some people to say, "God spoke to me." The phrase was, "My grace is sufficient for thee." It was at that moment that Nancy fell down the stairs.

"Good catch," she said with her slightly disoriented smile, because I was standing there on my weak legs, holding her like a doll. Grace easily vexes the laws of physics, so she seemed to weigh about what she might have weighed underwater. Then I gently put her down and reached for the handrail.

John Calvi, who's directing our workshop, talks about healing not as curing but as creating a space where healing can occur. Healing forces are at work everywhere within an organic system. As Galway Kinnell puts it in his poem, "St. Francis and the Sow": "Everything flowers from within of self-blessing." But when I'm cramped up with fear or anger or self-loathing, nothing can move. As the Sacred Harp text goes:

> I'm fettered and chained up in clay.
> I struggle and pant to be free
> I long to be soaring away—

Hindu cosmology teaches gardeners to create a wild space in the perennial bed where devas—angels—can multiply. They need such a lot of room.

Pearl of Great Price

THE YOUNG FARMER CALLED to say he had to refuse my offer on his farm, but could we all have dinner, it's been such fun—? I left this conversation light of heart, feeling that it's possible to negotiate and win or lose with reverence and kindness to all parties. I know my offer was low, though it was the best I could afford.

I love the parables of buying and selling in Matthew's Gospel:

> The kingdom of heaven is like a treasure
> hidden in a field; a man has found it and hidden it
> again and now, for joy, is going home to sell all that
> he has and buy that field; again the kingdom is like
> a merchant looking for rare pearls: and now he has
> found one of great price and has sold all
> that he has and bought it.

What attracts me about these stories is the clarity and lack of niggling that has to attend the great transactions of the soul. The merchants neither whine nor bargain, they just unload everything they've carried to that point, "for joy." On the one hand, everything you possess. On the other, your heart's desire. An easy choice. In the farm negotiations, however, I've weighed out everything I possess and come up forty thousand dollars short, though rich in a new friend, a warm feeling about the human condition, and better understanding of the zoning laws in Goodhue County.

These win-win negotiations are lessons in divine economics.

Dorothy Day, in her autobiography, *The Long Loneliness,* tells about an old custom of the early Catholic Worker movement. If they came up short of money for a project, they would give the rest of their money away. They had some notion that a generous action would prime the great pump of prodigality. Potlatching—when West Coast Indians pile up all their possessions and let the neighbors carry them away—seems to serve the same psychic purpose.

When I was more confined than I am now by Western thought systems, which mostly revolve around getting and keeping, these gestures used to strike me as superstitious, primitive, or merely foolish. Now they seem to me quite beautiful (though I have not the slightest inclination to potlatch my little bungalow); they honor our connection to each other and the essential richness we must know in ourselves in order to live gratefully in the world, rather than hunched over in miserly constriction.

My dear friend and *amachara,* Peter, used to teach me this over and over in the days when both our children were young and we would take car trips together. Peter's son would beg to stop at Toys R Us; my son and daughter would glare with disapproval. Peter would screech to a halt and let his son buy anything in the place; my children would be doled out their allowance.

"Peter," I would say. "You spoil him so terribly. He'll never learn thrift."

"I don't want him to learn thrift," Peter responded. "I want him to learn about love flowing out on your lap and rolling all over the ground."

I'm so glad I learned this, to the extent I learned it. It's what Natalia Ginsberg recommends in her dangerous essay, "The Little Virtues":

> As far as the education of children is concerned I
> think they should be taught not the little virtues
> but the great ones. Not thrift, but generosity and
> indifference to money; not caution but courage and
> contempt for danger; not shrewdness but frank-
> ness and a love of truth; not tact but love for one's
> neighbor and self-denial; not a desire for success
> but a desire to be and to know.

There are not many pages left in this book. Something dramatic
and splendid should happen, or something dramatic and terrible.
All narratives have an implicit quest structure, and a story should
not end with good-natured negotiations going nowhere. If this were
TV drama, I'd inherit forty acres just about now; if it were the kind
of fiction my creative writing students used to hand in, I'd be hit by
a tractor and wind up paralyzed. Students love irony. I don't; it demands too much mental action.

I went to work in the barn with a lot of ideas that clung to me
like damp feathers imported from academic life. When you work
with elemental creatures and machinery, though, your ideas quiet
down; this is good because mental constructions obscure a lot of
what we were put on earth to see and feel: the precise hang of a star,
the full heft of one's own body, the curious striations in a rabbit's fur
that, when distributed in miraculous order across the sweep of the
animal, account for his subtle coloration and camouflage.

But I didn't go to the barn to be infected with a mania for owning land. If I had a mania, these playful negotiations, the occasional
up-country jaunts to wave an auction card, would go better. As
Thoreau says, a poet gets the best part of any farm without the
bother of a mortgage. I don't want to own a farm so much as I want
plain work shared with others, the calming presence of animals, a

lot of silence, and a clear vista. Maybe I want (still) a monastic life. That's what I discovered, while trying not to discover much of anything.

Thoreau tells us he left Walden for as good a reason as he went there, which was one of his little jokes, like the one about traveling "widely in Concord."

Recently a group of teenagers invited me, a certified grownup, to their classroom for an interview about the meaning of life. They had prepared a list of questions.

"What interesting places have you been to?"

Oh dear, I think, *this* is an interesting place. I like this room a lot. I could travel widely in it.

"What big decisions have you made?"

If ever I saw a big decision coming, I would run for cover. So far, none has threatened me. I began to mumble about beauty.

Panic spread in the classroom. The teacher broke in—after all, he had young minds to mold. "How do you distinguish between your position and complete irresponsibility?"

I had no idea. The situation seemed to demand that I utter some cultural wisdom: Be kind! Tell the truth! Get your homework in on time! Remember that these agendas will be in eternal conflict! Fortunately, the bell rang. That's the kind of closure we get in real life, as opposed to fiction.

Pacem in Terris

MAYBE IT WAS MY LAST day at the barn that made me so sad, though that was lightened by its being Festival Day. Ben, graduated now, came "home." He and Marge, with the help of their parents, have bought a sheep farm in northern Minnesota. Both have good day jobs in agricultural extension, so, with some sixty hours of work per person per week, they're set to make it in farming. Robin and I played fiddle duets as background to the big lamb roast. There were hugs and food and a righteous lecture on scours from Lori.

But sicknesses of spirit come and go like illnesses of the body. Pervasive unexplainable depression arrived and lay on my stomach like an incubus. The incubus was not answering questions, however subtly asked. Then, after a couple of days, it rocked on its haunches and departed.

In this malaise, I said to myself: I have to spend more time in silence. I have to listen more. Twenty-four hours in a month is not too much. Last year, a group of disciples asked Thich N'hat Hanh if he couldn't reconsider the requirement for members of his Buddhist lay order—doctors, lawyers, farmers, etc.—to spend one day a month in seclusion. He thought about it quite awhile, then said, "I'm sorry. It just isn't possible to do the work without that."

It just isn't possible.

So, as the summer wanes, I have come to a hermitage called

Pacem in Terris, a cluster of little houses in the woods on a scrubby floodplain. A bad woods but, still, a good woods.

The hermitages are well-built structures, each with a tiny screen porch, bed, altar, rocking chair, propane stove. Bathrooms are outside, down the trail. Nobody is going to make me clean them. I got here this afternoon and have been sitting catatonic on the porch. At six, I ate some bread and cheese, cherries, a banana, and cookies sent by my sister, the bountiful.

I had wanted to come earlier in the day, but got caught in gridlock traffic in a terrible part of town. By "terrible" I mean a suburb. After moving one block in one hour, I realized that an accident was causing the traffic delay. As my Volvo balked and overheated, I glanced out the window to see a figure lying on the street covered by an inadequate plastic body bag, one leg protruding in a sandal: male or female, I don't know, but clearly a young person. A young mother stepping off the curb? Someone shot or thrown from a car?

I had to keep driving.

But here in the woods I am companioning this fellow traveler who died a few feet from my car.

It is too hot to dream of doing anything, but surely I came here to do something besides fall asleep, make slow careful walks through the woods covered in mosquitoes and deerflies, paint muddy pictures, and read in a desultory way from *The Cloud of Unknowing*. Maybe not.

This morning I startled a doe on my slow walk. She seemed to tumble through the underbrush head over white tail before collecting herself to leap and turn into a proper deer: at first I could not tell whose flight it was, a rattle and crash merely. Then along came a skunk, at the edge of the remnant prairie, quite sure of who he was.

Drawing bad pictures awakens both the desire to draw well and the impulse never to draw again. Praying badly creates the same bipolar impulse. But how does one pray well?

Beat ceaselessly on the cloud of unknowing and put all things, even stories about God, into a cloud of forgetting, the book says. It is like being on a mountain, cloud lowering above, everything familiar shrouded below. At that median elevation, we do not understand the nature of anything. The fourteenth-century author goes on, "You have awakened our desire, Oh God, and fastened it to a leash of longing." Those words again: longing, desire.

Thirty Hours

I HAVE SPENT THIRTY HOURS HERE, surrounded by the amorphous greenery of an undistinguished second growth forest—young oak, birch, and poplar with its undergrowth of fern and creeper. Now that it's time to leave, I could look at it all day, especially the odd disjunct dance of kinetic aspen leaves against the big solemn oak leaves that I have only just learned to look at, the shadow merely of a heron flying toward the wetlands below.

It stayed hot all night. I moved a rug onto the screen porch and lay there till my bones began to gnaw each other. It was pleasant to hear the wind, even a hot wind, stir, rise, and disappear in the odd way of winds.

Just at nightfall I had walked through the woods by moonlight all alone. The trail broke into a clearing—a pasture, still holding light like a bowl, though the sun was down—then dipped into the dark trees. Down at the lake at 9:30 P.M., the sky was still blue and the moon drawn in chalk. As I returned to the hermitage, I saw a sudden light in the woods where another hermit had lit up his little house. I don't use my propane lamp because I don't want the extra heat and because I love the darkness or candlelight. This other hermit is a strong presence to me, but I give him only darkness or a flicker of light in return.

Women can seldom spend time utterly alone in the woods. But even this safety is merely relative; I lock the inadequate screen door at night, a ritual rather than a gesture of real self-protection.

As I walk about, raccoons and mice lurch out of my way. Fear. Fear determines life in the woods. A biological recoil. Only one being, the skunk, stands like Gary Cooper on the trail, utterly competent if not without trepidation.

"Dove sta memoria?" — a tag end of Italian poetry. *Where is memory?* I write this story down, I guess, because it's evanescent, already slipping into ether. The barn itself is becoming a kind of Brigadoon — I do not mean this precisely in a metaphoric sense. It's an ugly old pole barn, indeed, but maybe it was built on a Native American holy site, or a ring of standing stones. Hank has been (so the rumor goes) nudged into retirement by factions that variously desire (1) land for a soccer field, (2) expanded hog facilities, and (3) the Platonic machine shed. The sheep, I read in the newspaper, are no more: sold downriver to Iowa. However, I stopped by a few days ago — traversed, without knowing it, liminal space — and found Hank shearing twenty Polypays. "Get a clippers, Mary," he growled. "Gimme a hand here." He has no idea I don't work there anymore. He has no idea he doesn't work there anymore. Maybe both of us *do* work there, in another dimension, forever. I fetched the clippers . . .

Tibetan Buddhists tell this story:

> Naropa's student Marpa, after laboriously collecting manuscript after manuscript in years of study in India, lost them overboard on his return journey home. He sorrowed, but then discovered that he had no need of them. He had only taken notes on what he did not understand. What he did understand had become a part of him . . .

In that spirit I leave these notes behind me on the trail. What we write about is what we do not understand.

Works Cited

p. 13   Galway Kinnell, "There Are Things I Tell to No One," in *Three Books* (Boston: Houghton Mifflin, 1993), 125–27. Copyright © 1993 by Galway Kinnell. Reprinted by permission of Houghton Mifflin Co. Previously published in *Mortal Acts, Mortal Words* (1980). All rights reserved.

p. 16   Henry David Thoreau, *Walden and Civil Disobedience* (New York: Viking Penguin, 1983), 135.

p. 18   Henry David Thoreau, *Walden and Civil Disobedience* (New York: Viking Penguin, 1983), 59.

p. 47   *The Sacred Harp: The Best Collection of Sacred Songs, Hymns, Odes, and Anthems Ever Offered the Singing Public for General Use,* ed. Hugh McGraw et al. (Bremen, Ga.: Sacred Harp Publishing Company, 1991), 269.

p. 47   *The Sacred Harp,* 49.

p. 48   *The Sacred Harp,* 547.

p. 49   *The Sacred Harp,* 236.

p. 50   *The Sacred Harp,* 384.

p. 53   Federico Garcia Lorca, *Deep Song and Other Prose,* ed. and trans. Christopher Maurer (New York: New Directions, 1980), 43, 46.

p. 56   *The Sacred Harp,* 278.

p. 62   Antoine de Saint-Exupery, *Terre des Hommes* (Paris: Gallimard, 1939), 7.

p. 62   Mary Oliver, "The Chance to Love Everything," in *Dream Work* (New York: Atlantic, 1986), 8–9.

p. 73   Olga Broumas, "Sweeping the Garden," in *Beneath a Single Moon: Buddhism in Contemporary American Poetry,* ed. Kent Johnson and Craig Paulenich (Boston: Shambhala, 1991), 37.

p. 74   *The Sacred Harp,* 271.

p. 83   Edward Abbey, *Desert Solitaire* (New York: Ballantine, 1968), x, 6.

p. 100   Olga Broumas, "Sweeping the Garden," in *Beneath a Single Moon: Buddhism in Contemporary American Poetry,* ed. Kent Johnson and Craig Paulenich (Boston: Shambhala, 1991), 38.

p. 101   Friedrich Nietzsche, *Beyond Good and Evil: Prelude to a Philosophy of the Future,* trans. R. J. Hollingdale (New York: Penguin, 1972), 84.

p. 103   Walt Whitman, *Leaves of Grass* (New York: Norton, 1973), 11.

p. 120   Richard Wilbur, "Two Voices in a Meadow," in *Advice to a Prophet and Other Poems* (New York: Harcourt, 1961), 11. Copyright © 1957 and renewed 1985 by Richard Wilbur. Reprinted with permission from Harcourt, Inc.

p. 135   Thich N'hat Hanh, *Cultivating the Mind of Love* (Berkeley, Calif.: Parallax, 1996), 92.

p. 165   Wallace Stevens, "Reply to Papini," in *The Collected Poems of Wallace Stevens* (New York: Knopf, 1969), 446.

p. 246   Flannery O'Connor, *The Habit of Being: Letters,* ed. Sally Fitzgerald (New York: Farrar, Straus and Giroux, 1979), 125.

p. 246   Jelalludin Rumi, *Open Secret: Versions of Rumi,* trans. John Moyne and Coleman Barks (Putney, Vt.: Threshold, 1984), 8. Reprinted with permission from Threshold Books.

p. 249   William Blake, "To the Christians," in *Blake's Poetry and Designs,* ed. Mary Lynn Johnson and John E. Grant (New York: Norton, 1979), 345.

p. 260   Lao Tzu, *Hua Hu Ching,* trans. Brian Walker (Livingston, Mont.: Clark City Press, 1992), 31.

p. 274   Robert Frost, "Mending Wall," in *Complete Poems of Robert Frost 1949* (New York: Henry Holt, 1949), 47–48.

p. 279   A. N. Wilson, *C. S. Lewis: A Biography* (New York: Norton, 1990), 127.

p. 288   Mark Doty, *Heaven's Coast* (New York: Harper, 1996), 260.

p. 289   Gretel Ehrlich, *The Solace of Open Spaces* (New York: Penguin, 1985), 52–53.

p. 296   Emily Dickinson, "A narrow fellow in the grass," in *The Complete Poems of Emily Dickinson,* ed. Thomas H. Johnson (Boston: Little, Brown, 1960), 459.

p. 297   *The Sacred Harp,* 61.

p. 297   *The Sacred Harp,* 569.

p. 299   Diane Arbus, quoted by Janet Malcolm, *New York Review of Books* 43, no. 2 (February 1, 1996), 7.

p. 303   Gerard Manley Hopkins, "Pied Beauty," in *The Poems of Gerard Manley Hopkins* (Oxford: Oxford University Press, 1970), 69–70.

p. 305   Adrienne Rich, "Natural Resources," in *The Fact of a Doorframe: Poems Selected and New 1950–1984* (New York: Norton, 1984), 260.

p. 308   Galway Kinnell, "St. Francis and the Sow," in *Mortal Acts, Mortal Words* (Boston: Houghton Mifflin, 1980), 126.

p. 308   *The Sacred Harp,* 384.

p. 311   Natalia Ginsberg, *The Little Virtues* (New York: Arcade, 1989), 97.

MARY ROSE O'REILLEY has taught English at the University of St. Thomas in St. Paul, Minnesota, since 1978. She has written for a wide range of academic, literary, and social-change publications and is the author of *The Peaceable Classroom* (Heinemann Boynton/Cook, 1993) and *Radical Presence* (Heinemann Boynton/Cook, 1998). Her recent awards include a Minnesota State Arts Board Grant, a Bush Artist's Fellowship, a Loft Mentor grant in poetry, a Sears Roebuck Foundation Award for Campus Leadership and Excellence in Teaching, and a Helen Hole Fellowship for Quaker teachers. She received her B.A. from the College of St. Catherine and her Ph.D. from the University of Wisconsin-Milwaukee.

When she can't be raising sheep, Mary Rose O'Reilley lives in St. Paul. Her activities revolve around music, gardening, and her two grown children. She is, at present, an apprentice in wild animal rehabilitation.

Taking Care:
Thoughts on Storytelling and Belief
William Kittredge

This Incomparable Land:
A Guide to American Nature Writing
Thomas J. Lyon

A Wing in the Door:
Life with a Red-Tailed Hawk
Peri Phillips McQuay

An American Child Supreme:
The Education of a Liberation Ecologist
John Nichols

Walking the High Ridge:
Life As Field Trip
Robert Michael Pyle

Ecology of a Cracker Childhood
Janisse Ray

The Dream of the Marsh Wren:
Writing As Reciprocal Creation
Pattiann Rogers

The Country of Language
Scott Russell Sanders

Of Landscape and Longing:
Finding a Home at the Water's Edge
Carolyn Servid

The Book of the Tongass
Edited by Carolyn Servid and Donald Snow

Homestead
Annick Smith

Testimony:
Writers of the West Speak On Behalf of Utah Wilderness
Compiled by Stephen Trimble and Terry Tempest Williams

Shaped by Wind and Water:
Reflections of a Naturalist
Ann Haymond Zwinger

Other books of interest to The World As Home reader:

Essays

Eccentric Islands:
Travels Real and Imaginary
Bill Holm

Children's Novels

Tides
V. M. Caldwell

The Monkey Thief
Aileen Kilgore Henderson

Treasure of Panther Peak
Aileen Kilgore Henderson

The Dog with Golden Eyes
Frances Wilbur

Children's Anthologies

Stories from Where We Live—
The California Coast
Edited by Sara St. Antoine

Stories from Where We Live—
The Great North American Prairie
Edited by Sara St. Antoine

Stories from Where We Live—
The North Atlantic Coast
Edited by Sara St. Antoine

ANTHOLOGIES

Urban Nature:
Poems about Wildlife in the City
Edited by Laure-Anne Bosselaar

Verse and Universe:
Poems about Science and Mathematics
Edited by Kurt Brown

POETRY

Turning Over the Earth
Ralph Black

Butterfly Effect
Harry Humes

Firekeeper:
New and Selected Poems
Pattiann Rogers

Song of the World Becoming:
New and Collected Poems
1981–2001
Pattiann Rogers

The World As Home, the nonfiction publishing program of Milkweed Editions, is dedicated to exploring our relationship to the natural world. Not espousing any particular environmentalist or political agenda, these books are a forum for distinctive literary writing that not only alerts the reader to vital issues but offers personal testimonies to living harmoniously with other species in urban, rural, and wilderness communities.

Milkweed Editions publishes with the intention of making a humane impact on society, in the belief that literature is a transformative art uniquely able to convey the essential experiences of the human heart and spirit. To that end, Milkweed publishes distinctive voices of literary merit in handsomely designed, visually dynamic books, exploring the ethical, cultural, and esthetic issues that free societies need continually to address. Milkweed Editions is a not-for-profit press.

Join Us

Milkweed publishes adult and children's fiction, poetry, and, in its World As Home program, literary nonfiction about the natural world. Milkweed also hosts two websites: www.milkweed.org, where readers can find in-depth information about Milkweed books, authors, and programs, and www.worldashome.org, which is your online resource of books, organizations, and writings that explore ethical, esthetic, and cultural dimensions of our relationship to the natural world.

Since its genesis as *Milkweed Chronicle* in 1979, Milkweed has helped hundreds of emerging writers reach their readers. Thanks to the generosity of foundations and of individuals like you, Milkweed Editions is able to continue its nonprofit mission of publishing books chosen on the basis of literary merit—of how they impact the human heart and spirit—rather than on how they impact the bottom line. That's a miracle that our readers have made possible.

In addition to purchasing Milkweed books, you can join the growing community of Milkweed supporters. Individual contributions of any amount are both meaningful and welcome. Contact us for a Milkweed catalog or log on to www.milkweed.org and click on "About Milkweed," then "Why Join Milkweed," to find out about our donor program, or simply call (800) 520-6455 and ask about becoming one of Milkweed's contributors. As a nonprofit press, Milkweed belongs to you, the community. Milkweed's board, its staff, and especially the authors whose careers you help launch thank you for reading our books and supporting our mission in any way you can.

Interior design by Donna Burch
Typeset in Granjon
by Stanton Publication Services, Inc.
Printed on acid-free, recycled 55# Perfection Antique paper
by Maple Vail Book Manufacturing